D0305987

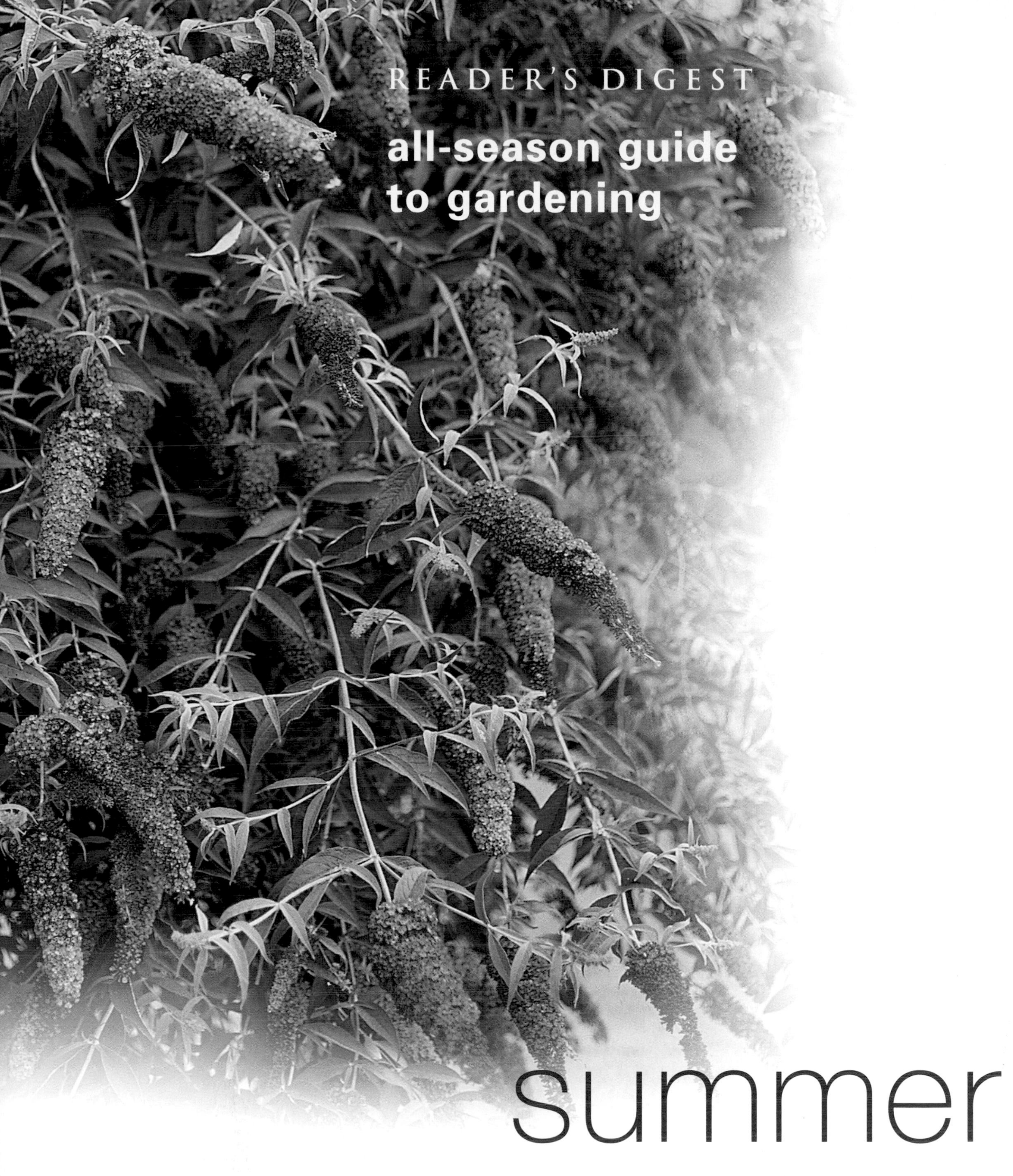

READER'S DIGEST

# all-season guide to gardening

# summer

READER'S DIGEST

# all-season guide to gardening

# summer

PUBLISHED BY
THE READER'S DIGEST ASSOCIATION LIMITED
LONDON • NEW YORK • SYDNEY • MONTREAL

# contents

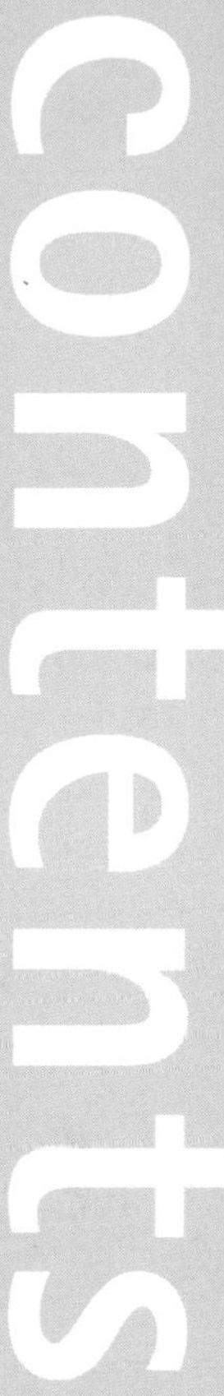

## *plant selector* 74

a photographic guide to the best plants in summer



## *garden projects* 120

ideas and practical instructions on ways to improve your garden



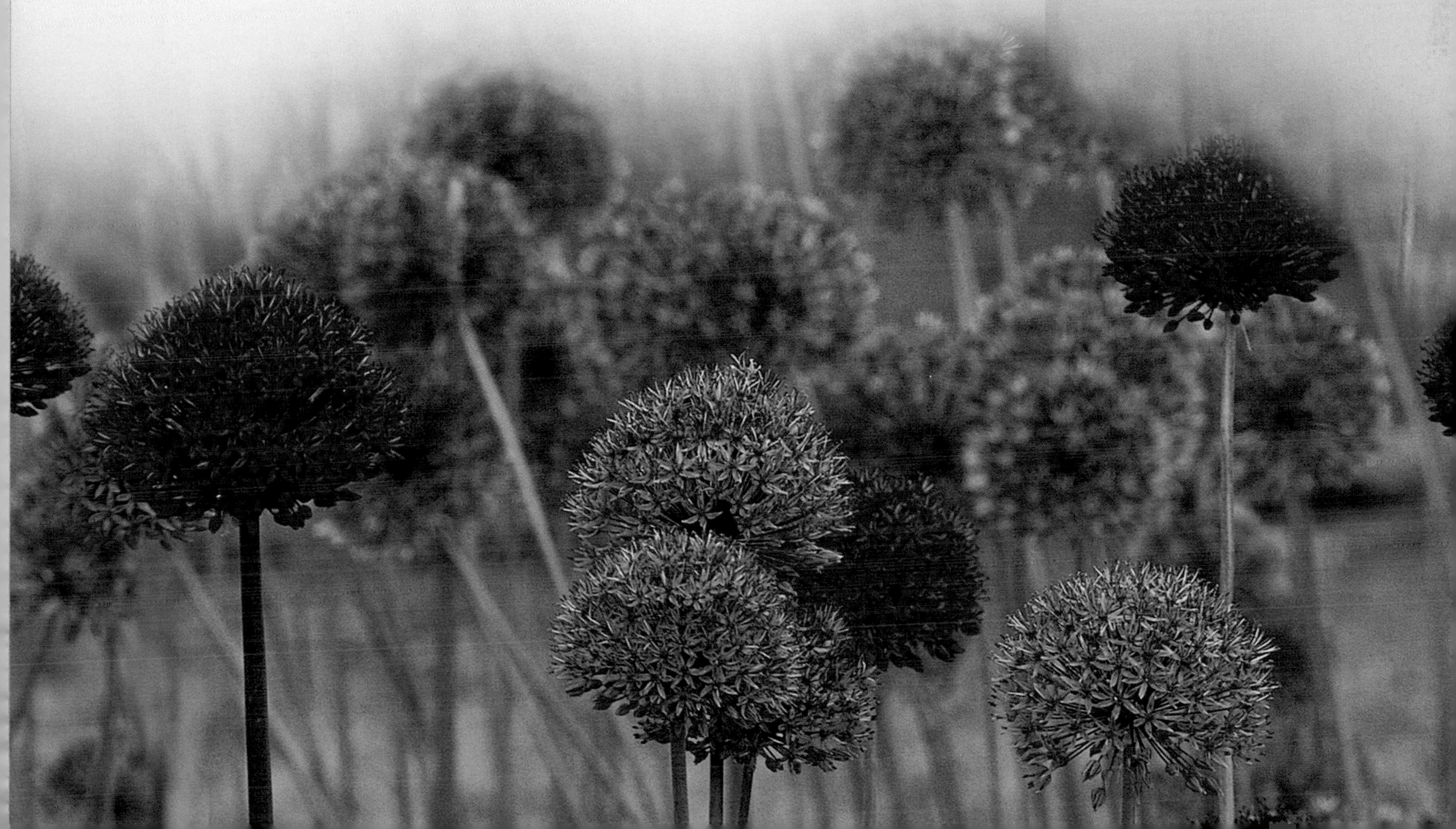

# contents

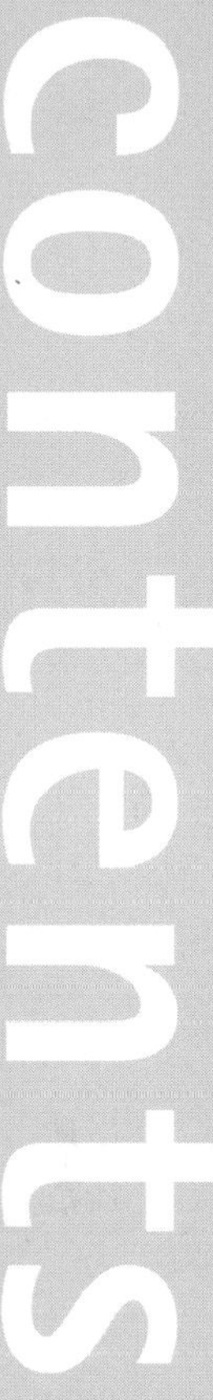

## *plant selector* 74

a photographic guide to the best plants in summer



## *garden projects* 120

ideas and practical instructions on ways to improve your garden



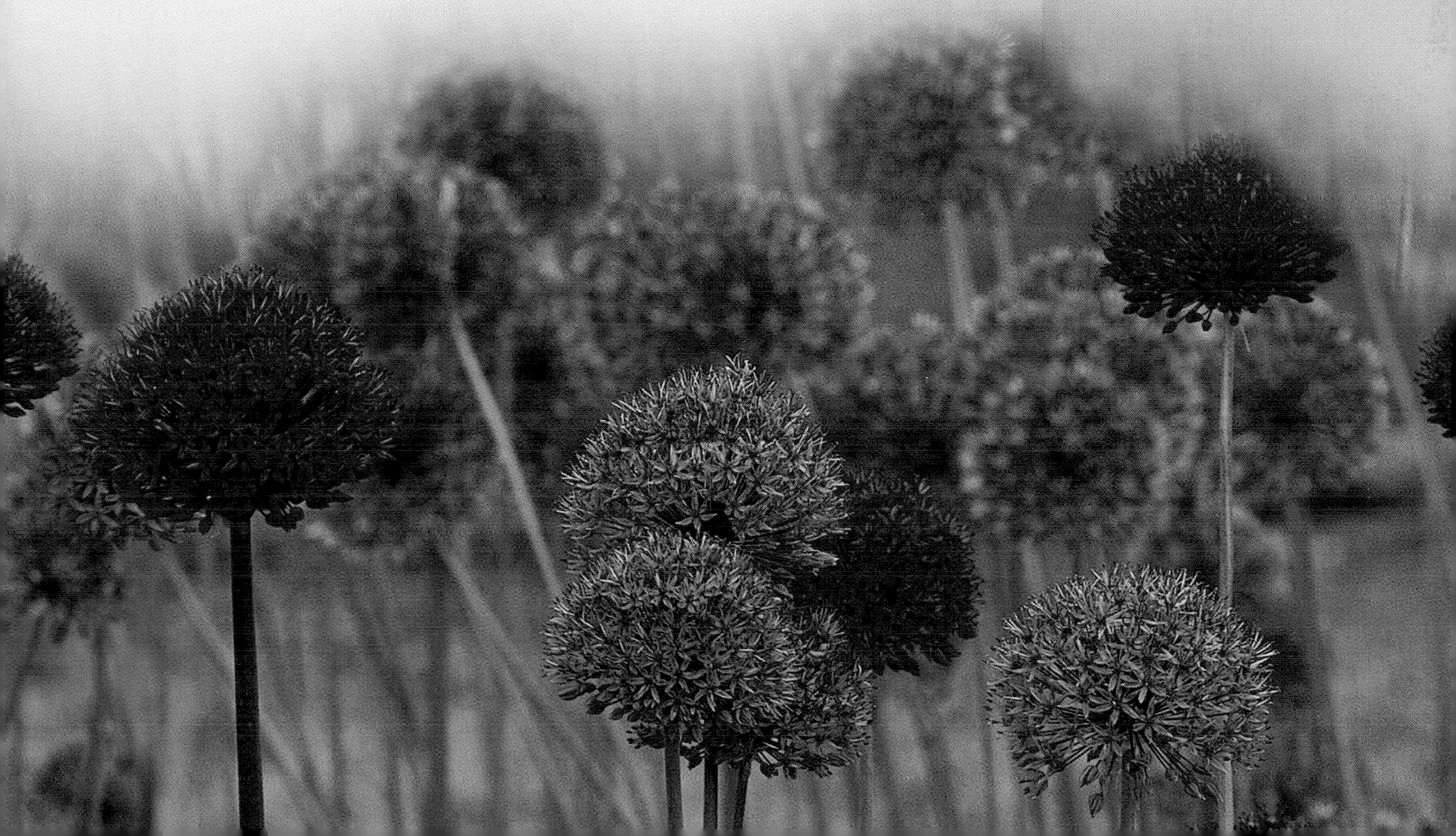

# foreword

The *All-Season Guide to Gardening* provides a complete practical and inspirational guide to making the most of your garden season-by-season, with year-round detailed information to help you plan, plant and enjoy the garden of your dreams. Each of the volumes is presented in four key sections:

*inspirations* offers a source of design and planting ideas taken from contemporary and traditional gardens photographed during the season. The plants featured have been identified to enable you to re-create or adapt the ideas to your own garden scheme.

*practical diary* is a guide to the most important tasks to be done in the garden at this time of year. The information is divided into subject areas – such as Perennials, Climbers, or Patios & Containers – that reflect particular gardening interests. The headings appear in the same order in every volume in the series, so you can easily find the information you need. Under each heading is a list of the season's main tasks. The most important jobs are then explained in more detail, with step-by-step photographs and expert tips. The Healthy Garden, at the end of the section, is a full checklist of priority seasonal tasks for the whole garden. Since many jobs require follow-up attention in a later season, a 'Looking

# useful terms

**alpine** Although this strictly refers to a mountain plant that grows naturally in free-draining soil at high altitude, the term is used by gardeners to mean any plant suitable for growing in a rock garden.
**annual** A plant that grows, flowers, sets seed and dies in one growing season.
**anther** The part of the flower that produces pollen.
**aquatic plant** In its widest sense, this can mean any water plant, but usually refers to plants such as water lilies that grow in deeper water, rooted in the bottom of the pond or in special baskets.
**bareroot** This refers to plants, usually trees and shrubs, that have been dug up and supplied to the customer without any soil on their roots. Roses are often supplied in this way.
**bedding (plant)** A plant used outdoors for temporary or seasonal display, often as part of a planned 'bedding scheme'.
**biennial** A plant that completes its life cycle in two growing seasons.
**biological control** The treatment or prevention of pests, diseases or weeds by natural, rather than chemical, methods, usually involving a naturally occurring parasite or predator.
**cloche** A glass or plastic cover used to shelter plants from cold or windy weather. Cloches are available as separate units or in tunnel form, often called 'continuous cloches'.
**coldframe** A low, unheated structure with a transparent top, in which plants can be grown in protected conditions.
**cordon** A plant restricted by pruning and training to a single, unbranching stem. Examples include apples, tomatoes and sweet peas grown on canes.
**corm** The swollen stem base of plants like crocuses and gladioli, where food is stored during winter. A new corm forms each year on top of the shrivelled remains of last year's.
**cultivar** A distinct, named plant variety that has originated in cultivation, rather than in the wild. Cultivars are often simply (but incorrectly) called 'varieties'.
**deadhead** To cut off the spent flowers.
**die-back** The result of attack by a fungal disease, which causes shoots or branches to die back from their tips.
**direct sow** To sow seeds in the ground where the plants are to grow, rather than starting them indoors or in a temporary seedbed for later transplanting.
**drill** A furrow or channel made in the soil at the correct depth for sowing seeds.
**ericaceous** Any plant belonging to the erica or heather family, for example pieris and rhododendrons. Also refers to the acid conditions these plants like and the special lime-free compost in which they are potted.
**espalier** A tree such as an apple or cotoneaster that is pruned and trained as a single upright trunk, with side branches extending horizontally to form symmetrical layers or 'tiers'.
**foliar feed** Liquid fertiliser sprayed or watered on the leaves of plants, usually applied for rapid results or when plants are not actively absorbing nutrients through their roots (after injury or in cold weather, for example).
**glyphosate** A chemical weedkiller that is absorbed through leaves and moves through the plant so that all parts, including roots, are killed (see systemic).
**habitat** The natural home of a plant growing in the wild. Not to be confused with habit, which is the typical form or shape of a plant.
**harden off** To gradually acclimatise a plant previously grown indoors to unprotected conditions outside in the garden.
**hardwood cutting** A piece of this year's shoot taken for propagation from a shrub, tree or climber during the autumn, when their stems are hard and ripe.
**heel** A small strip of bark torn from the main stem when a sideshoot is pulled off to make a (heel) cutting.
**heel in** To bury the roots of a plant in a temporary hole or trench when it is not to be planted immediately.
**humus** The dark, water-retentive component of soil that results from the decay of organic material.
***in situ*** Literally, in position, or where plants are to grow permanently.
**internodal cutting** A cutting that is trimmed midway between two leaf-joints, rather than immediately below the leaves.
**layering** A method of propagation in which a shoot is rooted while still attached to the

ahead' feature indicates when you will find details of follow-up action in another volume.

*plant selector* is a directory of the plants which are at their best at this time of year, as selected by our gardening experts. Within each subject grouping the plants are arranged by colour, and within each colour sequence they are generally listed alphabetically by botanical name. Each plant is shown in a photograph, with information supplied including the plant's common name, size, site and soil preferences, best uses, general care and suggestions for good companions. Each plant is also given a 'hardiness' rating:

- 'Hardy' plants can be grown outdoors in all parts of the British Isles.
- Plants rated 'not fully hardy' can be grown outdoors in milder parts of the British Isles but elsewhere will need some protection in winter.
- 'Half-hardy' plants can withstand temperatures down to 0°C (32°F). They are often grown outdoors in summer displays, but propagated and kept under glass between autumn and late spring.
- 'Tender' plants require protection under glass for all or part of the year.

At the end of the section, there are lists of the plants best suited to different garden conditions and soil types.

*garden projects* offers ideas and instructions for garden improvements, ranging from building a patio, pergola or raised bed to designing and planting up a new border or pond. Major DIY projects are illustrated with step-by-step photographs and all the projects are within the capabilities of a fit, practical person. Although some projects are specific to a season, many of them can also be undertaken at other times of the year.



parent plant. Rooting a branch where it touches the ground is called simple layering, while serpentine layering involves rooting a long flexible stem in several places; long stems can be tip layered by burying their growing tips.

**loam** A type of soil that contains a balanced mixture of sand, clay and organic material.

**marginal plant** A waterside plant that is grown at the edge of the pond, either in shallow water or on the bank.

**mulch** Any material used to cover and protect the soil surface. Organic mulches include straw, manure and lawn mowings, while polythene sheet and stones are examples of inorganic mulches.

**naturalise** To deliberately plant, or allow plants to grow and spread, as in the wild.

**node** The place on a plant's stem where a leaf forms.

**nursery bed** A piece of ground specially reserved for raising young plants.

**organic** This literally refers to any material derived from decomposed animal or plant remains. It is also used to describe a gardening approach that uses little or no obviously chemical substances such as fertilisers and pesticides.

**perlite** A granular, absorbent soil or compost additive made from expanded volcanic rock.

**perennial (correctly herbaceous perennial)** A durable non-woody plant whose soft, leafy growth dies down in winter, but grows again the following year.

**pinch out** To remove a growing tip, using finger and thumb.

**pot on** To move a potted plant into a larger container.

**pot (up)** To transfer a plant from a seedtray or open ground into a pot.

**prick out** To transplant seedlings from where they have been sown to a container or piece of ground where they will have more space to grow.

**rhizome** An underground root (strictly, a stem) that behaves like a bulb by storing food from one season to the next. Also used to describe the buried creeping shoots by which some plants, especially grasses, spread underground.

**rootballed** This describes plants packaged for delivery by wrapping their mass of roots and soil or compost in a net bag.

**rootstock (or stock)** The rooted portion of a grafted tree. This usually influences the habit and ultimate size of the selected variety joined onto it (the scion).

**seedbed** A piece of ground for raising seeds, specially prepared by removing all stones, weeds and large lumps of soil.

**semi-ripe cutting** A section of this year's stem cut off for propagation, usually during summer while the tip is still soft but the base has become firm and woody.

**softwood cutting** A cutting prepared from a portion of a young new shoot that has not started to harden.

**spit** A measurement of depth equal to the length of a spade-blade (about 25cm/10in).

**standard** A trained form of woody plant with a single upright stem that is clear of all leaves and shoots. Full standard trees have trunks about 2m (6ft) high, half-standards 1.2m (4ft). Standard roses are about 1m (3ft) high, while half-standards have 75cm (2ft 6in) stems.

**subsoil** The lower layer of ground below the topsoil (see below). Often paler and relatively infertile, this is usually coarser in texture and hard to cultivate.

**sucker** A shoot growing from below ground and away from the main stem of a plant, sometimes from its rootstock.

**systemic** A type of pesticide, fungicide or weedkiller sprayed onto leaves and absorbed into all plant parts in its sap.

**tender perennial** A plant that can live for several years but cannot tolerate frost or very cold conditions.

**thin out** To reduce the number of plants, buds or fruit so that those remaining have enough room to develop fully.

**tip cuttings** Softwood cuttings (see above) formed from the outer ends of young shoots.

**top dressing** An application of fertiliser, organic material or potting compost spread on the surface. Also refers to replacing the top layer of compost in a large container with a fresh supply.

**topgrowth** The upper, visible part of a plant above ground level.

**topsoil** The upper layer of soil, usually darker and more fertile than the layers below (see subsoil), and where plants develop most of their feeding roots.

**tuber** A fat, underground root (in dahlias, for example) or stem (begonias), constructed differently from a bulb or corm but used in the same way for storing food from one season to the next.

**variety** Botanically, a distinctly different variation of a plant that has developed in the wild, but commonly used to mean the same as cultivar (see left).

# inspirations

As the longest day approaches, growth in the garden reaches top speed. Newly opened blooms will delight you every day, their fragrances rich and heady, especially during still evenings. Tubs, pots and window boxes planted only a few weeks ago are filling out rapidly and increasing their flower power as the days grow warmer. In the borders there is competition from roses and early perennials such as peonies, oriental poppies and lupins, while among the lush green growth in and around pools and ponds, water lilies and irises provide bold colour highlights.

# enchanting beds & borders

*In almost every garden beds and borders look their best in the summer season. Foliage is still young, the colours are bright and every day brings the pleasure of new, pristine blooms.*

**This midsummer riot** (left) of perennial poppies, lupins, blue larkspurs and the sombre maroon *Lychnis coronaria* Atrosanguinea Group will intensify and run for weeks. Cut all faded flower stems back to encourage re-growth and later flushes of bloom.

*Dorotheanthus*

**Annuals** such as the white mignonette (*Reseda alba*) have been sown for a cool, calm display, albeit short-lived (below left). After flowering, replace them with temporary tender plants or with biennials such as canterbury bells.

**In cottage gardens**, colour schemes can be fairly random. Below, pink roses, white feverfew, yellow loosestrife and blue bellflowers make an eccentric, delightful mix.

**Foliage colour** plays as important a role as the flowers in this bed (above). The climbing golden hop contrasts with the bluish bracts of *Cerinthe major* and the strong blue of the pot. Later in the season, interest will come from the lilies and feathery bronze fennel.

**Purple alliums** and pale *Veronica gentianoides* provide a colourful early summer highlight (top right).

**A brooding collection** of reds (right) makes a contrast with cool blues and lush foliage. The hot-coloured cannas, salvias and *Phygelius capensis* are toned down by clear blue *Agapanthus* Headbourne hybrids.

# the fragrant garden

*A truly lovely garden must have fragrance as well as visual beauty. There are flowers with seductive perfume, aromatic herbs and scented foliage plants to choose from.*

**The sweet pea** (left) is bred in a huge range of colours and its unique fragrance and long stems make it ideal as a cut flower. Sow seed of this hardy climber in pots, in autumn or spring, and set the young plants outdoors when a few centimetres high.

**With its honey-scented blooms,** *Buddleja davidii* (left) is a magnet for butterflies and moths, which feast on the nectar-rich flowers for hours at a time. Prune these shrubs hard back in spring for best results.

**Grow scented plants** near a seating area where possible. Fragrant lavender mingles with scented climbing roses in this corner of a garden (below), making it a delightful place to sit in summer.

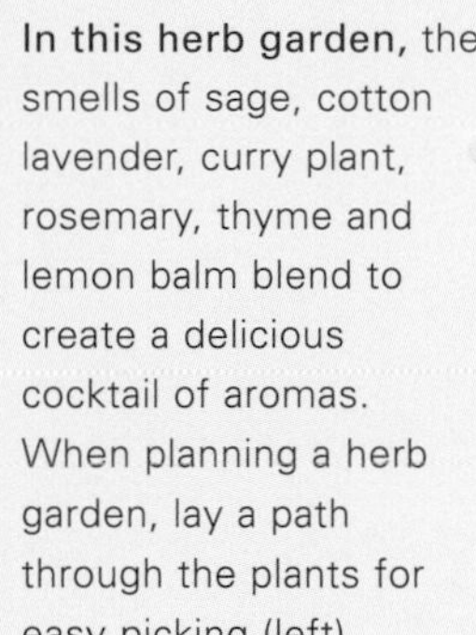

**In this herb garden,** the smells of sage, cotton lavender, curry plant, rosemary, thyme and lemon balm blend to create a delicious cocktail of aromas. When planning a herb garden, lay a path through the plants for easy picking (left).

*Lathyrus odoratus* 'Fragrant Ripples'

**A honeysuckle** (*Lonicera japonica* 'Halliana') turns a doorway into a special feature (left) with its sweet, slightly lemony fragrance and flowers that last from June until November.

**You can rely on lilies** to furnish a rich, sometimes heady, fragrance in summer (far left). Choose hybrids for scent but site them carefully if this might be overpowering.

**In a traditional** cottage rose garden (below left), clipped box hedges enclose a collection of old roses. Both the taller pink damask roses and the centifolias in the foreground ('Cardinal de Richelieu') flower once in summer, but their fragrance is intense.

**A tiny herb potager** (below) is planted with thymes, sage and lemon balm. Even a restricted area little more than a metre across can provide the site for an aromatic herb collection, provided it receives plenty of sun.

# the season's new crops

*As the year's first crops come to fruition, there is a great sense of anticipation. Waxy new potatoes, tender spinach leaves and crisp young lettuces taste all the better for being home-grown.*

**Swathes of lavender** (above) bring colour to a vegetable garden, together with young brussels sprouts and standard red currants.

**The greenhouse** is the key to sustaining productivity in this highly decorative garden (right). It is used to ensure a succession of crops to plant out as soon as others are harvested.

**Raspberries** are one of the most prolific and flavoursome fruits of early summer.

**Simple climbing frames** made from hazel wands are ideal supports for runner beans (below). Colourful marigolds also have a role to play: they attract hover flies whose larvae feed on aphids.

**A workmanlike kitchen** garden has been planted with rocket, spanish onions and lettuces, all at varying stages of development (right). Quick-growing lettuces make use of vacant ground between rows of longer-term crops.

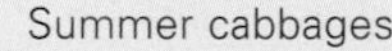

Summer cabbages

**This vegetable plot** (left) has been densely planted with courgettes, carrots, beet and lettuce as well as cornflowers and california poppies. The yields of vegetables will be low at this density, but the variety is rewarding.

**A modern design** (right) blends flowers and containers with a little food production, including broad beans and runner beans, in a garden that is both functional and ornamental.

# tubs, troughs & hanging baskets

*Containers can offer a good display at any time of year, but in early summer plant growth is rapid and sustained, providing new colour almost daily and building to a seasonal climax.*

**Trailing lobelias** come in a range of colours besides the familiar blue. This rich pink variety from the Cascade Series (above) may be grown from seed sown under glass in late winter.

**In a striking glazed pot** the dark form of *Aeonium arboreum* contrasts dramatically with the silver-green fronds of *Lotus berthelotii* (above, centre left). Both are easy to raise from cuttings, over-wintered in a frost-free place.

**A wicker basket** filled with trailing lobelias (above) hangs from the branch of a tree. Wicker containers must be lined with polythene, perforated at the base, before being planted up, to prevent the compost from being washed out.

**Diascias** (above, centre right) make superb container plants and, with protection, will last from one summer to the next. This is 'Blackthorn Apricot'.

**Generous clay pots** (left) are filled with tender coleus, annual busy lizzies and the perennial 'rabbit's tail' grass.

**Small fence-hung** pots carry summer colour in the form of purple lobelia, while in the bigger containers japanese anemones and a vine (*Parthenocissus*) will bring autumn interest. The dramatic olive jars are left empty.

**A majestic fan palm** (*Trachycarpus fortunei*) underplanted with argyranthemums makes a striking focal point with vivid red pelargoniums on a summer patio (below left). The fan palm must be given winter protection.

**Suspended from** the beam of a pergola, this large hanging basket is planted up with rooted cuttings of scented heliotrope, soft mauve petunias and *Tradescantia pallida* 'Purpurea'.

# ponds, pools & waterside planting

*Water brings life and movement to a garden, altering the light, changing perspective and reflecting images in its surface.*

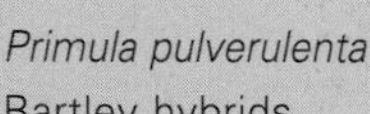

*Primula pulverulenta* Bartley hybrids

**The startling red** and lilac spikes of *Primula vialii* harmonise with hosta flowers by the waterside (right).

**A raised pond** (below) is constructed from dressed limestone. The handsome natural coping stones overhang the water, concealing the liner, but the water level is not allowed to reach the stone, which could perish if constantly wet.

**Recycled railway sleepers** have been used to create a pair of formal ponds (left) connected by a simple waterfall. The restrained planting is limited to grasses and hostas.

**A slate fountain** is a bold sculptural statement in this small circular pond with a paved surround (below). Behind is the tall grass, *Miscanthus sinensis*.

**Hostas and arums** offer bold foliage in this small cascade (left), while colour comes from japanese iris and primulas. When the flowers are over, the leaves of the iris will continue to provide architectural greenery.

**In a beautiful wildlife pond** (right) water lilies shade the water, keeping it cool and reducing blanket weed. Around the edge reeds, astilbes and irises offer cover for wildlife, while beneath the water oxygenating plants help to sustain aquatic life.

# flowering climbers

*Rosa* and *Clematis*

*Vertical planting provides an extra dimension, especially useful in a small garden. Doorways and arches as well as walls and fences can be framed and draped with foliage and flowers.*

**A brick wall** pierced by an arch is embellished by a collection of wall shrubs and climbers (above). The clematis blooms will have been preceded by the fragrant blossoms of the wisteria, whose foliage still makes a contribution. The pale blue ceanothus will have been blooming since spring.

**The rambler rose** 'Félicité Perpétue' flowers in perfect harmony with *Clematis* 'Comtesse de Bouchaud' (right). This rose does not repeat, but the clematis will bloom sporadically until autumn.

**Climbing rose** Bantry Bay has been teamed with the maroon clematis 'Royal Velours' (above). Select clematis that can be pruned hard in winter, when the rose is taken down for an overhaul.

**The potato vine** (*Solanum crispum* 'Glasnevin') will grow vigorously through summer, constantly in flower (above). To keep it within bounds, prune back to its main framework each year in spring, when frost is unlikely to damage the tender young growths.

**Clematis 'Comtesse de Bouchaud'** and *Rosa* 'Minnehaha' scramble together (below) without constraint, but each winter they must be unravelled and separately pruned.

**Unlike the annual sweet pea**, the everlasting pea (*Lathyrus latifolius*) is a long-lasting perennial that produces many stems from its rootstock every year (below).

# sun-loving perennials

*Cheerful perennials bring exuberance to the garden in early summer. Some, like oriental poppies, are soon over, but penstemons, cranesbills and diascias flower all summer.*

**Bright, strong colours** work best in strong sunlight, and these candelabra primulas, lupins and delphiniums make an ideal grouping for high summer (left). The primulas flower once only, but their spikes can be left to produce seed. Lupins and delphiniums, if cut back, will produce flowers again later.

**Try to introduce** plants with distinctive texture into a border (right). The spiky sea holly (*Eryngium* x *oliverianum*) contrasts strongly in texture and colour with yellow coreopsis, magenta lychnis and red crocosmia.

**Grassland plants** such as *Inula helenium,* helianthus and the double meadow cranesbill *Geranium pratense* (below right) blend with *Alchemilla mollis* to give a meadow-like impression. All these species would naturalise in a wild garden almost as easily as they grow in this flower border.

**A multicoloured group** of yarrows (*Achillea*) starts off brightly (above), but the blooms will later lose their intensity and present a more muted appearance.

*Aquilegia* McKana Group

**Softly contrasting colours** characterise this summer border (right), with blue *Campanula lactiflora*, white *C. latifolia* and the brighter yellow of *Anthemis tinctoria*. Though non-repeating, these flowers all have a long shelf life and will sustain the border for weeks.

**This vibrant planting** of summer perennials (right) holds plenty of flower – kniphofias, antirrhinums, poppies and penstemons – but there is a wealth of bloom yet to come.

# practical diary

In this season of rapid development the speed of plant growth is truly astonishing, and in dry weather plants will need frequent watering. Vigorous climbers spread luxuriantly to cover walls and pergolas, needing to be safely tied in. Your lawn will grow long again soon after mowing. The greenhouse feels like a tropical paradise at this time of year, and while peppers and tomatoes will revel in the sun, cucumbers and easily scorched plants like fuchsias will benefit from a little shade and higher humidity. The sun is warm, the evenings are long, and in early summer there is really no better place to be than a garden.

# perennials

Perennials are the mainstay of the summer border, and this is the time to increase the display by planting frost-tender varieties for guaranteed colour through to autumn. Keep all perennials at their best by paying attention to staking, thinning out and deadheading.

## *now is the season to . . .*

- **plant tender perennials** as early as possible so they establish quickly and start flowering. Make sure they are first acclimatised to outdoor conditions (hardened off) over a couple of weeks. Do this by standing plants outside during the day for increasing periods of time, eventually leaving them out at night unless frost is forecast.
- **check perennials raised from seed** in spring. Once they are well rooted, pot up into a minimum pot size of 8cm (3in).
- **water newly planted perennials** in dry spells. Soak them every few days, so water penetrates right through the rootball and roots are encouraged to reach down in search of moisture.
- **give regular attention** to perennials in containers. Water them daily, unless the weather is very wet. If they have not been fed so far this year, feed with a controlled-release fertiliser, which will last for the rest of the growing season. If any plant looks sickly, with pale or yellowing leaves, apply a liquid fertiliser first to give quick results.
- **deadhead all faded flowers** to prevent their seed from setting (see opposite).
- **thin overcrowded clumps** of perennials that missed being divided earlier in the year, to increase air circulation and to prevent the stems from flopping over. Cut out a quarter to a third of the stems at ground level.
- **stake tall-growing perennials** early in summer before they begin to flop, because once this happens the stems will never straighten properly (see opposite).
- **hoe and hand-weed** borders regularly. Hoeing off weeds as they germinate saves the more difficult job of tackling large, established weeds later on.
- **protect hostas** from slugs and snails throughout summer. Try growing them in large pots to keep these pests at bay.
- **avoid powdery mildew** on susceptible perennials, such as phlox and pulmonarias, by watering well during dry spells.
- **pick off leaves** affected by fungal disease and throw them away, but not on the compost heap, as disease spores will survive. Plants prone to infection include aquilegias, phlox and pulmonarias. Consider spraying with fungicide to prevent diseases from spreading.
- **propagate some perennials** by cuttings or division (see page 28).

*Astrantia major*

**Once they start to fade,** cut the flowered shoots of euphorbias to ground level; wear gloves when doing this as the milky sap can irritate the skin.

## staking

Stake tall-growing perennials early in summer using ready-made frames, canes or twiggy sticks. Stake individual stems of very tall plants, like those of delphiniums.

- **tailor-made supports** vary in style and are reusable. Many can be raised as the plants grow or may be interlinked to support clumps of different sizes.
- **place short canes in a circle** round the plant, with string run round and in between them.
- **poke in twiggy branches** of hazel, often referred to as 'pea sticks', round a perennial clump. If bent over at the top, these sticks will make a cage through which the plant will grow.
- **bamboo canes and soft string** or raffia provide reliable support for tall individual stems.

**Plant foliage** will soon hide tailor-made supports like this.

## deadheading

Removing dead or faded flowerheads encourages more blooms over a longer period of time. If this job is neglected, plants will set seed and flower less freely. With regular deadheading, tender perennials will flower well into autumn.

- **self-seeding perennials,** like lady's mantle (*Alchemilla mollis*) and bronze fennel (*Foeniculum vulgare* 'Purpureum'), can produce many seedlings informally throughout a border. To prevent this, cut off faded flowerheads before seeds ripen.
- **spring and early summer-flowering perennials** such as hardy geraniums and oriental poppies (*Papaver orientale*) should be cut back to ground level once they have finished flowering. Feed them with a general fertiliser and water in well, and they will soon reward you with a bushy mound of fresh foliage.
- **deadhead peonies,** but allow foliage to die back naturally.
- **for delphiniums and lupins** cut off dead flower spikes to encourage more flowers on shorter sideshoots.

**A low panel of woven willow** holds back leafy perennials and prevents them from flopping forwards onto a path or lawn.

# perennials/2

*Echinops ritro*

## *propagation*

Summer is the perfect time to make more plants by taking a variety of cuttings, by dividing and collecting seeds. Although spring is far away, now is also the time to divide polyanthus to ensure a good show of flowers next year.

### cuttings and divisions

- **take soft-tip cuttings of tender perennials** like pelargoniums in the cool of the morning (see below). Select strong, non-flowering shoots and cut a length of stem 10cm (4in) long from the top. Put the cut material straight into a plastic bag or bucket of cold water, to prevent it from wilting.
- **plant out basal cuttings** taken in late spring in a nursery bed, or move them into individual 8cm (3in) pots and grow on in a coldframe or sheltered area of the garden.
- **divide polyanthus** and double-flowered primulas after flowering. Dig up the clump with a fork and shake off any loose soil. Use a sharp knife to cut the clump into smaller pieces, each consisting of one or two shoots with plenty of roots attached. Plant out the divisions in rows, in a nursery bed or a spare corner of the garden, spacing them 15–23cm (6–9in) apart. Water them well.
- **split the rhizomes** of bearded irises in established clumps once flowering has finished (see opposite). Replant the divisions in full sun.
- **propagate pinks** (*Dianthus*) from 'pipings' (see opposite) taken from non-flowering shoots. After removing the lower leaves, treat as soft-tip cuttings (see below).

## *taking soft-tip cuttings*

1 **Make the cuttings** with a sharp knife by trimming the base just below a leaf joint.

2 **Carefully take off** the lower leaves and any flowers.

3 **Dip the base** of each cutting into hormone rooting powder before inserting round the edge of a 13cm (5in) pot filled with cuttings compost. Cover the pot with a polythene bag and place it in a shaded coldframe or sheltered spot outside. The exception is geraniums which should not be covered. Rooting usually takes about eight weeks, when the cuttings are potted up individually into 8cm (3in) pots.

## *dividing bearded irises*

1 **Lift the clump.** Cut off the younger, outer pieces of the thick fleshy rootstock, or rhizome, and discard the old central portion.

2 **Trim the leaves** so the plants are not rocked by the wind.

3 **Replant in groups of three** with the fans of foliage to the outside. The top of the rhizome must be just above soil level, as it needs exposure to sun in order to flower well. Feed with a low-nitrogen fertiliser and water thoroughly.

**Dianthus are propagated** from special cuttings (pipings). Pull out the tips of non-flowering shoots 10cm (4in) long, remove the lower leaves and insert in compost.

### collecting seed

Gather seed of spring and early summer-flowering perennials as soon as it is ripe, usually when the seedpods have turned brown. On a dry day cut the seed heads into labelled paper bags (see Late Summer) and place on a sunny windowsill. Once the seed heads are completely dry, tip them onto a sheet of newspaper, split open the pods and shake out the seed. Store in envelopes or empty film canisters, after writing on the plant name.

The seed of most perennials can be sown immediately, but a few, such as aconitums, meconopsis and primulas, need a cold period in order to germinate, and they should be left until autumn. The best place to store seed for any length of time is in moisture-proof containers in a refrigerator or other cool, dry place.

When you are ready, sow the collected seed thinly into pots of moist seed compost and cover with a thin layer of perlite or horticultural vermiculite. Stand the pots in a coldframe or other sheltered spot outside, and keep the compost moist.

### there is still time to . . .

- **take basal cuttings** of clump-forming perennials, such as lupins and delphiniums, before the end of June. Cut strong young shoots about 10cm (4in) long from the base of the plant and treat them as described for soft-tip cuttings (see opposite).

*looking ahead . . .*

☑ LATE SUMMER Pot up rooted cuttings of tender perennials.
☑ Transplant seedlings of early flowering perennials.
☑ AUTUMN Transplant polyanthus to their flowering positions.
☑ Plant out perennials raised from basal cuttings.

*plants* **that give good results from seed**

*Aconitum napellus* • *Alchemilla mollis* • *Aquilegia* • *Geranium* (some) • *Helleborus* • *Lychnis coronaria* • *Meconopsis* • *Polemonium* • *Primula*

Plants raised from species will resemble their parents, but the offspring of cultivated varieties, or cultivars, will produce plants of differing appearance. *Geranium renardii* is a species, while *Heuchera* 'Palace Purple' is a cultivar.

*Geranium* 'Ann Folkard'

# annuals & biennials

The flower garden becomes a celebration of colour as summer annuals take over from the recently cleared spring bedding. Continue sowing to prolong your display into autumn, and to bring on new plants for next spring.

## now is the season to . . .

- **finish hardening off** tender annuals, such as scarlet salvias and busy lizzies (*Impatiens*), and plant them out as soon as the frosts are over. Use them in formal and informal bedding schemes (see opposite).
- **give a weekly liquid feed** to pots and trays of bedding plants, and other seedlings that will flower, if their planting out has been delayed.
- **regularly water** any recently planted bedding and transplanted seedlings in dry weather. Feed annuals in containers with a dilute liquid fertiliser, every seven to ten days.
- **water and feed sweet peas** at regular intervals, and deadhead to prevent seeds from forming. Tie in the stems every two or three days when growing up vertical string supports as a cordon.
- **deadhead annuals,** such as pansies, marigolds, snapdragons and california poppies, to stimulate more flowers.
- **buy seedlings and plug plants** from the garden centre (see opposite).
- **cut flowers for drying** (see opposite).
- **transplant biennials** sown outdoors last month (see Late Spring) to a spare piece of ground, where they can mature until the autumn (see opposite).
- **pot up individual seedlings,** each in a 5–8cm (2–3in) pot, to make eye-catching feature plants for larger containers.
- **thin seedlings,** such as love-in-a-mist (*Nigella damascena*), sown in late spring where they are to flower, to 5–10cm (2–4in) apart according to vigour. Discard spare seedlings, or carefully transplant them and water immediately (see below).
- **keep weeding,** especially in beds of densely planted annuals, where weeds can flower and self-seed unnoticed.

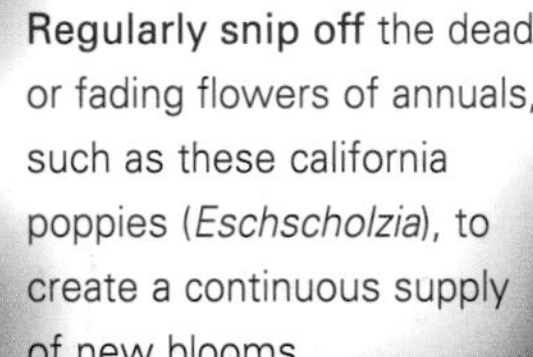

**Regularly snip off** the dead or fading flowers of annuals, such as these california poppies (*Eschscholzia*), to create a continuous supply of new blooms.

## transplanting seedlings

1 **Prick out seedlings** sown in seedbeds or trays in late spring. If they have been growing well they will now need much more space to develop. Handle them carefully by the leaves, and gently tease them apart so that you do not damage their roots. If they really are entangled, place a clump of seedlings with their soil in a large bowl of water; they should be much easier to separate.

2 **Sturdier seedlings can be moved** straight to their final flowering position, but the smaller ones, like these, are best grown on in a spare bed until they are larger. They will respond well to a warm, sheltered, sunny position; make sure that they never dry out.

## *cutting flowers* for drying

'Everlasting' flowers, with a long season, such as statice (*Limonium sinuatum*), helichrysum and helipterum (*Rhodanthe*), sown in March and April, will start to flower in July. Use the earliest young blooms for cutting and drying.

- **cut them off** with a good length of stem as soon as the petals are at their peak, and strip off some lower leaves. Tie in small bundles and hang upside down in a warm, airy place until dry and papery.
- **leave plants** with good seed heads, such as love-in-a-mist (right), until the seed heads form, before cutting.

- **protect young annuals** from slugs and snails, removing these pests by hand. Also deter red spider mites, which strike in hot, dry weather, by misting plants with water.

### planting formal bedding

Most flowers used for formal, organised summer bedding schemes are slightly tender, and cannot be safely planted outdoors until late May, after being acclimatised for a week or two. In an informal bedding scheme the flowers are planted in natural-looking groups and drifts. Work out your colour scheme, and the patterns or shapes you want to create, before preparing the ground.

- Clear the ground of any previous bedding and weeds, lightly fork it over and spread a dressing of granular or powdered general fertiliser. Rake this in, level the bed and remove any stones.
- First plant the tall, showy 'dot' plants, which dominate and catch the eye, where they will be the focus of the display, singly or in small groups, spaced about 1m (3ft) apart. Good examples include fuchsias, heliotropes and pelargoniums grown as standards, as well as cannas, cordylines, castor-oil plants (*Ricinus communis*) and variegated maize.
- Then plant the edging, using dwarf flowers spaced about 10–15cm (4–6in) apart. Try white alyssum, lobelia, marigolds, silver-leaved cinerarias (*Senecio cineraria*) and dwarf phlox.
- Finally, infill the space in between, using flowers of intermediate height, spaced 23–30cm (9–12in) apart, depending on size and vigour. Good plants include pelargoniums, petunias, salvias, bedding dahlias and coleus.
- Water in well after planting, adding a liquid fertiliser to give the plants a flying start.

### transplanting biennials

By July, seedlings of biennials such as wallflowers, forget-me-nots and foxgloves (*Digitalis*) sown in late spring will be clamouring for extra space. Now is the time to thin them out.

- **do this where they are sown**, first to 5cm (2in) apart and later to 10–20cm (4–8in).
- **for larger, sturdier plants,** you can transplant them to a spare, lightly shaded bed that has been forked over with added compost and a dressing of general fertiliser. Plant them in rows 23cm (9in) apart. Space hollyhocks (*Alcea*), foxgloves and other large plants 20cm (8in) apart, most other biennials 10–15cm (4–6in) apart. Pinch out the tips of wallflowers to encourage branching. Water in well, and keep moist during dry weather.

### buying seedlings

If you are not able to sow your own seeds, you can buy seedlings as plug plants from a garden centre. If the weather is warm enough, plant them straight out where they are to flower, or transplant them into individual pots where they can be kept for two weeks before planting them in the ground. Scattering a layer of horticultural grit on the soil surface of seedlings in coldframes deters pests and keeps the soil surface dry, thus eliminating moss.

**Snapdragon seedlings** grown as plugs

### there is still time to . . .

- **sow fast-growing annuals.** Candytuft (*Iberis*), linaria, night-scented stock and annual chrysanthemums will provide an autumn display if sown where they are to flower or grown in a spare piece of ground for transplanting later.
- **sow spring-flowering biennials,** especially brompton stocks (*Matthiola incana*), forget-me-nots and dwarf varieties of wallflowers. Start them off in a spare bed, then plant out in late September.
- **clear away exhausted spring bedding.** Weed and lightly fork the soil, and rake in a dressing of fertiliser. The bed is then ready for summer.

# bulbs & tubers

Summer is a busy bulb season. Some spring bulbs require dividing or storing; summer bulbs need tending; and autumn-flowering bulbs need planting. You can also sow many bulb seeds now, for example if you would like to create your own bluebell wood.

## now is the season to . . .

- **lift, dry and store hyacinths,** tulips and, occasionally, daffodils in a cool, dry place (see below).
- **dig up and divide** overcrowded clumps of daffodils (see opposite) once their foliage has completely died down.
- **plant autumn bulbs** such as colchicums (often called autumn crocuses, which is a misnomer, as they are not crocuses), saffron (*Crocus sativus*) and real autumn-flowering crocuses (see opposite).
- **plant autumn-flowering** *Amaryllis belladonna* 5–8cm (2–3in) deep, close to a warm, sunny wall.
- **plant out young begonias** grown from tubers or cuttings taken in late spring, as soon as the frosts are over.
- **plant out dahlias** grown from seed or cuttings, and mulch.
- **plant out arum lilies** that have flowered indoors, for their annual rest. Stand those grown in pots outdoors in a shallow pool for the summer.
- **feed summer-flowering bulbs** planted in pots and keep moist.
- **water summer bulbs,** such as gladioli, during prolonged dry spells, and mulch them to keep the soil moist.
- **stake large-flowered gladioli** in windy gardens, individually or in small groups (see page 27), particularly if you are growing them for cut flowers.
- **watch for early signs** of pests and diseases, especially serious ailments such as narcissus eelworm, which causes stunting, and lily viruses, signalled by failed flowers and mottled foliage.
- **gradually reduce the water** given to amaryllis (*Hippeastrum*) in pots, to allow the bulbs to rest.
- **hand-weed** between groups of lilies and other bulbs that seed freely, to keep them in large clumps rather than letting them spread. Hoe around clumps to create a dust mulch.
- **start planning** next spring's bulb displays. Since bulbs such as daffodils benefit from being planted in August or September, be ready to order them when the bulb catalogues appear in midsummer.
- **sow bluebells** (*Hyacinthoides*) and other bulbs that grow well from seed, in trays or in a nursery bed (see opposite).

## and if you have time . . .

- **continue deadheading late spring bulbs** as they fade – unless you want to grow more from seed.

## lifting, drying and dividing bulbs

Bedding hyacinths and most hybrid tulips need to be dug up and dried in summer to keep the bulbs in peak condition to replant in autumn. Daffodils benefit from being lifted every few years to prevent overcrowding and reduced flowering.

**One of the earliest lilies to bloom,** *Lilium martagon* var. *album* makes a fantastic clump of startling white flowers. It grows up to 2m (6ft) high, even in light shade, and is trouble free. Weed the surrounding soil well.

**Large clumps** of daffodils can be lifted with a fork and either divided into smaller clusters and replanted immediately, or separated into individual bulbs and dried for storing.

- Once the foliage has completely died down and shrivelled, carefully lift the bulbs with a fork; insert it well away to avoid spearing the bulbs.
- Rub off as much soil as possible, then spread out the bulbs on trays or in shallow boxes lined with newspaper. When they are quite dry, with withered roots and papery skins, trim the roots and remove any loose skin.
- Store the sound bulbs in paper bags or boxes in a cool, dry place. Discard any damaged, soft or discoloured bulbs, as well as very small, young bulblets.

BULB TIP Many daffodil varieties have multiple 'noses' – small offset bulbs produced at the side of the parent. These can be left in place or carefully removed for storing until autumn, when you can plant them in rows in spare ground. Leave until they are larger and have reached flowering size.

## planting autumn bulbs

The small range of autumn-flowering bulbs provides a welcome late show of colour in beds, borders and containers. Plant them in July, 10cm (4in) deep, in informal groups. The soil should have been well forked over, and fed with plenty of garden compost or a high-potash fertiliser for good flowers.

- **colchicums** have large white or mauve, crocus-like blooms; the large leaves appear in spring. The best is *C. speciosum*.
- **autumn crocuses** flower in shades of lilac, blue, purple and white. The leaves appear in spring. *Crocus speciosus* and its varieties are excellent, but there are many other terrific species, such as the scented, lilac *C. goulimyi*.
- **the brilliant, golden-yellow** crocus-like flowers of *Sternbergia lutea* appear in September and October, accompanied by dwarf, strap-shaped leaves.

SAFFRON TIP You do not have to buy expensive saffron – you can grow your own. It comes from *Crocus sativus*, which has rich purple flowers with bright, orange-red stamens that are harvested to produce saffron. This bulb likes very rich conditions and is traditionally grown along the edges of well-manured vegetable beds or fertile herb borders.

## *disbudding* a dahlia

If you have any dahlias with spectacular flowers, it is well worth looking to see if there are smaller buds to each side of the main bud. Removing them channels the plant's energy into making fewer, larger flowers. Subsequent deadheading of faded blooms stimulates further flowering.

If you have any dahlias still at the seedling stage, try pinching out their growing tips to produce bushy plants.

## growing bluebells from seed

Bluebells set masses of black seed, which can be gathered in midsummer from their open seed capsules.

- Sow the seed immediately in rows in a nursery bed, specially created for young plants, or in shallow trays of soil-based compost in a coldframe. Water regularly when dry.
- Prick out the seedlings when they emerge in late winter, or transplant them during spring, about 2–3cm (1in) apart.
- Grow them for another year, then when the leaves die down in their second autumn, plant them out permanently in a moist, shady position.

## there is still time to . . .

- **plant winter-flowering** *Anemone coronaria*, outdoors in mild areas, or in pots or coldframes elsewhere. Bury the bulbs individually, or in small groups, 5cm (2in) deep and 10cm (4in) apart.
- **plant autumn-flowering nerines** (cultivars of *Nerine bowdenii*) just below the surface in a warm, sheltered spot.

## *other bulbs* to sow now

• camassia • crocus • foxtail lilies (*Eremurus*) • fritillaries • *Lilium regale* • lily of the valley (*Convallaria majalis*) • sisyrinchium • snowdrop (*Galanthus nivalis*) • tulips

The lovely *Camassia cusickii* flowers in early summer – and sometimes in a warm late spring too.

# roses

Summer is the season when roses take centre stage. From late June onwards you can enjoy all the different kinds, including those that flower just once a year. All roses need some attention now – especially those that will carry on blooming.

*Rosa* 'Francis E. Lester'

## now is the season to . . .

■ **tie the stems** of young climbing and rambler roses temporarily to supports. This prevents wind damage and keeps the plants tidy. They can be secured permanently in late summer or autumn.

■ **deadhead blooms** as soon as they fade (see below), unless hips are required later in the season.

■ **water newly planted roses** if the weather is dry for more than two weeks. Give each plant 5 litres (2 gallons) of water. Established roses are deep-rooting and relatively drought-tolerant.

■ **regularly water all container-grown roses,** checking the compost daily during hot weather. Add a dilute liquid fertiliser every seven to fourteen days.

■ **apply a summer dressing** of rose fertiliser and lightly hoe or rake it in (see opposite). Do this soon after the longest day. Do not feed roses after the end of July.

■ **disbud hybrid tea** and floribunda varieties for better flowers (see right).

■ **propagate your favourite varieties** from bud cuttings during July (see opposite).

■ **keep weeding,** especially around new roses. Hoe and hand-weed, but avoid forking near plants in case you injure the roots and cause suckers to appear.

■ **remove suckers** immediately, if they appear (see opposite).

■ **spray** a combined insecticide-fungicide at fortnightly intervals if you wish, or need, to take preventative measures against a range of potential problems. In any event, watch out for any signs of mildew, black spot, rust and aphids (see page 72).

■ **move roses in pots outdoors** so that they can rest after flowering. Stand them in a sunny, sheltered place, or put each pot in a planting hole so that the compost will not dry out too rapidly.

■ **cut blooms for indoors** from late June onwards. Remove only from established, strongly growing plants, and cut off no more than a third of the stem, with a sloping cut, just above an outward-facing bud.

## and if you have time . . .

■ **harvest fragrant roses** at their best, then dry the petals in layers in a warm, airy room. Use them as the basis of a potpourri.

■ **remove all fading and fully open flowers** before going on holiday. This prevents hips from developing while you are away, and wasting the plant's energy.

## disbudding roses

Disbudding is the best way to produce top-quality flowers. On hybrid tea varieties cleanly pull off or pinch out the small buds that can form around a central bud. Do this as early as possible to divert all the plant's energy into the single remaining flower and you will get large, fully formed blooms.

Another good idea is to pinch out or snip off the central bud in the flower trusses of floribunda and modern shrub roses. This encourages most of the other buds to open together, creating a better, showier display, and it helps to reduce overcrowding.

## deadheading

The removal of faded blooms is a form of light pruning that prolongs flowering on repeat-flowering roses. It also stops roses from making seed, so do not deadhead species roses and once-flowering roses that produce attractive hips.

• **cut off complete floribunda trusses** with a good length of stem to prevent the bushes from producing numerous thin, unproductive shoots.

Use sharp secateurs for deadheading and make an outward-sloping cut.

• **on hybrid tea roses** remove the faded blooms with a portion of the stem. Cut the stem two to three leaves down from the flower and just above a strong leaf bud. Never remove more than half the shoot because this can delay further flowering.

## feeding roses

While it is not essential to feed roses to get a good display, they will be healthier and more resistant to disease if you do. So give all roses a summer dressing of high-potash or rose fertiliser, sprinkled evenly around the base of the plant. This is the second of two annual feeds (the first being in early spring), and should be given in the first half of July; later feeding causes soft growth, which will not ripen before autumn frosts.

EXTRA FEEDING TIP You can give young roses, and those growing on 'hungry', light soils, an additional liquid boost one month before the main summer feed. Apply onto the soil, or spray as a foliar feed on a cloudy day when it will not immediately evaporate, nor scorch the leaves.

## propagation

Most roses are propagated commercially by budding. This delicate operation joins a bud from a chosen variety onto a wild rose root system (rootstock), which guarantees vigorous growth. This technique requires a lot of skill.

Most gardeners prefer easier methods using cuttings. Many shrub, climbing and rambler roses can be layered or grown from semi-ripe cuttings in summer (see page 43), and most kinds, except hybrid teas, can be grown from hardwood cuttings in September or October (see Late Summer). But you can also try bud cuttings, taken now from most varieties. It takes two years to make substantial young plants and a further season to flower (see above right).

After planting, stand the pots in a coldframe, water well and close the lid. Shade from bright sun, mist the cuttings weekly with water, and give a liquid feed every four to six weeks until late autumn. Keep in the coldframe over winter, and pot up individually into 8cm (3in) pots when growth revives in spring. Water and feed regularly. In early summer, transplant them 30cm (12in) apart in spare ground, and grow for one or two seasons until they are large enough to plant out.

## taking bud cuttings

1 **Cut off a young shoot** about the thickness of a pencil and slice it into sections: cut just above each leaf to produce a number of short pieces, each with a leaf and bud near the top.

2 **Shorten each leaf** to leave just two to three 'leaflets', then dip the base of the cutting in rooting hormone. Insert in a mixture of equal parts grit and perlite with the bud just below the surface. Space four or five cuttings round the edge of a tray or 8cm (3in) pot, without touching.

## there is still time to . . .

• **mulch warm, moist soil** around established rose plants, using a 5–8cm (2–3in) layer of rotted manure, garden compost or lawn mowings that are free from weedkillers.

## dealing with rose suckers

1 **Clear away soil** at the base of the rose to trace a sucker to its origin on the roots. Suckers are vigorous shoots that grow from below ground on grafted roses, and also from the stems of standards.

2 **Tear off the sucker** to prevent regrowth. Cutting with secateurs would only stimulate the rose to produce more suckers.

# climbers

Climbers and wall shrubs grow fast at this time of year, and the fresh new shoots need tying in regularly. Pruning may be necessary to keep plants tidy and encourage more flowers. This is also a good time to raise more of your favourites by taking cuttings.

## now is the season to . . .

- **train and tie in climbers** regularly to produce an attractive display, otherwise many rapidly form a tangled bird's nest of stems that can never be unravelled. Prime candidates for attention are those that climb by means of tendrils or twining leaf stalks, such as clematis, particularly *C. armandii*, and sweet peas (*Lathyrus odoratus*). Use soft string for tying in, not wire.
- **water container-grown climbers** daily unless the weather is very wet. Add a liquid fertiliser to the water once a week over summer, or add slow-release fertiliser to the compost.
- **check climbers against buildings:** even when established they may need watering if the structure keeps off most of the rain.

*Clematis* 'Jackmanii'

The golden hop (*Humulus lupulus* 'Aureus') is a vigorous perennial climber that will quickly clothe a trellis or fence in summer.

- **prune climbers** that have already flowered if next year's blooms are carried on stems produced this summer.
- **plant permanent climbers** and wall shrubs, but remember to water them regularly during dry spells until the autumn.
- **propagate climbers** and wall shrubs (see opposite).
- **pot up rooted cuttings** taken in spring.
- **watch out for clematis wilt.** This disease causes part or all of the clematis to collapse suddenly. You can help your plant to survive an attack by planting it deep, so that the surface of its compost is about 8cm (3in) deep (buds below ground usually survive to shoot and provide replacement growth). Cut back any affected stems to healthy growth.

## pruning

Many climbers and wall shrubs need pruning now to keep them within bounds and to encourage prolific flowering.

- **cut back** *Clematis montana* and its cultivars to keep them within their allotted space. Shorten stems as soon as possible after flowering because next year's blooms are carried on growth produced this summer. To avoid having to prune these rampant climbers, plant the compact cultivar 'Primrose Star', which grows to only 3m (10ft) high.

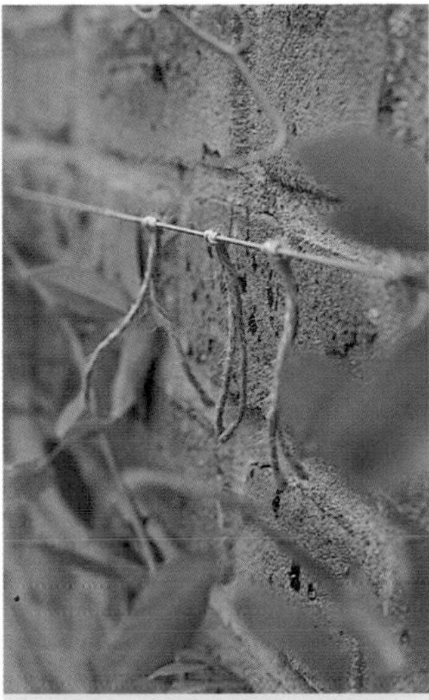

TYING-IN TIP Speed up the training process by attaching string ties to the wires before you start. Move them along as required.

- **prune early flowering honeysuckles,** such as *Lonicera periclymenum* and its cultivars, immediately after flowering. Cut back the flowered stems to strong, young growth to keep the plant neat and bushy.
- **train firethorn** (*Pyracantha*) and flowering quince (*Chaenomeles*) close to their supports. Prune them, and other wall-trained shrubs, immediately after flowering. Cut back all outward-facing shoots to two or three buds and tie in the others.
- **prune wisteria** twice a year, in midsummer (see below left) and again in winter.

## summer-pruning wisteria

1 In midsummer, prune young shoots and any long, whippy growths not required to make new branches, to leave five or six buds.

2 This tidies the overall shape of the wisteria, after which the winter prune reduces sideshoots, leaving three buds on all growth that has appeared since the summer pruning. This pruning regime creates a neat shape and plenty of flowers.

## propagation

Take advantage of the abundant young growth on climbers and wall shrubs to raise new plants from cuttings.

- **propagate small and large-flowered clematis** (but not the very large kind) by taking 8cm (3in) leaf-bud cuttings (see Late Spring). Make the cut between leaf joints, instead of immediately below them as with most other plants.
- **take soft cuttings** of climbers and wall shrubs in early June for the best results (see Late Spring). They should be 10cm (4in) long and have two or three pairs of leaves. Pinch out the top growth, just above a pair of leaves, and remove the lowest leaves. Plant round the edge of a 13cm (5in) pot, filled with cuttings compost, so that the first pair of leaves is just above the surface.
- **pot up any cuttings** taken in late spring once they have rooted. Grow them for six to twelve months in containers, before planting them out.

## there is still time to . . .

- **prune spring-flowering clematis** such as *C. alpina* and *C. macropetala*, if necessary.
- **plant bought annual climbers** such as *Cobaea scandens* or morning glory (*Ipomoea*), though you can easily grow them from seed next spring.

*looking ahead . . .*

☑ LATE SUMMER Pot up cuttings of large-flowered clematis.

☑ WINTER Winter-prune wisteria.

# shrubs & trees

Most trees and shrubs are now covered in bright fresh foliage and, in many cases, are in full flower. To keep them in peak condition, maintain a regular routine of watering, weeding, pruning and pest control.

## now is the season to . . .

- **trim fast-growing hedges** such as privet and lonicera regularly for an immaculate finish.
- **uncover tender shrubs** after the last expected frost, and move outdoors those given winter shelter under glass.
- **water and feed** during prolonged dry weather. Concentrate on freshly planted shrubs and trees, and those being grown in containers (see opposite).
- **eradicate weeds** by hoeing and hand-weeding, particularly around new plants and hedges.
- **support and tie in** the new growth of plants being trained against a wall or trellis.
- **prune shrubs** such as broom (*Cytisus*) and flowering quince (*Chaenomeles*) as soon as they finish flowering (see page 40).
- **prune ornamental plums,** cherries and almonds for shape once they are in full leaf. If you do it when they are dormant they are more susceptible to disease.
- **remove the flowers** from grey-leaved shrubs, like senecio or helichrysum, grown for their foliage or as formal hedges.
- **spur prune** wall-trained chaenomeles and pyracantha in July (see page 41). This thins out any congested tangles of spurs – the clusters of mini branches off the main branches – where the flowers grow.
- **thin out the crowns** of congested broad-leaved trees such as crab apples (*Malus*) and acers that heavily shade plants beneath them (see page 41).
- **pot up or transplant seedlings** from earlier sowings, giving them more space to develop.
- **pot up rooted soft-tip cuttings,** and take more if required using the young sideshoots on established plants.
- **start taking semi-ripe cuttings** from conifers using the mid or late summer growth (see page 43).
- **continue layering plants** such as the smoke bush (*Cotinus*) and magnolias (see Late Spring).
- **watch out for** early signs of pests and diseases, and treat them now before they get serious.

### and if there is time . . .

- **feed hardy fuchsias** once or twice with a high-potash fertiliser to encourage prolific flowering.
- **gather lavender flowers** for drying. Hang the stems up in bundles, or spread on trays of absorbent paper in airy shade.
- **protect exposed hydrangeas** from hot, dry winds with a screen of net curtaining or a similar fine material.

*Robinia pseudoacacia* 'Frisia'

**Slate fragments** make a decorative and effective mulch for trees grown in large pots, reducing moisture loss.

■ **move camellias in containers** out of bright sunshine into partial shade.

■ **start deadheading lilac** (*Syringa*) and later flowering rhododendrons before new shoots begin developing behind the withered flowers.

## watering

Regularly check shrubs, trees and hedges planted earlier in the year, and water if necessary, especially during prolonged dry or windy weather. Limp or lacklustre foliage, and wilting tips, indicate that they desperately need a drink.

- **when watering,** thoroughly soak the ground right round the base of the plant, ideally following with a thick mulch to 'lock' the moisture in the soil. Water early in the morning, or from late afternoon onwards, to avoid the risk of scorching on splashed leaves.
- **add a liquid fertiliser** at the recommended rate when watering new plants, and any that have been hard-pruned or which show signs of poor growth. Apply a foliar feed to the leaves after sunset to give a quick tonic to ailing plants.
- **check plants in containers** daily and move them to a sheltered, lightly shaded position if they dry out rapidly; a mulch of pebbles or gravel helps to prevent moisture loss.

## providing support

Tie in the new growth on plants trained up walls, wire or trellis. This is particularly important for young plants still forming their framework of main branches. Space the main stems out evenly, and secure them with soft string. Also ensure that the shoots are pointing in the right direction; pinch off any that are misplaced before they get too long.

## weeding

Continue to eradicate weeds by hoeing and hand-weeding. This applies particularly to the immediate area around new shrubs, trees and hedges, as they need a couple of seasons without any competition. Keep at least $1m^2$ (1 sq yd) around the base of the plant weed-free by hoeing, spraying or laying a woven mulching mat.

If you plan to make a new bed or border this autumn, it is best to clear the site now and spray it with glyphosate, or a similar chemical, to kill perennial weeds. This gives surviving roots and weed seeds time to regenerate, and be forked out before planting. The traditional, non-chemical method of getting rid of weed roots is to dig the area thoroughly, removing by hand every trace of weeds, including all root fragments.

## acclimatising plants

Now that there is no longer any risk of a late, damaging frost, there are plenty of things to be done.

- **leave the fleece off cold-sensitive shrubs** that were protected from frost at night, now that temperatures are rising.
- **move outdoors any tender shrubs** in containers, such as citrus or oleander (*Nerium*), that were kept under glass during winter. Give them a sunny, sheltered position.
- **check these plants** for any injured or dead stems. Cut them off, together with any unshapely growth.
- **hoe or lightly fork** round the plants, and scatter a balanced fertiliser on the soil surface. Fork it in.

## pests and diseases

Watch out for early signs of pests and diseases, and tackle them before they take hold. Look out for aphids on young conifers, beech (*Fagus*), box and camellias, scale insects and mildew on hebes, blackfly on cherries, and red spider mite on a number of shrubs in very dry weather (see page 72).

**Silver birches look** their best in naturalistic settings, as here in an area of long grass.

# shrubs & trees/2

The beauty bush (*Kolkwitzia*) makes a magnificent early summer display. After flowering it will benefit from having about a third of its growth removed by pruning.

## pruning early flowering shrubs

Shrubs and informal hedges that flower in May and early June, on stems produced the previous year, need annual pruning. This prevents twiggy growth, and sparse blooms next year. It is best done immediately after flowering to allow plenty of time for new growth to develop and ripen before the end of the season. How hard you prune depends on the age, size and condition of the shrub.

### formative pruning

For the first two to three years of a shrub's life, pruning helps form a strong framework of branches and a balanced shape.

- **after planting,** remove any damaged or weak, spindly growth, and lightly trim back the shoot tips to a strong bud, or pair of buds.
- **in the autumn,** cut out any weak shoots and those that unbalance the overall shape.
- **repeat this formative pruning** for the next two years, when you must also prune in midsummer those shoots that carried flowers; cut them back to about 5cm (2in) long.

### renewal pruning

This is the simplest way to maintain a compact shape and a vigorous supply of young, floriferous growth on shrubs that are over about three years old. It is often called the one-third prune (see below).

## early flowering shrubs to prune now

• beauty bush (*Kolkwitzia*) • *Berberis darwinii* • ceanothus (evergreen) • chaenomeles • cytisus • deutzia • escallonia • flowering currant (*Ribes*) • kerria • Mexican orange blossom (*Choisya*) • mock orange (*Philadelphus*) • pyracantha • winter-flowering viburnums • weigela

## the one-third prune

1 **As soon as the flowers fade,** it is time to prune away a third of a leafy overgrown shrub.

2 **Cut out any weak,** spindly shoots and stems that cross or crowd each other out. Use a sharp pair of secateurs.

### spur pruning chaenomeles and pyracantha

When trained on a wall, either growing freely or pruned as a fan or espalier, these shrubs will need spur pruning. This maintains their shape and maximises flowering.

- **about two weeks before midsummer,** remove all crossing or inward growing shoots, and shorten those growing away from the wall, to leave four to six leaves. This encourages the formation of flowering shoots and, in the case of pyracantha, exposes the colourful berries.
- **in early autumn,** further shorten the pruned shoots, leaving two to three leaves on each.

### pruning broom

If broom (*Cytisus*) is left unpruned it becomes top-heavy and short-lived. It is best to prune young plants in early summer.

- **pinch out the growing tips** of young plants to keep them bushy and cut back the current year's growth by half immediately after flowering to control the shrub's size. Never prune into woody growth as this can kill the plant.

### pruning evergreen ceanothus

Evergreen varieties are often injured by frosts unless grown against a sunny, sheltered wall, where they need regular pruning to maintain their shape and vigour. The majority bloom in spring or early summer, and need pruning immediately afterwards.

- Trim back the shoots growing away from the wall, on which the flowers have just finished, to about 10cm (4in) from their base. Where they meet older main branches, do not cut into these because the main branches do not readily produce new shoots.
- Tie any stems growing sideways against the wall.
- Check again in early autumn, and shorten any excessively long new shoots.

3 **Remove a proportion** of the oldest branches just above ground level or to a low, strong sideshoot. You may need to use a pruning saw for this.

4 **Aim to remove a third** of the growth annually, so that no branch on the shrub is more than three years old. This will admit light to the shrub and maintain a good shape.

### *pruning* Viburnum plicatum 'Mariesii'

With its branches arranged in horizontal tiers, *Viburnum plicatum* 'Mariesii' needs careful pruning to maintain its striking architectural shape.

- **as soon as** the flowers fade in early summer, cut off any dead or injured growth.
- **then remove** any misplaced branches growing up or in towards the centre of the shrub, to create clear layers.
- **shorten sideshoots** on the main branches, to leave two to three leaves on each.

## crown thinning

A broad-leaved tree with a dense or cluttered canopy of branches may cast so much shade that little will grow beneath it. The technique of crown thinning is used to remove several branches, creating greater penetration of air and light, without altering the tree's size and shape.

Tall trees should be thinned by a qualified tree surgeon, but on a smaller tree you can do this yourself. Do the work in midsummer to assess how much the shade is reduced, and because re-growth will be less vigorous than after winter surgery. The following winter, check to see whether further light pruning is needed to improve the balance and symmetry of the bare branches.

- Start by cutting out dead, damaged and diseased wood, followed by any branches that cross or rub against each other. Also cut out branches that grow across or into the centre of the tree.
- Reduce pairs of branches that form narrow angles to a single, strong branch. If necessary, trim back any low branches creating an obstruction at head height, and any that are too long, unbalanced or too close to others.
- Aim to remove no more than a third of healthy branches.

# shrubs & trees/3

## propagation

Close to midsummer, the garden will be full of young growth that can be used as cuttings, creating new plants by autumn or the following spring. You can take several kinds of cuttings, while many shrubs can be layered where they grow by pegging branches down in the soil (see Late Spring).

### soft-tip cuttings

These are the soft tips taken from main stems and sideshoots. They may be rooted in covered pots or trays, in the greenhouse or on a windowsill (see Late Spring).

### semi-ripe cuttings

The sideshoots on shrubs that started growing early in the season are forming woody tissue at their base by midsummer. You can feel this as a slight firmness when you gently bend a shoot with your fingers. Cuttings from these shoots take a little longer to root than soft cuttings, but are less likely to dry out or to rot if conditions are too wet.

Semi-ripe cuttings are normally prepared with the aid of rooting hormone powder or liquid, and are grown in containers or in the ground under a cloche or in a coldframe. Choose a warm, sunny or lightly shaded position. A sheet of bubble polythene makes an excellent cloche cover. Alternatively, coat glass cloches and glazed coldframes with a thin speckling of greenhouse shade paint.

### shrubs to propagate under cloches

• box • buddleja • deutzia • elaeagnus • escallonia • flowering currant (*Ribes*) • forsythia • hebe • hyssop • kerria • potentilla • privet (*Ligustrum*) • st john's wort (*Hypericum*) • tamarisk • viburnum • weigela

• **fork over the soil** where the cuttings are to go. Remove all weeds and stones, rake level and cover the surface with a 2–3cm (1in) layer of grit and perlite, in equal parts. Mix this into the top 5cm (2in) of soil with a hand fork. Prepare and plant the cuttings (see opposite), then cover them with a cloche or close the coldframe.

• **check after four to six weeks** to see if there is rooting and new growth. If there is, raise the lid or side of the cloche a little to let in some air. Keep the cuttings moist by watering, and mist occasionally with a spray in very hot weather. Rooted cuttings that are growing vigorously may be moved to a 'nursery bed' or spare

**Closely planted rows of semi-ripe cuttings** – from left, senecio, euonymus, yew and box – ready to overwinter in a coldframe.

## *taking semi-ripe cuttings of lavender*

1 **Prepare the cuttings** by gently pulling off 10cm (4in) long sideshoots. This will leave a short 'heel' of tissue at the base, where it is torn from the main stem. Trim the heel with a sharp knife to give a clean edge, and remove all except the top five to ten leaves. Dip the base of the cuttings in hormone powder, and shake off any surplus.

2 **Use a dibber** to make holes in the soil or cuttings compost. Insert the cuttings, 5cm (2in) deep and 5cm (2in) apart, in rows in the ground, or round the rim of a 13cm (5in) pot; firm in.

3 **Water in well,** and cover with a cloche or the lid of a coldframe or propagator. Keep closed, but check weekly to see that the soil is not drying out.

piece of ground in autumn, but it is generally safer to wait until next spring before replanting the cuttings 30cm (12in) apart. Plant the young plantlets out permanently the following autumn.

### conifer cuttings

Conifers are also easily raised by semi-ripe cuttings. Follow the technique below.

• Take semi-ripe cuttings, 5–8cm (2–3in) long, each with a 'heel'. Nip off the sideshoots from the lower half of the cutting, and carefully trim the bark from one side of the lower 2–3cm (1in) with a sharp knife.

**Conifer cuttings** planted up into cans.

• Root them with the aid of hormone powder and plant 1cm (½in) deep in small pots filled with a mixture of equal parts grit and perlite.

• Keep the cuttings covered in a propagator, or with a clear plastic bag, and stand them in a warm but shady part of the greenhouse or on a windowsill. New growth should be visible by mid autumn. If they have failed to root, a further batch of cuttings may then be taken in exactly the same way.

### azalea cuttings

Some lime-hating plants need slightly different treatment when it comes to propagation. Follow this easy approach for acid-loving plants such as japanese azaleas, enkianthus, gaultheria, kalmia, vaccinium and pieris.

• Take cuttings of 5cm (2in) sideshoots and root in a coldframe or gently heated propagator in a greenhouse.

• Prepare them as for other semi-ripe cuttings (see left) and insert them 1cm (½in) deep in small pots filled with a mixture of equal parts lime-free grit and perlite.

• Water well and keep in a closed coldframe or lidded propagator until late autumn. Then transfer to a cool but frost-free bench in the greenhouse.

• Feed with a high-potash liquid fertiliser in early spring. When new shoots appear in early summer, pot them up individually in lime-free compost.

## there is still time to ...

• **prune forsythia,** cutting the flowered shoots almost back to their base. Thin out the older, overcrowded stems on more mature plants.

• **plant container-grown shrubs and trees,** but try to do this before the weather really heats up.

### *success* with rooting hormone

• **never dip cuttings** into the main container: pour a little of the hormone into a dish, and discard any left over after use.

• **keep rooting powder** or liquid in the fridge for prolonged life, and replace annually with a fresh supply.

• **insert only the bottom tip** of the cutting in the hormone, shaking or tapping off any surplus.

# alpine gardens

Summer is a relatively quiet time in the alpine garden, enabling you to enjoy its beauty without having to work too hard. Most tasks consist of tidying and deadheading, but summer is also an excellent time to try propagating some of your favourite alpines.

## *now is the season to . . .*

■ **tackle any potential weed problems** immediately, before they begin to spread, set seed, and start to detract from the display (see below).

■ **keep deadheading** to promote a longer show of flowers. Remove faded blooms and, if plants have become 'leggy', with thin, gangly bare stems, cut them off completely to promote fresh, replacement growth. If you plan to collect seed later, leave some stems untouched to allow their capsules to ripen.

In this small rock garden, dwarf conifers create the framework while flowering plants include meconopsis, aubrieta and gentians.

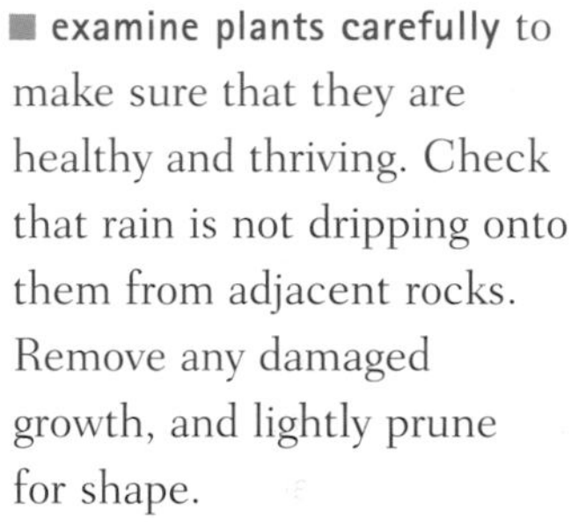

■ **examine plants carefully** to make sure that they are healthy and thriving. Check that rain is not dripping onto them from adjacent rocks. Remove any damaged growth, and lightly prune for shape.

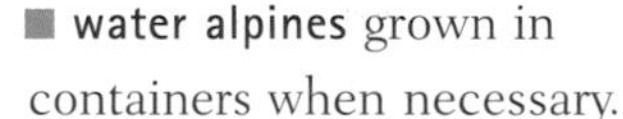

■ **water alpines** grown in containers when necessary.

■ **increase the shading** if you are growing alpines under glass, as the summer temperatures rise.

Houseleeks (*Sempervivum*) are easy to propagate from individual rosettes.

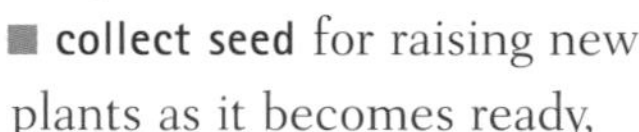

■ **collect seed** for raising new plants as it becomes ready, enabling you to build up a good show of your favourites (see opposite).

■ **take cuttings** to raise more new plants (see opposite).

■ **pot up young plants** grown from cuttings in spring.

■ **fill any gaps** with colourful pinks (*Dianthus*) and houseleeks (*Sempervivum*).

### and if you have time . . .

■ **occasionally, lightly feed alpines** growing in containers.

## eradicating weeds

To a great extent, alpine gardening is small-scale precision gardening, and the rocks, stones and plants need to be thoughtfully placed to produce a good show. But that display can easily be ruined by an invasion of weeds. It is vital that you tackle troublesome weeds promptly, not least because if they scatter their seeds the problem will become even worse. Remove any weeds on the surface compost of containers too.

• **the small, virulent hairy bittercress** can easily lurk behind rocks or under the leaves of plants, so keep an eye out for this. Its tiny, explosive pods scatter seed surprisingly widely, and each seed germinates, grows and flowers within a few weeks. A single plant can cause a widespread infestation in a frighteningly short time.

• **troublesome perennial weeds** pose another problem because their roots run deep, sometimes beneath the rocks, making them difficult to eradicate. Wild species, such as ground

### *taking soft-tip* cuttings of alpines

Remove healthy, non-flowering stem tips, up to 8cm (3in) long. Cut them off just below a leaf joint or node, and trim off their lower leaves. If you have a propagator, rooting will be quick, but at this time of year it is easy to root most potted cuttings in any sheltered spot.

Fill a 9cm (3½in) pot with an equal mix of free-draining compost and horticultural grit or perlite, and insert the cuttings around the sides (see page 43). Water thoroughly and leave them in a warm place; with luck, the cuttings will root in about six weeks.

elder, lesser bindweed and celandine, are problematic, but certain cultivated rock plants can be equally annoying unless carefully controlled. Consequently, plants with creeping stems or rootstocks, such as acaena, some of the campanulas, particularly *C. poscharskyana*, and creeping jenny (*Lysimachia nummularia*), need to be grown with care, keeping their spread under control.

WEED CONTROL TIP Handle free-seeding weeds, such as groundsel, gently, to avoid accidentally spreading the seed, and do not let them hang over the sides of your wheelbarrow or gardening trug when transporting them away.

## watering and feeding

It is unnecessary to water a rock garden in all but the driest years, but the compost in pots holding alpines can dehydrate. Give them an occasional, thorough soaking. Intervals between watering will vary according to weather conditions, but once a week should be enough, even in the driest summer.

In the wild, alpines grow in rocky crevices or in poor soil and do not respond well to feeding. But container-grown alpines might benefit from minimal feeding once a year, using slow-release fertiliser or a light dressing of a high-phosphorous fertiliser, such as bone meal.

## propagating alpines

The propagation of alpines and rock garden plants can be enormously satisfying and is by far the most economical way to produce more stock.

- **some plants, such as pinks,** primroses (*Primula*), and aquilegias are easy to grow from seed. Check the ripening seed capsules and, when a couple have begun to open, remove the whole stem and place it headfirst in a clean, dry envelope: as the other capsules open, the seed collects in the envelope. Store in a cool, dry place and sow either straight away or in early autumn.

SEED TIP A good way to keep seeds is in the small, semi-transparent envelopes used by stamp collectors. These envelopes can be sealed and inserted into larger ones to keep out light; write on the plant's name and the date.

- **spring and early summer** are excellent seasons for taking soft-tip cuttings from alpines such as penstemon, viola and anthemis (see left).
- **when dividing** certain alpines, such as campanulas, pinks and *Daphne cneorum*, it is best to separate them in autumn, but get them off to a good start now by applying compost to stimulate extra root production at the base of the stems on the parent plant.

**Put a handful of** gritty compost all round the base of clumps to be divided later.

### *potting up young plants*

**1 Cuttings taken in spring** should be ready for potting up now. Remove them from the propagator and gently separate the rooted cuttings.

**2 Transplant each plant** into its own pot, filled with free-draining compost. Choose a pot that comfortably matches the size of the plant's rootball – with alpines that is unlikely to exceed 8cm (3in). Stand hardy plants outdoors, ready for planting in a few weeks.

# water gardens

Ponds and other water features are at their most enjoyable in early summer. This is the best time to divide water lilies and introduce fish, but blanket weed and duckweed need to be controlled.

## now is the season to . . .

■ **deadhead flowering plants** in pond and bog gardens once a week, and remove any yellowing leaves. Gather up the debris so it does not rot down and pollute the pond.
■ **weed bog gardens regularly,** by hand rather than by hoe so primulas and other plants can self-seed.
■ **control blanket weed and duckweed,** which grow very fast in warm weather (see opposite).

■ **raise submersible pumps on bricks** to prevent them from sucking up debris from the bottom of the pond.
■ **clean pump filters** every couple of weeks by removing them and rinsing in clean water.
■ **top up ponds** and other water features in hot weather. Use collected rainwater if possible rather than nutrient-rich tap water, which will encourage undesirable green algae.
■ **thin oxygenating plants** by cutting back growth little and often. Pile the trimmings by the pond's edge for a few days so pond creatures can creep back into the water.
■ **add tender floating plants** such as water chestnut (*Trapa natans*) and water lettuce (*Pistia stratiotes*). If these are introduced into the pond before June they may suffer damage from cold and frost.
■ **lift and divide water lilies and irises.**
■ **deal with 'green water'** if this condition, caused by algae, persists. It commonly occurs in late spring, but usually disappears in summer once plants are growing strongly. If it does not, try adding more plants, primarily water lilies, to shade about a third of the pond's surface, and oxygenating plants to take up nutrients that the algae would otherwise feed on. Take care not to over-feed fish, which would add surplus nutrients to the pond.
■ **introduce fish** in summer when the water is warm (see page 133). Float the bag of newly purchased fish in the pond for half an hour so the temperature inside the bag stabilises to match that of the pond. Open it to let some pond water in, and allow the fish to swim out a few minutes later.
■ **give fish somewhere to hide** from predators by putting one or two lengths of drainpipe in the pond.
■ **feed fish daily,** giving only as much food as they will eat in about half an hour.

## water lilies

At this time of year, water lilies need extra attention and may suffer from several problems. Catch these early by inspecting leaves regularly. You can divide water lilies now (see opposite).

- **thin overcrowded leaves** using secateurs. If the leaves are being pushed out of the water, the variety is too vigorous for the size of pond. Water lilies vary enormously in vigour, from dwarf varieties suitable for a container pond to fast-growing ones that need a small lake.
- **continue to lower baskets** of water lilies planted in late spring until they sit on the bottom of the pond.

**Water-lily leaves** shade the pond surface while a variety of flowering and foliage plants, including a variegated iris, bring interest and colour.

## keeping the pond clear

Duckweed and blanket weed spread rapidly in warm weather. Blanket weed, resembling green cotton wool, looks unsightly and chokes water plants. Duckweed becomes hazardous if it is allowed to cover the water completely; apart from blocking light and oxygen, it appears to be a firm surface. Try these methods to keep the water clear.

**Sink pads** of barley straw or lavender stalks in the water; they will slow weed growth as they rot down. Use straw in small ponds and lavender in large ones.

**Thin out** any overgrown plants on the pond's surface by hand, so sufficient water is left clear. The oxygenating canadian pondweed (*Elodea*) helps control blanket weed but can spread rapidly.

**Pull blanket weed out** by hand or by carefully twirling it round a rake or bamboo cane.

**Use a net,** such as a child's fishing net, to remove duckweed from the surface of the pond.

- **look out for** water-lily aphids and water-lily beetle. The beetle comes in two forms: brown adults, 1cm (½in) long, and black grubs. Control these pests by removing the worst affected leaves. Then weigh down the remaining leaves with pieces of wood sufficiently heavy to hold the leaves under the water, so that pond creatures can feast on the pests.
- **water-lily leaf spot** may appear during warm, damp weather. These spots will eventually rot away, leaving holes in the leaves. Control the disease by removing the affected leaves.

*looking ahead . . .*

☑ LATE SUMMER Top up water during hot weather.
☑ Thin out overcrowded marginals and oxygenators.

### propagation

Early summer is the time to split and rejuvenate some of the most popular pond plants.

- **lift and divide water lilies** that are several years old (see Late Spring). Carefully remove them from their baskets and wash any soil off the fleshy rootstock. Cut the outer branches off the rootstock using a sharp knife and discard the old central portion. Dust cut surfaces with yellow sulphur powder to prevent fungal infection. Plant the divisions individually in mesh baskets lined with hessian, or fine-mesh baskets that do not need lining, and filled with aquatic compost. Top with a layer of fine gravel to prevent the soil from floating away. Water well by soaking in a bowl of pond water until no more air bubbles are produced, before replacing in the pond.
- **divide irises** that have formed large clumps, immediately after flowering.

### there is still time to . . .

- **feed established pond plants** with aquatic fertiliser if this was not done in spring.
- **put in new plants** by midsummer.

*Trollius chinensis*

# patios & containers

This is the season to enjoy your patio. Rearrange the containers to create different colour combinations, give scented plants a prominent position, and make sure there is room for exciting last-minute purchases.

## *now is the season to . . .*

- **hang up baskets** and stand out pots of tender bedding, but make sure they are acclimatised (hardened off) first.
- **water all plants in containers,** and mulch raised beds to conserve moisture (see page 150).
- **keep deadheading** for prolonged flowering (see below).
- **regularly feed plants** in hanging baskets and other containers for optimum performance (see opposite).
- **give all plants a regular check,** even if it means getting on your hands and knees, to make sure they really are healthy. Look under the leaves where aphids might be lurking, and examine the stems closely.
- **check under large planters** from time to time to see that ants are not marching in through the drainage holes, creating nests in the compost.
- **group together pots** and tubs of flowering plants, to create eye-catching combinations.
- **put scented plants** in a sheltered, sunny position by seating areas or near open windows.
- **remove a paving slab** on a patio for planting scented herbs, such as thyme (see right).
- **leave room for impulse buys** to jazz up a raised bed or a container grouping (see right).
- **fill any unintentional gaps.**

For an extravagant globe of colour, water hanging baskets daily and feed weekly. In hot weather they dry out very quickly and may need watering twice a day.

## planting thyme

Plant a few permanent thymes in full sun in the patio itself. Their essential oils will be released when they are trodden on.

- **lift a slab** and dig out the soil to a spade's depth. Replace it with a mix of topsoil, compost and horticultural sand for good drainage.
- **plant spreading,** creeping thymes (which can also be planted in the cracks between paving) or taller species that can be pruned to give a rounded shape. Arrange the container-grown plants behind the thymes.

**Plant creeping thyme** between the slabs in a paved patio; they will release their scent when walked over.

## impulse buys

When planting up a patio scheme for containers or a raised bed, do not worry if there are gaps. You will always find a special plant to tempt you at the garden centre or a flower show, possibly something tender or quite flamboyant.

If you buy a tender plant, such as a lemon tree, bear in mind that the conditions on your patio might be cooler and windier than the protected environment in which the plant has been growing and you should acclimatise it gradually.

CITRUS TREE TIP To encourage young potted lemon trees to build up a good framework of branches, remove the flower buds. If they are allowed to flower, the seed heads will develop into lemons and the plant will put all its energy into fruit production, whereas in these early years you want the plant to extend its root, stems and leaf growth. When it has reached a decent size, allow it to produce one lemon, then, as it gets bigger, a few more. When it has reached the height you require, let it flower and fruit all it wants.

## deadheading

Promptly snipping off fading or dead flowers does two things. It gets rid of insipid colours that detract from the overall display, and it ensures that plants channel their energy into creating more beautiful flowers instead of developing the seed heads.

- **deadhead patio roses** quite severely after blooming, removing entire flower sprays.
- **radically cut back violas, most geraniums,** campanulas and convolvulus to promote a second flush of bloom.

REVIVAL TIP After cutting the growth back, give the plants a thorough watering and a light application of plant food, such as a dilute liquid feed. This will stimulate new growth and plenty of flowers.

## feeding container plants

Regular summer feeding is essential for plants growing in containers or they will develop pale leaves and, ultimately, perform badly.

- **if you have not added a slow-release** fertiliser at planting time, start feeding now, every 7–14 days. Use a high-nitrogen fertiliser for newly planted baskets and containers (see page 152). Swap to a tomato feed after three weeks, to encourage flowering until autumn. Do not exceed the manufacturer's recommended dose, or the concentration of chemicals will do more harm than good.
- **use a liquid feed** or slow-release fertiliser sticks or capsules.

## watering and mulching

Plants in pots and raised beds need regular watering.

- **soak pots and baskets** at least once a day in warm weather, until the water runs out of the drainage holes.
- **use a moisture-retaining gel,** available from garden centres, to help prevent the compost in pots and baskets from drying out too quickly. The gel holds water which is then available when the plant needs it.
- **conserve moisture in raised beds,** where the soil can remain dry to a surprising depth, by adding a thick layer of mulch (see Late Spring). Use home-made garden compost, especially if it is bulky and fibrous. Grass clippings are an alternative, though they may look rather too unsightly for use on a patio. If you do not have a source of home-produced mulch, most garden centres sell bags of bark chippings and coco husks. Thereafter check to see when watering is required. Organic mulches are porous and let rain through.

**Brighten up container displays** with floriferous bedding plants such as pelargoniums, penstemon, verbena or phygelius, which will provide pretty colours right through to autumn.

**This all-green patio planting** displays an astonishing range of shapes and leaf textures. A pair of standard catalpas rise above clipped box, ferns, grasses and the dramatic ornamental rhubarb.

# lawns

As the days become warmer and longer, the lawn demands more of your time to keep it green and lush, with mowing the dominant task. The key to easy mowing is frequency: little and often gives the best results.

## now is the season to . . .

- **increase mowing** to about twice a week, as the grass will be growing rapidly (see opposite).
- **control lawn weeds** by raking or applying a weedkiller (see opposite).
- **clear moss** early in the season with an application of lawn sand containing sulphate of iron. In dry weather, water the lawn first so the lawn sand will stick to the moss. As it dies the moss will turn black then brown, at which stage you can rake it out using a fan-shaped rake. Burn or bin the dead moss; do not compost it.
- **trim lawn edges** after mowing. Use a pair of long-handled shears or an electric edger to save bending and to cut close to the lawn edge, removing the untidy fringe of grass.
- **feed the lawn regularly** to compensate for frequent mowing, which can starve the grass. In summer give an application of high-nitrogen fertiliser to keep the grass green, healthy and growing rapidly. Two days after mowing, and when the soil is moist, apply a granular feed and water it in (see page 152).
- **water the lawn** in dry periods (see opposite).
- **scarify the grass** if it feels soft and spongy to walk on; this is usually a sign that a layer of dead grass and clippings, or 'thatch', has formed. Use a fan-shaped rake in a vigorous combing action to clear off the dead material so that water and fertiliser can penetrate to the grass roots.

**However small the lawn,** regular mowing, watering and feeding are essential to keep the green sward looking its best.

**Move objects** standing on the lawn often to prevent pale patches from forming.

## mowing

When you mow, aim to remove only the top third of the growth. Fine lawns need frequent mowing, with a cutting height of about 1–2cm (½–¾in). Regular close mowing keeps out the coarser grass and weeds that could otherwise smother fine grasses.

• **change direction** each time you mow to prevent the mower from forming ruts and ridges in the lawn. This will also make it easier for you to mow off taller weeds and any grass flower stalks.

• **in dry conditions** let the grass grow longer, and raise your mower blade to a slightly higher setting, 2–3cm (1in) for fine lawns. The extra length will help to shade grass roots and reduce stress due to water loss.

• **during long periods** of dry weather mow less frequently – about once every seven to ten days should suffice. By leaving a greater leaf area on each plant you are reducing the pressure on it to produce more growth in order to feed itself.

MOSS TIP Moss in the lawn is usually a symptom of poor drainage, heavy shade, an acid soil or of mowing too closely and leaving bare patches, where moss will quickly establish. Killing the moss is only a temporary measure, because if you fail to resolve the original source of the problem, the moss will always return.

## weeding

The best way to eradicate spreading weeds, especially over a large area, is to make regular applications of lawn weedkiller in conjunction with frequent mowing. Remember that plants 'drink', rather than 'eat', so any product not already diluted must be accompanied by sufficient liquid to enable it to be taken up through the roots. For this reason water your lawn thoroughly after each application if no heavy rain falls within two to three days. Other useful techniques include:

• **before mowing, rake the grass** to lift weeds like speedwell and yarrow. This enables the cutting blade to slice off their top growth.

• **dig out tap-rooted weeds,** like dandelions, with an old knife or a special tool known as a grubber, to a depth of at least 7–8cm (3in) below soil level. Alternatively, spot-treat such weeds with a herbicide stick.

**Sprinklers look effective** but can be wasteful and imprecise, whereas a hose (inset) delivers water exactly where it is needed.

## watering

Turf can lose about 2–3cm (1in) of water every square metre over a period of one week in hot summer weather. To replace this you need to apply about 25 litres (4 gallons) of water for every square metre of lawn. Using a lawn sprinkler is inexact in delivering water and can be wasteful in view of the volume lost to evaporation. A more effective method is to place a seep or soaker hose on the lawn, connected to a tap, and leave it oozing water for at least half an hour (an hour in dry weather). Then move it to another site 1m (3ft) away and repeat the process. This allows water to penetrate the soil to a good depth, encouraging the grass to root down. If you can, water in the evening to minimise what is lost through evaporation.

*looking ahead . . .*

☑ AUTUMN Improve poor drainage by aerating and top dressing.

☑ WINTER Lime lawns on acid soil if required.

# fruit

This is the season for soft fruit, with luscious strawberries, raspberries and currants ripening on a daily basis. Enjoy the harvest, but do not overlook the routine jobs of weeding, watering, mulching and problem control.

## now is the season to . . .

- **water all kinds of fruit** except the largest trees, and mulch to conserve moisture.
- **check ties and supports** on all tree fruit. Stems swell quickly during summer, and ties may need loosening to prevent constriction.
- **keep newly planted fruits** free of weeds by hoeing, hand-weeding or spraying. Those planted in grass establish faster if surrounded by clear soil for the first two years.
- **clear up** and dispose of any fruitlets that fall prematurely, especially if they have holes or signs of damage, as these are probably victims of pest attack.
- **summer-prune** fruits trained as cordons, fans and espaliers, starting with gooseberries and red currants in late June, and finishing with apples at the end of July (see page 54).
- **prune wall-trained figs** by shortening half of all new sideshoots to about six leaves and tie in to training wires those left unpruned. Rub or nip off any shoots growing towards the wall, and shorten the breastwood (shoots growing out from the wall) to three leaves.
- **train grape vines** by tying in new growth to training wires. On fruiting vines, pinch out shoot tips two leaves beyond a truss of flowers or fruit, and the tips of any further sideshoots after one leaf.
- **stop picking rhubarb** by mid July, to give plants time to recover before winter.
- **thin heavy sets of fruit** to prevent overcropping and the risk of breaking laden branches (see page 54).
- **cover ripening fruit with nets** to guard against birds and squirrels, unless already protected by a fruit cage.
- **watch for pests and diseases** and treat them at the first signs, or use appropriate deterrent measures to keep them at bay (see pages 54, 55 and 73).
- **feed alpine strawberries** every two or three weeks with a high-potash fertiliser once they start cropping.

### and if you have time . . .

- **propagate blackberries** and hybrid berries in July by layering new canes. Bury the tip of a cane in the soil and peg down with a wire loop. Keep moist, and layers should be ready for transplanting in autumn.

**Pick cherries** as soon as they ripen, before the birds eat them.

*harvesting* now

• blackcurrants • early peaches and nectarines • early plums • gooseberries • raspberries • red currants (above) • late rhubarb • strawberries • sweet cherries • white currants

## harvesting fruit

• **check ripening fruits regularly** and harvest while they are dry and in peak condition, preferably in the morning. This is particularly important for strawberries, but any over-ripe or rotting fruit encourages diseases.

• **strawberries crop** from late May to late July, according to variety. They ripen very quickly in hot weather, so check daily and gather all berries that are fully coloured. Pick them with the stalk, and avoid handling the berries as they bruise easily. Remove all diseased and damaged fruits.

• **gooseberries need thinning** during June, so pick green fruits for cooking until well-spaced berries ripen, from early July onwards. Pick fully ripened berries carefully, as they are soft and burst easily. Crops ripen unevenly, so check over the bushes several times a week.

• **red and white currants ripen** from early July, when they are shiny and with a good colour. Pick whole strings of fruit and remove individual currants back in the kitchen with a table fork. You may need to go over the plants two or three times. In cool, dry weather the ripe berries will often hang quite happily on the bushes for several weeks without deteriorating.

• **blackcurrants** are ready from early or mid-July, when the fruits are a shiny blue-black. Either pick individual currants or wait a week or so, then harvest clusters as for red currants.

• **raspberries** start to ripen during July. They are ready to pick when they are well coloured and part easily from the remains of the flower. Handle with care for these fruits are soft and easily damaged.

• **sweet cherries** are ripe in June. Harvest as soon as they are fully coloured, but test one or two first for flavour. Pick with the stalk, using scissors or secateurs, and use immediately.

• **the first plums** ripen towards the end of July. Test well-coloured fruits to see if they come away easily from the stalk and then check every two or three days, as crops do not ripen all together.

• **early peaches and nectarines** are ripe in July. Check if the flesh around the stalk is soft, then lift the fruit gently in the palm of your hand. If ready, it will come away easily from the stalk. Fruit ripens progressively over several weeks.

## there is still time to . . .

• **tuck straw or mats** round strawberry plants before their ripening fruit can touch the soil.

• **mulch gooseberries** as a precaution against mildew.

**A heavy crop of** raspberries can be supported on a wooden frame.

# fruit/2

## *special fruit care*

The best-quality tree fruits are the result of careful thinning and summer pruning, which aids ripening as well as next year's cropping potential. Now is also the time to clear up strawberry beds and prepare new ones.

### tree fruit

- **apples** and, to a lesser degree, pears shed some surplus fruits in late June and early July, the so-called 'June drop'. Further thinning is usually necessary to ensure large, good quality fruit. Snip off misshapen and damaged fruits with scissors in mid June. After the June drop, thin the remaining fruits to leave one or, at the most, two fruits in each cluster, to achieve a final spacing of about 10cm (4in) apart for dessert varieties and 15cm (6in) for culinary kinds.

**Twist the stems** to remove damaged and surplus apples, to leave two in each cluster.

- **thin plums** to 5–8cm (2–3in) apart in early June, and prop up heavily laden branches to prevent breakage.

**Use secateurs** to shorten the sideshoots on trained apples and pears in mid to late July.

- **summer-prune apples and pears** trained as bushes, cordons, espaliers and fans, to keep the branch structure open and stimulate next year's fruit buds. Shorten new sideshoots growing from main branches to about five leaves, and those emerging from existing fruit spurs to one leaf; leave the growing tips at the end of branches untouched. Prune pears in mid July and apples slightly later.
- **prune plums and sweet cherries** trained on walls between late June and late July. Shorten new sideshoots by a third, but leave shoots at the ends of branches unpruned. After fruiting, these pruned shoots should be further shortened to three leaves.
- **hang pheromone traps** in apple and plum trees to help to control and monitor various moth pests.

### bush fruit

As crops of gooseberries and currants develop, avoid overwatering as this can cause fruit to split, but make sure the plants do not suffer from drought. Mulching the plants is a sound precaution against drying out.

- **start summer-pruning gooseberries** and red or white currants in early or mid June. This opens up plants to fresh air, exposes fruit to sunlight and removes soft tips that attract aphids and mildew. Shorten all new sideshoots to about five leaves, but leave the main growing tips unpruned.
- **prune blackcurrants** after the last fruits are picked, or delay until winter. As the best crops are borne on young stems, encourage new growth by cutting out some of the old branches, to just above ground level or to a strong low sideshoot. Aim to remove a third of the branches each year, starting with the oldest and darkest.
- **watch out for reversion** of blackcurrants, indicated by a thick crop of coarse, narrow nettle-like leaves with fewer points on their edges than normal. This is an incurable virus infection, and bushes must be dug up and burned.
- **check gooseberries** for the small 'looper' caterpillars of sawflies. Spray with insecticide or hose off with water.
- **cut off gooseberry shoots** that show signs of mildew.

### cane fruit

- **keep cane fruits under control,** otherwise they can get untidy and spread where they are not wanted.

**Early plums** will need further pruning after they have fruited.

• **tie in new canes of blackberries** and hybrid berries in a temporary bundle (see below).

• **tie in canes of autumn-fruiting raspberries,** spacing them about 10cm (4in) apart on their wires, either individually or by looping a continuous length of string round each cane and over the wire.

• **pull out raspberry suckers** growing out of line while they are small.

• **raspberry beetles** can be troublesome when the maggots hatch out in blackberries and hybrid berries, as well as raspberries. Treat with derris, spraying in the evening when bees are not about. Spray blackberries and hybrid berries when their flowers open, and raspberries when the first berries start to colour and again two weeks later.

*looking ahead . . .*

☑ LATE SUMMER Plant new strawberries in prepared ground.
☑ AUTUMN Sever and transplant rooted tip layers of blackberries and hybrid berries.
☑ Dig in green manures where fruit has been harvested.

## care of blackberries

1 Tie in the new canes, which will bear next year's fruit, in a central 'column'. This will keep them tidy and separate from the current year's fruiting canes, and help to prevent damage from wind.

2 Once the blackberries have fruited, remove the old fruiting canes at ground level using secateurs.

## strawberries

• **clear up strawberry beds** once fruiting has finished.

• **shear off foliage** about 8cm (3in) above ground. Cut off runners unless required for new plants; alternatively, tuck them into rows of two-year-old plants to produce a heavy yield of small fruit for jam-making in the bed's third and final year.

• **dig up three-year-old plants** and burn. Prepare the vacant ground for a late vegetable crop or sow a green manure.

• **remove fruiting mats** and rake off straw for burning.

• **prepare a new strawberry bed for planting** in late summer. Choose a sheltered site that is sunny or lightly shaded, where strawberries have not grown for several years. An area 1.2m (4ft) wide will accommodate two rows spaced 75cm (2ft 6in) apart. Remove all weeds, including perennial roots, before forking in garden compost or rotted manure, one large bucketful a square metre. In heavy clay dig in plenty of grit or coarse compost to improve drainage. Rake the soil roughly level and leave undisturbed for a month before planting the newly rooted strawberry plants.

**Root runners** for replacement plants by pegging down the small plantlets in the soil or in plunged pots of compost. Perpetual varieties are well worth rooting – these types are best replaced every year because quality deteriorates in subsequent seasons.

# vegetables

The vegetable garden is a busy but wonderfully rewarding place at this time of year. Early crops of peas and cabbages are ready to harvest, while later crops need sowing, thinning and planting out. Watering is critical for many vegetables and routine weeding is essential.

## *harvesting* now

- asparagus • asparagus peas
- baby sweetcorn • beetroot
- broad beans • calabrese
- chard and spinach beet
- early carrots • early potatoes
- french beans • globe artichokes • kohl rabi • lettuces and salad leaves • peas and mangetout • radish • shallots
- spinach • spring onions
- summer cabbage • summer cauliflower • summer squash
- turnips

**A collection of beans** including french, runner and flageolet beans.

## *now is the season to . . .*

■ **sow more seeds** for succession in drills (short single rows) or small blocks, to ensure a continuing supply of fresh vegetables later in the year (see opposite, and pages 58 and 60 for individual crops).

■ **thin seedlings** in stages, rather than all at once. If you have space, transplant a few strong thinnings elsewhere. Water the row after thinning to settle the soil so that the remaining plants grow rapidly.

■ **watch for slugs** and other pests and diseases. Take action immediately.

## watering

Vegetables grow rapidly at this time of year, and plants require plenty of water to sustain them. Ideally, use a method to get water straight to the plant roots, rather than wastefully spraying it over the leaves.

- **lay a seep hose** alongside plants, so water oozes onto the soil exactly where it is needed and loss due to evaporation is minimal. In this way, soil between the rows and pathways remains dry, and weed seeds are not encouraged to germinate.
- **seedlings and crops recently transplanted** or thinned need watering so that they do not dry out and their growth can continue unchecked.
- **leafy vegetables,** such as lettuces and members of the cabbage family, need at least 2 litres (½ gallon) a plant each week to keep growing unhindered in dry weather.

WATERING TIP To increase yields apply water generously at the following times:

- peas and beans at flowering and when the pods begin to swell
- onions as the bulbs start to develop
- carrots, turnips and other roots as they begin to swell
- potatoes when the tubers begin to form
- courgettes, marrows and squashes as fruits start to swell.

## controlling weeds

Hoeing with a Dutch hoe (see page 71) is the most effective way to control weeds in vegetable beds, but it must be done with care so as not to disturb crop plants and seedlings.

**The first french beans** appear while the plant is still flowering.

- **run the hoe blade** just below the surface, no deeper than 1cm (½in). This severs seedling weeds from their roots and minimises moisture loss and soil disturbance, which in turn helps to prevent more weed seeds from germinating.
- **hoe on a hot,** sunny day, so that weeds quickly wilt and die.
- **in wet conditions** rake off the weeds or they will reroot. Leafy annual weeds can be added to the compost heap.

## peas and beans

Plant runner beans in early June (see below). Make further sowings of dwarf french beans at three-week intervals. Space seeds 15cm (6in) apart in rows 20cm (8in) apart, as well as using them to fill in the gaps of any plants that failed to grow.

- **harvest peas** sown in spring when the pods are well developed but before they become tightly packed with seeds.
- **sow peas in a broad drill** at three-week intervals. Space the seeds 3–5cm (1–2in) deep in two or three rows 8cm (3in) apart. Sow early varieties for harvesting in late summer and maincrop varieties for harvesting in autumn.

## cabbages and calabrese

- **transplant brassicas firmly** to prevent them from drying out and to help their root systems establish. After transplanting, tug one of the larger leaves; if the plant pulls out of the ground, replant and firm in thoroughly with your knuckles.
- **transplant savoy and winter cabbages** to their growing positions at a minimum spacing of 30 x 30cm (12 x 12in), for harvesting from late autumn through to mid spring. Closer spacing will result in more but smaller heads.
- **harvest summer cabbages** when they have developed a good solid heart. Use a sharp knife to cut through the main stem just above the oldest leaves. Leave stalks in the soil and make two cross cuts at right angles; new leaves will sprout from this stump to produce a crop of greens later in the year.
- **early summer cauliflowers** are ready to harvest once the heads have swollen and the outer protective leaves open to show the white curd inside. Cut the head first, then clear the remaining stem and outer leaves.
- **cut broccoli** before the flowers show. Remove the central head with about 15cm (6in) of stem. This encourages smaller sideshoots to develop for harvesting later.
- **sow spring cabbage** in July to transplant later in the year.

*looking ahead . . .*

☑ LATE SUMMER

Transplant spring cabbages sown this season.

☑ Continue picking peas and dwarf french beans.

## there is still time to . . .

- **sow beetroot,** carrots, courgettes, dwarf french beans, kohl rabi, lettuce, mangetout and peas, outdoor cucumbers, radish, runner beans, swedes and turnips.
- **transplant brussels sprouts** and winter cauliflowers.

**Twiggy hazel 'pea sticks'** protect peas and dwarf beans from birds and give the plants some support.

## *planting runner beans*

1 **Plant beans sown under glass** in spring 15cm (6in) apart in double rows 60cm (2ft) apart.

2 **Install a sturdy cane support** structure and secure it well before the beans start to grow tall.

3 **Start guiding the stems** up a line or wigwam of bamboo canes from inside the structure.

# vegetables/2



## *harvesting shallots*

Shallots planted in winter are ready for harvesting as early as late June if the weather has been warm, dry and sunny. Summer sunshine ripens the bulbs as well as extending their storage life.

- **as the leaves die down,** gently lift each clump of shallots with a border fork. Allow the bulbs to dry in the sun.
- **store bulbs** once the skins are thoroughly dry and the remains of the tops pull off easily. Lay the bulbs in wooden or cardboard trays in a dry, cool, dark, frost-free place until they are required; shallots should keep for up to a year in the right conditions.

**Leeks and parsley** growing in their final spacings; chives edge the bed.

## *onions and root vegetables*

By now the onion relatives, shallots, sun-ripened and firm, are ready to lift, and it is time to enjoy the first crop of carrots and new potatoes. Meanwhile, earth up maincrop potatoes to prevent them from greening, and pull baby beetroots and turnips to make space for later, larger roots.

### transplanting leeks

Leeks sown in spring are ready to transplant when they are about 20cm (8in) tall.

- **lightly trim off** the tops of the leaves and the bottoms of the roots, and drop each young plant into a 15cm (6in) deep hole made with a dibber. Space holes 15cm (6in) apart.
- **water each plant.** There is no need to firm as the soil soon collapses in around the roots, filling the hole.

### sowing and harvesting root vegetables

Make several small sowings every few weeks to spread harvesting over a long period. This method of successional sowing goes a long way towards avoiding the peaks and troughs in availability caused by changeable weather during the growing season. Another way to avoid gluts and gaps is to thin in stages, first harvesting baby vegetables to leave more growing space for later, larger roots.

- **sow kohl rabi** at three-week intervals throughout early summer. Sow seed 1cm (½in) deep and thin to a final spacing of 20cm (8in) apart in rows 30cm (12in) apart. Green-skinned types take about eight weeks from sowing to harvest, and mature faster than those with purple skins.

Kohl rabi

- **baby turnips** are ready to eat six weeks after sowing. Try out different cultivars by sowing a different one every three weeks throughout summer. Sow seed 2–3cm (1in) deep and thin to a final spacing of 15cm (6in) apart in rows 25cm (10in) apart.
- **sow round beetroot** at three-week intervals until mid July. Sow seed 2–3cm (1in) deep and thin to a final spacing of 5–8cm (2–3in) apart in rows 30cm (12in) apart; baby beets are ready to pull in eight to ten weeks.
- **carrots sown late in June** are less vulnerable to carrot fly than earlier sowings. Sow seed 1cm (½in) deep, and thin to 10cm (4in) apart in rows 15cm (6in) apart. Extend the

## *potatoes*

The most reliable indication that early potatoes are ready for harvesting is when the flowers have opened.

- **lift early potatoes** as required with a border fork. Drive the fork under the line of the ridge and gently shake the soil to expose the tubers. For the best flavour, harvest only what you need and use them as fresh as possible, leaving the rest of the crop growing *in situ* until required.
- **if potato blight has been a problem** in previous years, cut off and dispose of the leaves and stems, and harvest the entire crop early to prevent the disease re-establishing or spreading.
- **in warm, humid conditions, spray potatoes** with a copper-based or other suitable fungicide. This may prevent potato blight becoming established. Coat both sides of the leaves completely with fungicide for it to be effective.
- **earth up maincrop potatoes** when the plants are about 25cm (10in) high (see right), but first hoe between the rows to loosen the soil surface and remove any weeds. Earthing up keeps the young tubers moist and growing rapidly. More important, it prevents them from turning green and becoming poisonous.

## *earthing up* maincrop potatoes

- **use a rake** to pull the loose soil from the centre of each row into the potato plants, covering the bottom half of each stem.
- **make sure the soil** is in close contact with each stem so that the stems are growing from the top of a soil ridge.
- **firm the sides** of the ridge with a spade blade and leave the top flat so that rain can soak down to the plant roots.

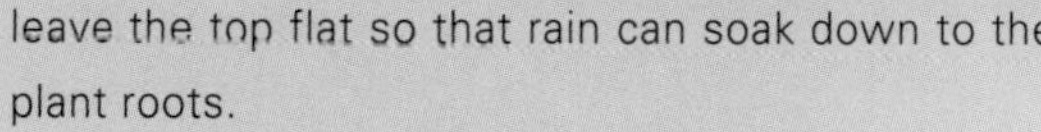

harvest by sowing early varieties, ready in eight weeks, then maincrop varieties, which mature in 10–12 weeks.

- **harvest finger-sized carrots** sown in early to mid spring. Ease the roots with a fork and pull them up by their tops.
- **try not to disturb carrots** more than you need while thinning or harvesting as this releases a scent attractive to carrot root flies. To prevent flies from laying eggs, protect rows of young carrots with insect-proof netting tucked securely in the soil.

**The white flowers of garlic** open in summer. Unlike onions and shallots, garlic flowers have no adverse effect on the bulbs underground.

**Neat blocks of vegetables** – radishes, carrots, lollo rosso lettuce and parsley – are planted here in raised brick beds, divided by driftwood. Behind them, seedlings and leeks await their turn to be planted out.

# vegetables/3

## *salads and other crops*

Finish planting tender crops like sweetcorn, tomatoes, ridge cucumbers and courgettes once the danger of frost has passed. Globe artichokes are ready to pick, and salads and cut-and-come-again crops, like spinach, need regular harvesting or they may run to seed.

### salad crops

- **keep up the supply** of quick-maturing salad leaves by sowing in small batches at two to three-week intervals. Ensure that while one crop is ready for picking, others are at different stages of maturity. Sow seed 1cm (½in) deep.
- **thin lettuces in stages** to 25cm (10in) apart in rows 30cm (12in) apart. Do not transplant thinnings in hot, dry weather as they will run straight to seed.
- **sow radishes and spring onions** in short rows, so as not to produce more than you need. Sow seed 1cm (½in) deep and very thinly indeed.
- **continue to water** at regular intervals if there is no rain, so that leafy salad crops like rocket do not run to seed.

**Red and green lettuces** grow in timber-edged beds with seedling rows of spring onions and herbs. Pick alternate heads of lettuce for eating while young and leave the rest to hearten up. Spring onions take up little room and are the ideal vegetable for growing between rows of other crops.

**Once asparagus** has finished cropping and the ferny foliage is growing strongly, apply a granular or liquid feed to the base of the stems two or three times at 10–14 day intervals. This will improve the quality of next spring's crop.

## perennial crops

- **pick globe artichokes** from established plants when they are plump and just about to open. Cut them with about 15cm (6in) of stem, to encourage secondary, smaller heads to develop three to six weeks later.
- **feed globe artichoke** plants after harvesting the first crop. Apply a liquid fertiliser round the base of the plants and repeat two or three times at 10-day intervals, to improve the size and quality of a second crop.

## tender crops

It is safe to plant tender crops in colder areas now that the danger of frost has passed, but do this early in June to give them as long a growing season as possible.

- **plant tomatoes and peppers** outside in growing bags or fertile soil. Feed and water regularly.
- **support tall-growing cordon tomatoes** and peppers with a stout cane driven in close to each plant. Tie in the stems at intervals of 20–30cm (8–12in) with raffia or soft string to avoid bruising the stems; do not tie too tightly (especially near the base) as this could constrict the stem as it swells.
- **plant out sweetcorn plants** 35cm (14in) apart in blocks (not rows), to aid pollination by the wind (see below).
- **harvest immature 'mini-corns'** from sweetcorn sown under cloches in May or in pots indoors in April. Cut off these young, unpollinated cobs when they are about 10cm (4in) long; the plants are too soft for them to be pulled off like mature cobs.
- **sow courgettes, marrows and ridge cucumbers** in well-drained fertile soil. Dig holes 1.2m (4ft) apart, as deep and as wide as a spade blade. Half-fill with well-rotted organic matter and top with soil to leave a slight mound. Sow three seeds onto the top of each mound; they should germinate in seven to ten days. Allow only the strongest seedling to grow to maturity and remove the other two.
- **plant squashes and pumpkins** in well-drained fertile soil, prepared as described for courgettes and marrows (see above).
- **train squashes** to prevent their vigorous stems becoming a tangled mass. Remove the tip of the main stem once five leaves have developed. This will encourage four or five sideshoots to sprout; as they grow spread them out like the spokes of a wheel.
- **hand-pollinate squash and pumpkin flowers** to ensure good cropping, especially in cool summers (see right). The plants have separate male and female flowers and will produce fruits only if they are cross-pollinated. You can recognise the female by the tiny fruit behind the flower; male flowers have only a thin stalk.

## *planting* sweetcorn

**Plant sweetcorn seedlings** in a block, 35cm (14in) apart in each direction.

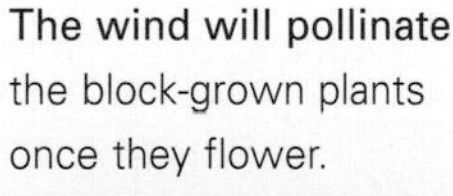

**The wind will pollinate** the block-grown plants once they flower.

## *pollinating* squashes

When the flowers are fully open, test a male flower with your fingertip. If pollen grains stick, it is ready to use.

- **pick the flower** and carefully strip off the petals. Gently push the male into the centre of a female flower to transfer the pollen. Use one male flower to pollinate up to four females.
- **repeat** this process three or four days running to ensure that pollination has taken place.
- **for large fruits,** allow only one flower to develop on each stem, and remove all flowers once the required number of fruits start to form.

# herbs



Herbs are at their most flavoursome now, so pick them regularly for immediate use and to encourage fresh tasty growth. Take special care of tender herbs like basil and don't let vigorous mint plants get out of control.

## now is the season to . . .

- **nip out the growing tips** of bushy herbs, such as basil, savory and marjoram, for kitchen use and to encourage plenty of new sideshoots.
- **thin or prick out seedlings** sown in late spring before they are too large, and pot up a few for the kitchen windowsill.
- **plant out tender herbs,** such as basil and lemon verbena, into permanent positions as soon as late frosts are over and young plants are acclimatised to outdoor conditions.
- **water recently planted herbs** in dry weather, and check those in containers regularly. Chervil, parsley, coriander and sorrel need regular watering, but avoid over-watering basil.
- **keep on top of weeds,** especially in new beds and borders where herbs are still establishing.
- **pinch out parsley flowers** forming now on older plants to encourage more leaves, but allow one or two to flower and self-sow to provide seedlings for transplanting in autumn.
- **gather and dry flowerheads** of chamomile, hyssop and sweet woodruff, as well as lavender and pot marigolds (*Calendula*), to add colour to potpourri.

## and if you have time . . .

- **feed herbs in containers** and perennial herbs planted outside this year, using a high-potash fertiliser.

**Shear off the flowers** of bushy herbs such as marjoram to promote new leafy growth and prevent seeds from setting.

**Against a background of ferns,** sage, mint, thyme, parsley and marjoram are grown in pots. They need regular clipping to maintain their rounded shape.

## mint

Most mints are vigorous and spreading. To prevent their running roots from invading neighbouring plants, grow them in containers or confine them in open ground by planting in an old bucket or plastic bag. Make sure the container has plenty of drainage holes in the bottom and plunge it in the border soil.

Growing mint in a container is one way to restrain its roots.

- **trim back any wandering roots** once or twice during summer.
- **as mint starts to flower** in July, the quality of the foliage deteriorates. So cut down a proportion of the tall stems to just above soil level, water well and feed with a high-nitrogen fertiliser to stimulate a second crop of young, full-flavoured leaves.
- **watch for mint rust,** distinguished by pale, swollen or distorted stems that later develop dirty orange spots on the leaves. Cut off all affected growth to ground level and burn or dispose of it promptly.

## success with basil

To grow well basil needs warmth and shelter, a free-draining rich soil and regular feeding. For these reasons do not plant or sow outdoors until after the last frosts. For a longer cropping period grow basil in a fertile greenhouse border or in 15–20cm (6–8in) pots of soil-based compost with a layer of coarse grit in the bottom for drainage purposes.

- **stand the pots in a warm, sunny corner,** protected from the wind.
- **water before midday** whenever the compost is dry, but avoid overwatering.
- **feed every 10–14 days** with high-nitrogen liquid fertiliser.
- **pinch out the growing tips regularly,** starting while the plants are still small, to encourage bushy growth and prolong the life of the plants by suppressing flowering.

*looking ahead . . .*

- ☑ AUTUMN Pot up parsley plants and move under cover.
- ☑ Scorch beds of mint affected with rust, to kill the spores and sterilise the soil.
- ☑ Transplant self-sown parsley seedlings.

## propagation

A variety of herbs are sown at this time, including a final and generous sowing of parsley for use in autumn from the open garden. With care this sowing should also see you through the winter – some plants can be potted up in September and grown under cover or indoors.

- **sow parsley seeds** sparingly in rows in a warm, sheltered part of the garden in mid July. When the seedlings are large enough to handle, water them well and thin out to leave plants 8cm (3in) apart. Water again to firm.
- **sow basil outside** once the danger of frost has passed.
- **continue to sow annual herbs,** such as chervil, dill and coriander, outdoors, to ensure a continuous harvest all season.
- **sow chives, fennel, winter savory** and other biennials and perennials under glass or in a seedbed outdoors.
- **divide mature clumps of mint** for new plants. After flowering lift ageing clumps and chop them into pieces with a spade. Transplant the younger, outer pieces into a fresh site, where they will grow more vigorously. Discard the exhausted central portion.
- **take semi-ripe cuttings** of woody herbs during July. The sideshoots of bay and rosemary will provide suitable material (see page 43).

**Try out a variety of different herbs** in their pots before planting up a large container or window box for kitchen use.

## there is still time to . . .

- **take soft cuttings** of marjoram, mint, rosemary, sage, thyme and tarragon, and root in a propagator or in a pot on a windowsill (see Late Spring).
- **layer low branches** of thyme and rosemary by pinning them down in the soil, but keeping the tips above ground (see Late Spring). They should have rooted by winter.

# herbs/2

## harvesting herbs

Many herbs reach perfection around midsummer, when their foliage is still fresh and unblemished, and their flavour peaks just before flowering. This is the time to harvest large quantities that you can preserve for winter use.

### now is the season to . . .

- **gather herbs for preserving** on a dry morning, ideally when it is slightly cloudy or before the sun reaches the plants. Harvest only as much as you can deal with straightaway and select only clean, healthy growth. Keep different herbs separate at all times to avoid cross-flavouring.
- **water and feed herbs** after each mass harvest. Annuals should regrow to supply a second harvest later in the summer and perennials will give another cut or two.

**Chop parsley** finely, place in ice-cube trays and top up with water – or freeze sprigs.

**Preserve borage flowers** in ice to float in summer drinks. This works well with other plants.

### freezing

This is the best way to preserve the full flavour and colour of most leafy culinary herbs. Freeze them singly or in mixtures, as bouquets garnis, for convenience.

- **pick small sprigs of foliage,** wash in cold water and shake well. Do not pat them dry, as this can bruise the leaves. Place small bunches loosely in plastic bags and freeze.
- **when fully frozen** crush the leaves in their bags, working quickly before they thaw, and pack the bags in a labelled container to save space.
- **alternatively, chop leaves finely** after washing and pack them into the sections of ice-cube trays. Top up with water and freeze. Store the cubes in the trays, or pack them in bags or containers. Use this method to preserve borage flowers and the leaves of variegated mint, lemon balm or scented-leaved pelargoniums for adding to cold drinks.

### drying

Dry herbs quickly to retain as much of their colour and their volatile oils as possible. They are ready for storing when crisp, but not so brittle that they crumble to dust. Store dried herbs whole or crushed in airtight, dark jars or tins in a cool place.

- **dry naturally** in a warm, dark and well-ventilated place, such as an airing cupboard, spare room or

**Tie the stems** of thyme, oregano, sage, rosemary and lavender together with soft string before hanging them up to dry.

## *preserving* herbs

| HERB | PART | METHOD |
|---|---|---|
| BASIL | leaves | freeze;<br>infuse in oil or vinegar |
| BAY | leaves | dry;<br>infuse in oil or vinegar |
| BERGAMOT | flowers, leaves | dry |
| CHAMOMILE | flowers, leaves | dry |
| CHERVIL | leaves | freeze |
| CHIVES | flowers<br>leaves | dry<br>freeze; make butter |
| CORIANDER | seeds | dry |
| DILL | leaves<br>seeds | freeze; infuse in vinegar<br>dry |
| FENNEL | leaves<br><br>seeds | freeze;<br>infuse in oil or vinegar<br>dry |
| HYSSOP | flowers, leaves | dry; infuse in oil |
| LEMON BALM | leaves | dry; freeze;<br>infuse in oil or vinegar |
| LEMON VERBENA | leaves | dry;<br>infuse in oil or vinegar |
| MARJORAM | flowers<br>leaves | dry<br>dry; freeze;<br>infuse in oil or vinegar |
| MINT | leaves | dry; freeze; infuse in oil<br>or vinegar; make jelly |
| PARSLEY | leaves | freeze; mix with butter;<br>infuse in vinegar |
| POT MARIGOLD | flowers | dry |
| ROSEMARY | leaves | dry;<br>infuse in oil or vinegar |
| SAGE | flowers<br>leaves | dry<br>dry;<br>infuse in oil or vinegar |
| SAVORY | leaves | dry;<br>infuse in oil or vinegar |
| TARRAGON | leaves | freeze;<br>infuse in oil or vinegar |
| THYME | leaves | dry;<br>infuse in oil or vinegar |

dry shed. For best results, spread the leaves and stems in a single layer on trays or drying racks and turn several times during the first few days. When the leaves snap easily, they are dry enough to store in airtight jars, tins or wooden boxes in total darkness.

- **alternatively,** tie stems into small bundles and suspend these from hooks or coat hangers to dry gently.

**Oven-dry sprigs** of rosemary and thyme. Sage and mint can also be oven-dried.

- **oven-drying** speeds up the process. Spread the herbs on trays lined with greaseproof paper and place them in an oven, set at a very low temperature with the door slightly open. Turn and check frequently, making sure the herbs do not get too hot.
- **microwave-drying** is the quickest method, but the trickiest. First remove all stems, which sometimes spark or burn. Spread the leaves on kitchen paper on the turntable with an eggcupful of water in the middle. Dry on full power in 30-second bursts, stirring around and testing after each session. Stop when the leaves are just dry: thyme and other small-leaved herbs take about one minute, large leaves three or four minutes. Leave in the microwave for a few more minutes to complete their drying.
- **allow seeds to dry** for a few days, then store them in airtight jars or tins (see Late Summer).

### infusions

Infuse the fresh taste of leafy herbs in a medium, such as oil, vinegar, butter or jelly, by first pounding them in a pestle and mortar.

- **add the pulp to an oil** (olive or sunflower), white wine vinegar or cider vinegar and allow to infuse for two to three weeks. Strain out the herbs and bottle the oil or vinegar in a clean bottle or jar with a fresh sprig of the particular herb.
- **blend pounded herbs** with unsalted butter and store in the refrigerator. Basil, oregano and chives are all suitable for this method.
- **make herb jellies** by combining pounded mint leaves, for example, with the cooking apples or crab apples used to make 'jam' or jelly.

# the greenhouse

Even though many plants have now been moved outdoors, there is still plenty to get on with. Propagators and coldframes are filling up with seedlings and cuttings, while greenhouse crops need daily attention.

## now is the season to . . .

■ **take leaf cuttings** of gloxinias and african violets (*Saintpaulia*) (see below) and *Begonia rex* (see right). Take soft-tip cuttings of busy lizzies, houseplant ivies and tuberous begonias (see page 28).

■ **take semi-ripe cuttings** of climbers and shrubs (see page 43). Propagate sturdy sideshoots of hydrangeas to root in individual 8cm (3in) pots, making flowering container plants for next year.

■ **sow large-flowering cyclamen** to bloom in 18 months, and gently start watering last year's corms after their dormant period (see opposite).

■ **sow winter-flowering pansies,** primroses and polyanthus (both *Primula*) in trays in early June. Keep them in a shady part of the greenhouse or in a coldframe, and prick out into small pots when large enough.

■ **sow tender perennials** such as gloxinias, tuberous begonias and streptocarpus in early June, and pot up seedlings to make sturdy young plants for keeping over winter.

■ **prick out seedlings of cinerarias** (*Pericallis* x *hybrida*), calceolarias and other greenhouse flowers sown in late spring. Transfer them to individual cell-trays or 6cm (2½in) pots. When they fill their containers, move to larger pots and stand in a shady place outdoors.

■ **pot up soft cuttings** started in May (see Late Spring) when new growth indicates successful rooting. Transfer them individually to 8cm (3in) pots, and keep lightly shaded for the first few days.

■ **cut back regal pelargoniums** in July after flowering, and reduce watering to allow plants to rest.

■ **train tomatoes**, cucumbers and melons as they develop (see page 68), and feed regularly (see page 152). Where necessary, pollinate open flowers by hand. Pick tomatoes as they ripen.

■ **thin out fruit on grape vines** to prevent overcrowding (see page 68). Watch out for mildew, and treat it by increasing the ventilation and spraying with fungicide.

■ **check plants daily for watering,** more often in hot weather, or use an automatic system (see page 151). Also feed pot plants regularly, starting about six weeks after potting.

■ **keep temperatures stable** under glass by a combination of shading, ventilation and damping down (see page 68).

■ **inspect plants regularly** for the first signs of pests and diseases, and use biological controls as necessary (see page 69).

■ **move greenhouse shrubs,** such as azaleas and camellias,

## taking leaf cuttings/1

1 **For african violets** and gloxinias, pull or cut off a leaf stalk and shorten to about 2–4cm (1–1½in) long.

2 **The leaves will root easily** in cuttings compost or a mix of equal parts of grit and perlite, with the base of each leaf just buried. Either cover with a clear plastic lid or stand in a closed and lightly shaded propagator. You can also root african violets by standing the leaves, with their stalks intact, in a jar of water.

## taking leaf cuttings/2

1 **A single colourful leaf** of *Begonia rex* can produce several plants when laid on the surface of compost. Cut off a leaf, then make cuts straight across the strongest main veins in a number of places, on the underside, using a sharp knife.

2 **Spread the leaf,** facing up, on the surface of a tray filled with cuttings compost or a grit and perlite mix. Weigh down with pebbles and keep warm and moist in a propagator. Young plants will soon appear where the cuts are in contact with the compost.

**It is not too late** to take soft-tip cuttings of perlargoniums, such as this delicate angel pelargonium grown under glass.

outdoors. Stand or plunge their containers in deep sand or leaves, ideally in a coldframe, to keep them cool and moist (see page 69). Christmas cacti (*Schlumbergera*) can spend the summer outdoors in light shade.

■ **clean and store away** all heating equipment now that it is no longer needed.

### and if you have time . . .

■ **pot up leftover bedding plants** for indoor colour. Ageratum, coleus, dwarf asters, *Begonia semperflorens* and heliotrope all make attractive windowsill plants in 13cm (5in) pots.

■ **clean out an empty coldframe** and plant with 'self-blanching' celery for late summer and early autumn crops.

■ **scrub out pots** as they are emptied, when the plants are put out. Before re-use, rinse them in a sterilising solution.

## leaf cuttings

Some plants, such as *Begonia rex* (left) and streptocarpus, can be grown from a leaf, or portions of it, and they can be propagated during summer. For streptocarpus, choose healthy, full-size leaves that are not too old and insert them vertically in pots or trays of moist cuttings compost (see below). They will root in a few weeks. Pot up new young plantlets individually when large enough to handle.

## sowing cyclamen

The best time to sow seed of indoor cyclamen (*C. persicum*) is between June and August, when you should also kick-start last year's corms back into growth.

**Streptocarpus can be propagated** in much the same way as *Begonia rex* leaf cuttings (see opposite), or you can slice the leaf sideways into several pieces, then bury the lower edge (the one nearest the parent plant) of each strip in the compost. Young plants will then grow from the cut veins.

- Soak the seed in water for 24 hours. Then space them 2–3cm (1in) apart and just cover with compost, in trays or pots of moist seed compost.
- Cover the trays or pots with a sheet of newspaper so that the seeds are completely in the dark, and keep at 13–18°C (55–64°F) for several weeks.
- Move them into the light when seedlings emerge, and when large enough to hold, prick them out individually into small pots. Keep in bright light and pot on as necessary, feeding them every 10–14 days. They will usually grow right through the first winter if kept at 10°C (50°F), and flower a year later in 13–15cm (5–6in) pots.
- To restart cyclamen corms after their early summer rest, remove them from their pots and clean off all the old compost and as many of the dried roots as possible. Choose a pot that is just a little wider than the corm, fill it with fresh compost, and plant the corm so that its rounded base faces downwards, with its top at surface level and protruding above the compost. Keep it in a warm, shady place, and water whenever dry, either from below or into the compost around the corm. Feed regularly in late summer and autumn.

### there is still time to . . .

- **take soft-tip cuttings** of pelargoniums, marguerites and fuchsias (see page 28). Grow them initially in small pots covered with clear plastic bags; prune the tallest cuttings to a single vertical stem if you wish to train them into standards next summer.
- **sow cinerarias** and greenhouse primroses such as *P. obconica*, to flower next spring.

# the greenhouse/2

## crop care

All greenhouse crops need special care to control their growth and maximise fruiting.

### training

Train the following vegetables and fruit in different ways to ensure maximum production.

#### cucumbers

- **train all-female varieties** in the same way as cordon tomatoes (see Late Spring). Tie the main stems to canes, or train them up and around vertical string for support; remove any sideshoots that form at the base of leaves.
- **with other varieties,** suspend a wide-meshed net from the roof to provide support, and train the main stem vertically up it, pinching out the tip when it reaches the roof. Tie in the sideshoots to grow horizontally, and pinch out their tips two leaves past a fruit. Remove all the male flowers; they grow on simple stalks, unlike the female flowers which have a tiny cucumber-like swelling behind the petals.
- **for all varieties:** keep the compost moist at all times, damp down daily by spraying to maintain high humidity, and feed like tomatoes (see right).

A fruiting ridge cucumber trained on a string.

A truss of orange tomatoes 'Golden Delight' begins to ripen.

#### tomatoes

- **spray the open flowers** with water or tap the plants sharply to encourage fruit to set. Water consistently because irregular watering can cause blossom end rot when a sunken patch develops at the base of young fruit.
- **feed every two weeks** with a tomato or high-potash fertiliser.

#### melons

- **melons enjoy** the same conditions as cucumbers. Train as single-stemmed cordons (see Late Spring) up vertical nets, keeping the main stem upright, and stop it at the roof.
- **train sideshoots horizontally,** pinching them out or stopping them after five leaves. They then produce flowering sideshoots, which should be stopped two leaves past a female flower (recognised by its swollen stalk, like a tiny fruit).
- **pollinate each female** with an open male flower (which has a simple stalk), by removing its petals and pushing the pollen-bearing tip into the centre of the female flower (see page 61).

### summer care of grape vines

- **pinch out the growing tips** of sideshoots two leaves past a flower truss, and any sideshoots that form later to one leaf.
- **help pollinate the open flowers** by sharply tapping the stems daily with a cane.
- **thin the small fruits** while you can still see their stalks. Use long-bladed scissors to nip off the inside berries first, then the smallest of the remainder. Do not touch the grapes with your hands.
- **water each week** in hot, dry weather, and feed with high-potash fertiliser every fortnight. Stop feeding and reduce watering when the grapes show signs of ripening, because the soil and air should then be kept dry.
- **check every week** for split or mouldy grapes, and cut them off. Watch out for mildew, and spray with fungicide when first signs appear.

### good growing conditions

Plants under glass often grow at an astonishing rate during summer, and need continuous care for the best results.

- **check their watering needs** morning and evening, more often in hot weather.
- **feed every seven to ten days** with a dilute liquid fertiliser.
- **on hot days, reduce temperatures** and keep the humidity high (see Late Spring) by damping down (wetting) the staging and floor with a hosepipe or watering can, by fitting blinds or painting the glass with white shading, and by opening ventilators and leaving the doors open for longer.

**Paint the glass** with special greenhouse window paint to reduce temperatures.

**Suspend a sticky card** from the roof to catch flying insects such as whitefly.

## biological control

In the concentrated warmth and humidity of summer, pests and diseases can multiply rapidly under glass, so stay alert for early signs and take prompt action. Simple precautionary measures include keeping the greenhouse atmosphere humid to prevent red spider mites from spreading, hanging up sticky yellow cards as traps (see above), and keeping your plants in peak condition.

Aphids, whitefly, scale insects, red spider mites and vine weevils are the commonest greenhouse pests. They can be kept at acceptable levels by introducing a specific parasite or predator (see top right).

Biological controls are effective all season, but only if the pest is already present and the temperatures are high enough, so wait until you see the first signs in early summer. And remember, you cannot combine biological control with conventional spraying because the biological control will be killed by insecticides.

## using coldframes in summer

Once you have finished hardening off tender plants, a coldframe remains a valuable asset all summer.

### in June . . .

- **use it as a seedbed** for sowing biennials and perennials, and as a nursery bed for raising transplanted seedlings.
- **revive the soil** with compost or decayed manure, and plant 'self-blanching' celery, or melons or cucumbers 'on the flat', training their stems out from the centre, across the surface, to each corner.

### *biological control* methods

| TO CONTROL: | YOU NEED: |
|---|---|
| • aphids | • *Aphidius* parasite |
| • red spider mite | • *Phytoseiulus* parasite |
| • scale insect | • *Metaphycus* parasitic wasp |
| • vine weevil | • *Heterorhabditis* nematodes |
| • greenhouse whitefly | • *Encarsia* parasitic wasp |

- **partially fill with leaves,** compost or sand to make a 'plunge bed' in which to stand, and keep cool, greenhouse pot plants when they are moved outdoors for the summer.

### in July . . .

- **use it to house young cinerarias,** primroses and other winter pot plants. Keep the lid shaded, or filter sunlight with a screen of horticultural fleece.
- **make it into a propagating bed** for soft-tip cuttings (see page 28), semi-ripe cuttings (see page 43) and divisions of perennials (see Late Spring).
- **sow parsley,** endive and oriental vegetables.
- **dry garlic, shallots and onions** that overwintered in the ground, during a wet season.

**Aubergines are in flower now.** Pinch off some of the blooms if you do not want the plant to set too many small fruit. When the plant becomes heavy, support it with twiggy sticks.

# the healthy garden

Hopes, plans and preparations come to fruition in summer as the garden fills with flowers and produce. Keep the momentum going right through the season, by watering, weeding and taking steps to improve displays.

## summer checklist

Use this checklist to make sure you have not overlooked any seasonal jobs.

- **water outdoors in hot, dry weather,** targeting plants most in need (see right).
- **feed plants in containers** at regular intervals, and check their watering needs daily (see page 152).
- **weed regularly** (see opposite).
- **plant out tender annuals and perennials** in June, as soon as frosts are over. Keep some in reserve to fill any gaps that may appear in beds and borders.
- **harvest vegetables and fruit** as they reach their prime.
- **clear vegetables after harvesting** and sow or plant a different crop in their place.
- **continue successional sowings** of vegetables and annual herbs outdoors.
- **prick out, transplant or thin seedlings** as soon as you can handle them, so that they have plenty of room to develop.
- **lift and dry spring-flowering bulbs;** tidy those that you leave in the ground.
- **plant autumn-flowering bulbs** in June (see page 33).
- **cut off dead blooms** to prolong flowering, and disbud where larger flowers are wanted.
- **top up water features** and aerate for fish in hot or windy weather; control algae (see page 46).
- **keep the greenhouse cool** by shading, ventilating and damping down (see page 68).
- **mow lawns frequently,** reducing the cutting height to summer levels, and trim edges regularly.
- **clip hedges and topiary,** particularly those of conifers and evergreens.
- **take precautions** against pests and diseases (see page 72).
- **pick herbs regularly,** and harvest larger quantities for preserving (see page 64).
- **start sowing biennials and perennials** under glass or outside.
- **take soft-tip and semi-ripe cuttings** to root under glass (see pages 28 and 43).

## watering

Treat watering as a top priority, especially for plants in containers. Outdoor plants can also have huge water requirements for steady growth, especially on light soils and in exposed gardens. On average, 2.5cm (1in) of rain every eight to ten days is needed to keep soils moist. Annually working in large amounts of organic material such as garden compost and well-rotted manure helps the soil to retain moisture, as does mulching the surface when the soil is thoroughly moist. When you do water, give substantial and regular amounts rather than an occasional light sprinkling, and continue until there is prolonged rain.

- **water in dull weather,** in the early morning or during the evening.
- **concentrate on vulnerable plants:** leafy vegetables, flowering and maturing fruit, seedlings and plants that have been recently planted or moved, and those growing near walls or in containers.
- **direct water to the roots** of thirsty plants by burying pots or sections of drainpipe close by and filling these, or by creating a depression around the plant to hold water.
- **check plants in pots,** window boxes, hanging baskets and greenhouses at least once a day as the weather begins to get hotter and drier.
- **explore the range** of automatic watering aids available that can save time and effort (see page 151).

**Use external blinds to shade** the greenhouse in hot weather.

- **stand pots in trays** lined with capillary matting, immersing one end in a reservoir of water (see right). In this way plants are kept moist for several days.
- **collect rainwater in butts** and other containers as a useful precaution if drought threatens, and as a reservoir of soft water for lime-hating plants, such as camellias and rhododendrons.
- **remember the birds,** and provide a shallow dish or bowl of water for them to bathe in and drink.

**Capillary matting** draws up water from the reservoir, reducing the need to water manually.

## weeding

Many weeds, particularly small annuals such as groundsel, bittercress and shepherd's purse, grow fast in hot summer weather. If allowed to flower, they scatter thousands of seeds in a few weeks. In dry weather and where soil is covered with a weed-suppressant mulch, there should be few weeds and these are easily hoed or pulled out by hand.

- **hoe bare soil regularly,** ideally while weed seedlings are small and the soil is dry.
- **pull up large annual weeds** before they flower and add to the compost heap, or dispose of them.
- **never leave weeds lying on moist ground,** where they may continue to ripen and shed seeds.
- **fork up perennial weeds** while small or spot-treat with a systemic weedkiller.

**Run the Dutch hoe blade** just below the soil surface to cut through weed seedlings. Remove them to a compost heap or destroy.

## improving displays

As summer advances plants concentrate their energy on setting seeds or surviving heat and drought, but you can encourage them to produce new growth.

- **before dryness at the roots** checks growth, provide plants with regular and adequate supplies of water.
- **feed plants in containers** every 10–14 days, starting about six weeks after planting, unless the compost contains controlled-release fertiliser.
- **water and feed all plants** after major pruning.
- **remove dead flowerheads regularly** unless seeds or decorative seed heads are wanted in preference to flowers.
- **cut out completely exhausted flower spikes** from plants such as delphiniums, lupins and foxgloves to encourage later flowers on sideshoots.
- **trim back early flowering perennials** like hardy geraniums, and feed to stimulate new growth.
- **pinch out the growing tips** of fuchsias, marguerites (*Argyranthemum*) and other tender perennials to encourage fresh bushy growth.
- **propagate short-lived shrubs,** such as lavender, and perennials for a supply of young, vigorous replacement plants.

**A pelargonium** enjoys the shower from a watering can.

# the healthy garden/2

## *holiday and greenhouse care*

In summer pests and diseases can become established quickly, so keep your eyes open, act fast and consider taking preventative action of the organic kind. You also need to make provision for plants while you are on holiday.

### coping with pests and diseases

This is the main growth or migration time for many pests and diseases, with conditions just right for their rapid establishment, so take every precaution to avoid or prevent trouble.

- **inspect plants regularly** for the first sign of problems; hand-pick caterpillars, and collect slugs and snails late in the evening after rain.
- **practise good hygiene** by clearing up fallen fruit, dying leaves and other plant debris that can harbour pests and disease. Burn or dispose of affected material, but not on the compost heap.
- **use mechanical and biological controls** where possible (see page 69).
- **if you need to spray,** use a chemical specifically targeted at a particular pest or disease; always follow the manufacturer's instructions exactly. Afterwards, wash your hands and face, and all equipment, and dispose of any leftover solution safely on a vacant, out-of-the-way patch of soil.
- **never spray in bright sunshine** or windy weather; avoid spraying open flowers or wet leaves, and do not spray when bees are around.

**Leaf cutter bees** leave a distinctive hole in foliage. They do not harm the plants, and will help with pollination.

**Snails** congregate in empty containers and cool corners where plant debris has been left to rot.

### holiday tips

Before you go on holiday take precautions to prevent problems while you are away.

- **thoroughly water everywhere** the night before you leave if the weather is dry.
- **mulch drought-sensitive plants** after soaking them.
- **water and feed greenhouse plants,** and move them away from sunny windows to stand in self-watering containers or a bowl or sink of shallow water.
- **mow the lawn.**
- **deadhead all fading flowers** and remove dying leaves, especially from plants in pots.
- **gather ripe fruit and vegetables,** together with any that are nearly ready.
- **get up to date with pricking out** and potting on so that young plants continue growing unchecked.
- **in the greenhouse** ensure there is adequate shading, and invest in an automatic ventilator and watering system.
- **arrange for a neighbour or friend to water** while you are away, and to pick ripening fruit and vegetables.

**Mulching the surface** of the compost helps to stop it from drying out.

### greenhouse plants

Many greenhouse or conservatory plants grow rapidly and need more attention as temperatures rise, which makes early summer a good time to sow seed and root cuttings.

- **regularly water and feed** plants that are in active growth.
- **water cacti and succulents regularly** and stand outdoors if you can, desert species in full sun and forest kinds such as christmas cacti in light shade and with shelter from wind.
- **winter and spring-flowering bulbous plants,** such as lachenalias, hippeastrums and cyclamen, begin to die down and rest in summer, and require little watering.
- **mist leafy plants regularly** to increase humidity; a dry atmosphere encourages red spider mites, which are difficult to control once established.
- **watch out for aphids,** whitefly, mealy bugs and vine weevils, and treat at the first sign. Open windows may admit pests and diseases that readily colonise soft young growth.
- **deadhead plants regularly** and remove all dying leaves to prevent fungal diseases from taking hold.

**Group containers** together and plunge them into the soil when you go on holiday, to conserve moisture.

- **sow perennials** such as strelitzia, gloriosa, clivia and tender ferns in pots of seed compost and stand on a warm windowsill; they should germinate quickly in the summer heat and make strong seedlings before the winter.
- **take root cuttings** of callistemon, bougainvillea and similar tender woody-stemmed plants. Take soft-tip cuttings from non-flowering shoot tips (see page 28), and semi-ripe cuttings from sideshoots (see page 43).

## the organic approach

This puts the emphasis on feeding the soil, raising its fertility with compost, manure and other organic materials, so that plants grow stronger and are better able to cope with problems. Converting to organic gardening methods takes time. You can make the change gradually, by reducing the use of chemical fertilisers, insecticides, fungicides and weedkillers year by year as you introduce these organic practices.

- **recycle vegetable waste** from both kitchen and garden to make compost.
- **seek out local supplies** of rotted animal manure, spent mushroom compost and composted bark.
- **sow green manures** on an empty piece of ground for digging in later to improve the soil (see Late Summer).
- **choose plant varieties** that are resistant to pests and diseases and that enjoy the conditions found in your garden; sow or plant them at the right time; and tend them regularly so that they never lack for food, water and growing room.
- **cover the soil** with a 5cm (2in) mulch of rotted compost, composted bark, manure or other organic material to control weeds, conserve moisture and improve the soil structure.
- **feed plants with organic fertilisers** based on dried poultry manure, fishmeal, calcified seaweed or dried blood. Or use a liquid 'tea' made from composted plant materials.
- **avoid pest and disease problems** with good growing methods, a diversity of plants, physical barriers such as fleece, short-lived sprays of plant origin such as derris and pyrethrum, and biological controls like pheromone traps and parasites (see page 69).
- **encourage natural predators,** such as ladybirds, hover flies, toads, ground beetles, hedgehogs and bluetits, into the garden. Create suitable habitats, like a pond; provide cover and overwintering sites, such as a log pile; and leave food in strategic places.

**Brightly coloured flowers** attract hover flies, whose larvae feed on aphids.

# plant selector

Herbaceous plants, including climbers such as clematis and jasmine, are reaching the first of their flowering climaxes, with poppies, foxgloves, geraniums and bellflowers all looking their best. Summer is also the season of roses. With high summer the species roses come into bloom, followed a little later by a vast range of garden hybrids, from small-flowered patio gems to old-fashioned shrub roses and modern hybrid teas. Penstemons, pinks and delphiniums will soon brighten borders while the blooms of early annuals such as cornflowers, larkspurs and bright orange marigolds make the garden sparkle.

*Clematis* 'Jackmanii'

# perennials

Although a few are evergreen, most durable non-woody plants are herbaceous, that is they die down in winter and re-emerge in spring. Plant when dormant, in autumn or early spring.

1

## purple, blue and violet

### 1 Anchusa azurea 'Loddon Royalist'
Alkanet
Usually short-lived plant worth growing for the intense blue of its saucer-shaped flowers, which are carried in upright open sprays. May need to be staked. Hardy.
**Height:** 1m (3ft) **Spread:** 30cm (12in)
**Site:** Sun. Moist but well-drained soil
**Use:** Sunny border
**Good companions:** *Geum rivale* 'Leonard's Variety', *Hemerocallis lilioasphodelus, Iris sibirica* 'Ego'

### 2 Campanula lactiflora 'Prichard's Variety'
Milky bellflower
Through summer the leafy stems are topped by crowded sprays of starry bell-shaped flowers. These are usually blue or violet, although the soft pink of 'Loddon Anna' makes a useful exception; 'Prichard's Variety' has rich violet flowers. In exposed gardens it may need to be staked. Hardy.
**Height:** 1.5m (5ft) **Spread:** 60cm (2ft)
**Site:** Sun, partial shade. Fertile well-drained soil
**Use:** Sunny or lightly shaded border
**Good companions:** *Geranium* x *magnificum, Phlox paniculata* 'Fujiyama', *Rosa* Graham Thomas, *Thalictrum flavum* subsp. *glaucum*

### 3 Campanula latifolia
Pointed leaves diminish in size up erect stems that are topped by loose spikes of pale blue to deep violet or white narrowly tubular bells. The flowers of 'Brantwood', which grows up to 75cm (2ft 6in), are deep violet. Hardy.
**Height:** 1.2m (4ft) **Spread:** 60cm (2ft) or more
**Site:** Sun, partial shade. Well-drained soil.
**Use:** Sunny or lightly shaded border
**Good companions:** *Achillea* 'Taygetea', *Crocosmia* 'Lucifer', *Hemerocallis* 'Stella de Oro'

### 4 Campanula persicifolia
Peach-leaved bellflower
From an overwintering rosette of narrow toothed leaves rise wiry stems that support nicely spaced outward-facing bells. These are in shades of blue or white, and self-seeding populations produce a happy mixture. 'Telham Beauty' has light blue flowers. Those of 'Chettle Charm' are white with a purplish blue edge. There are also doubles in both blue and white. Hardy.
**General care:** Cut down stems of faded flowers.
**Height:** 75cm (2ft 6in)
**Spread:** 20cm (8in)
**Site:** Sun, partial shade. Well-drained soil
**Use:** Sunny or lightly shaded border, woodland garden
**Good companions:** *Achillea* 'Taygetea', *Anthemis tinctoria* 'E.C. Buxton', *Lupinus* 'Chandelier'

### 5 Delphinium Belladonna Group 'Atlantis'
Belladonna Group delphinium
Belladonna Group delphiniums form clumps of dark fingered leaves from which rise branched wiry stems that support spurred single flowers in shades of blue. The velvet flowers of 'Atlantis' are rich violet-blue. Hardy.
**General care:** To prolong the flowering season, remove stems of faded flowers promptly.
**Height:** 1m (3ft) **Spread:** 45cm (18in)
**Site:** Sun. Fertile and well-drained soil
**Use:** Sunny border
**Good companions:** *Geranium psilostemon, Incarvillea delavayi, Paeonia lactiflora* 'Festiva Maxima'

### 6 Festuca glauca 'Elijah Blue'
Fescue
Evergreen grass that forms a bristling blue-grey tuft of needle-like leaves. In late spring and early summer purplish green flowering spikelets stand above the foliage. Hardy.
**Height and spread:** 30cm (12in)
**Site:** Sun. Dry and well-drained soil
**Use:** Gravel garden, front of sunny border, raised bed, rock garden, ground cover
**Good companions:** *Campanula carpatica, Euphorbia myrsinites, Geranium cinereum* 'Ballerina'

### 7 Geranium 'Johnson's Blue'
Cranesbill
This forms a spreading clump of lobed leaves with notched and cut fingers. It creates a dense ground cover from spring to autumn, when the leaves take on warm tints. The production of light blue saucer-shaped flowers reaches its peak in midsummer. Hardy.
**Height and spread:** 40cm (16in)
**Site:** Sun, partial shade. Well-drained soil
**Use:** Ground cover, sunny or lightly shaded border
**Good companions:** *Ceratostigma willmottianum, Euonymus fortunei* 'Emerald 'n' Gold', *Muscari armeniacum, Sisyrinchium striatum* 'Aunt May'

2

### 8 Geranium x magnificum
Cranesbill
This forms a good clump of foliage that is mid-green in summer then develops warm tints in autumn. The rounded leaves are cut into several lobes and are hairy. The violet-blue of the glossy flowers is intensified by the darker colour of the many veins. The blooms are produced abundantly in midsummer. Hardy.
**Height and spread:** 60cm (2ft)
**Site:** Sun, partial shade. Well-drained soil
**Use:** Sunny or lightly shaded border
**Good companions:** *Clematis* 'Perle d'Azur', *Clematis* 'Royal Velours', *Hemerocallis* 'Stella de Oro', *Rosa* Graham Thomas

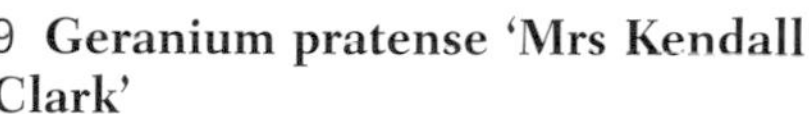

### 9 Geranium pratense 'Mrs Kendall Clark'

**Meadow cranesbill**

The lobed and cut leaves make attractive and effective ground cover from spring to autumn, when they take on warm tints. For several weeks in early and midsummer the foliage is topped by sprays of grey-blue flowers that may be tinted with palest pink. Hardy.

**Height and spread:** 60cm (2ft)

**Site:** Sun, partial shade. Moderately moist but well-drained soil

**Use:** Sunny or lightly shaded border, woodland garden

**Good companions:** *Anemone hupehensis* 'Hadspen Abundance', *Aster* x *frikartii* 'Mönch', *Polygonatum* x *hybridum*

### 10 Hosta 'Halcyon'

**Plantain lily**

A silvery blue foliage plant with elongated, heart-shaped leaves that are thick and waxy and overlap to form an impressive mound. In summer, smoky mauve flowers stand clear of the foliage. Needs some shade for best leaf colour. Hardy.

**Height:** 40cm (16in)

**Spread:** 75cm (2ft 6in)

**Site:** Partial shade. Fertile and moist but well-drained soil

**Compost:** Soil-based (John Innes No. 2) with added leaf-mould, or soil-less

**Use:** Container, ground cover, lightly shaded border, waterside

**Good companions:** *Cardamine pratensis* 'Flore Pleno', *Geranium macrorrhizum*, *Pulmonaria* 'Mawson's Blue'

### 11 Iris 'Jane Phillips'

**Tall bearded iris**

This long-established bearded iris retains its popularity, despite waves of new introductions, on account of its shapely blooms. The clear blue flowers have elegantly ruffled petals with dark veining around the white beards. They are vanilla scented. Hardy.

**General care:** Do not allow other plants to overshadow the roots (rhizomes). Divide these every three years.

**Height:** 1m (3ft): **Spread:** 25cm (10in)

**Soil:** Sun. Light and well-drained soil. Good on lime

**Use:** Sunny border

**Good companions:** *Clematis alpina* 'Frances Rivis', *Erysimum cheiri* 'Ivory White', *Paeonia lactiflora* 'Bowl of Beauty', *Tulipa* 'Queen of Night'

### 12 Iris sibirica 'Ego'

**Siberian iris**

Nicely shaped rich blue flowers flutter above a clump of grassy leaves. This iris thrives in reliably moist ground, but is also remarkably tolerant of drier conditions. Hardy.

**Height:** 1m (3ft) **Spread:** 20cm (8in)

**Site:** Sun. Fertile and moist but well-drained soil

**Use:** Sunny, moist border, waterside

**Good companions:** *Aquilegia* 'Hensol Harebell', *Euphorbia palustris, Trollius europaeus*

## purple, blue and violet (continued)

### 1 Meconopsis betonicifolia
Himalayan blue poppy, Tibetan blue poppy

At their peak these short-lived plants present a pyramid of open saucer-shaped flowers. These consist of blue petals and yellow stamens around a central cone. The blue is best when the plant is grown in cool conditions. The erect flower stems and the blue-green leaves are covered with rust-coloured hairs. Hardy.

**General care:** To extend the life of plants prevent flowering in the first year by removing buds.
**Height:** 1.2m (4ft) **Spread:** 45cm (18in)
**Site:** Partial shade. Lime-free, humus-rich and moist but well-drained soil
**Use:** Woodland garden
**Good companions:** *Kirengeshoma palmata, Rhododendron luteum, Trillium grandiflorum*

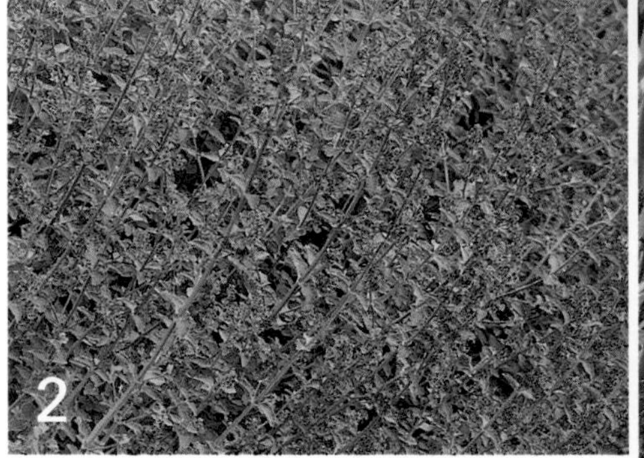

### 2 Nepeta 'Six Hills Giant'
Catmint

Numerous large sprays of mauve-blue flowers emerge from a grey-green clump of small aromatic leaves. This plant blends with a wide range of colour schemes. Hardy.

**General care:** To encourage renewed flowering in late summer, trim away spent sprays of the first display.
**Height:** 75cm (2ft 6in) **Spread:** 60cm (2ft)
**Site:** Sun, partial shade. Well-drained soil
**Use:** Edging, front of sunny border, gravel garden, ground cover
**Good companions:** *Achillea* 'Taygetea', *Allium cristophii, Anthemis tinctoria* 'E.C. Buxton', *Verbascum* Cotswold Group 'Gainsborough'

### 3 Salvia x sylvestris 'Mainacht'
Sage

This softly hairy plant has crinkled leaves and produces numerous dark stems that are crowded with violet-blue hooded flowers from early to midsummer. These emerge from reddish bracts, which remain colourful after the flowers have fallen. Hardy.

**Height:** 60cm (2ft) **Spread:** 45cm (18in)
**Site:** Sun. Well-drained soil
**Use:** Gravel garden, sunny border
**Good companions:** *Papaver orientale* 'Black and White', *Stipa gigantea, Verbena bonariensis*

### 4 Veronica austriaca subsp. teucrium 'Kapitän'
Speedwell

Hummock-forming perennial that produces many upright stems set with small flowers of intense blue. 'Crater Lake Blue' also has vivid blue blooms, but is shorter and has a slightly later flowering season. Hardy.

**Height and spread:** 40cm (16in)
**Site:** Sun. Well-drained soil
**Use:** Front of sunny border, raised bed, rock garden
**Good companions:** *Campanula garganica, Dianthus* 'Gran's Favourite', *Diascia barberae* 'Ruby Field', *Festuca glauca* 'Elijah Blue'

### 5 Veronica gentianoides
Speedwell

Mat-forming plant with glossy dark green leaves arranged in rosettes. Graceful spires of pale blue flowers may first appear in late spring. Hardy.

**Height**: 35cm (14in) **Spread:** 45cm (18in)
**Site:** Sun. Well-drained soil
**Use:** Front of sunny border, gravel garden, raised bed, rock garden
**Good companions:** *Achillea* 'Taygetea', *Euphorbia polychroma, Helianthemum* 'Wisley Primrose'

## pink and mauve

### 6 Acanthus spinosus
Bear's breeches

Substantial foliage plant with deeply cut spiny leaves. In late spring and early summer the glossy dark green leafy base is topped by spires of white flowers that are hooded with purplish pink petal-like bracts. Attractive seed heads follow. The Spinossima Group has smaller plants with grey-green leaves that are almost reduced to veins and spines. Hardy.

**Height:** 1.2m (4ft) **Spread:** 75cm (2ft 6in)
**Site:** Sun, partial shade. Well-drained soil
**Use:** Gravel garden, sunny or lightly shaded border
**Good companions:** *Allium hollandicum* 'Purple Sensation', *Euphorbia characias* subsp. *wulfenii, Stipa gigantea*

### 7 Dianthus 'Gran's Favourite'
Modern pink

The Modern pinks are evergreen perennials that produce single to double flowers in two or three, flushes between early summer and autumn. Most have prettily fringed petals and some are strongly scented. 'Gran's Favourite' has white double flowers with a purplish mauve centre and

5 6

7

petal margins, and is clove scented. Hardy.
**Height:** 30cm (12in) **Spread:** 40cm (16in)
**Site:** Sun. Well-drained soil, preferably limy
**Use:** Edging, front of a sunny border, raised bed, rock garden
**Good companions:** *Gypsophila repens* 'Rosa Schönheit', *Lavandula angustifolia* 'Nana Alba', *Sisyrinchium striatum* 'Aunt May'

### 8 Erysimum 'Bowles' Mauve'
Wallflower

Shrubby evergreen perennial with grey-green foliage and in spring and summer numerous spikes of four-petalled mauve flowers. Although unscented and often short-lived, it warrants a place for its extended flowering. Hardy.
**Height:** 75cm (2ft 6in) **Spread:** 60cm (2ft)
**Site:** Sun. Well-drained soil, preferably limy
**Use:** Gravel garden, large rock garden, sunny border
**Good companions:** *Artemisia ludoviciana* 'Valerie Finnis', *Eryngium* x *tripartitum*, *Lavandula* x *intermedia* Dutch Group

### 9 Geranium psilostemon
Armenian cranesbill

With above average foliage, this plant makes a large clump of deeply cut leaves that in autumn are randomly tinted red. Arresting, dark-eyed magenta flowers are produced freely throughout summer. Hardy.
**Height:** 1m (3ft) **Spread:** 60cm (2ft)
**Site:** Sun, partial shade. Well-drained soil
**Use:** Sunny or lightly shaded border, woodland garden
**Good companions:** *Anemone* x *hybrida* 'Honorine Jobert', *Aquilegia vulgaris* 'Nivea', *Polemonium* 'Lambrook Mauve', *Viburnum opulus* 'Compactum'

### 10 Hemerocallis 'Catherine Woodbery'
Daylily

Evergreen daylily with narrow linear leaves and mauve-pink starry blooms that are wide petalled, slightly ruffled and sweetly scented. Although individually short-lived, these are borne over several weeks from midsummer. Hardy.
**Height:** 75cm (2ft 6in) **Spread:** 60cm (2ft)
**Site:** Sun, partial shade. Fertile and moist but well-drained soil
**Use:** Sunny border
**Good companions:** *Campanula lactiflora*, *Geranium* 'Johnson's Blue', *Monarda* 'Prärienacht'

### 11 Incarvillea delavayi

Rich pink trumpet-shaped flowers, several per sturdy stem, stand above a rosette of divided leaves. The flared mouth of each flower is surrounded by five wavy lobes. Hardy.
**General care:** Mark the position of the plant as it is late coming into growth.
**Height:** 60cm (2ft) **Spread:** 30cm (12in)
**Site:** Sun. Fertile and moist but well-drained soil
**Use:** Rock garden, sunny border
**Good companions:** *Galtonia candicans*, *Liatris spicata*, *Polemonium* 'Lambrook Mauve'

### 12 Iris 'Pearly Dawn'
Tall bearded iris

Like most of the tall bearded irises, this has a flowering season that spans late spring and early summer. The gauzy ruffled petals are delicate shades of creamy pink. Hardy.
**Height:** 75cm (2ft 6in) **Spread:** 20cm (8in)
**Site:** Sun. Well-drained soil, preferably neutral
**Use:** Sunny border
**Good companions:** *Campanula lactiflora*, *Lupinus* 'Chandelier', *Paeonia mlokosewitschii*, *Rosa* 'Nevada'

8

9

10

11

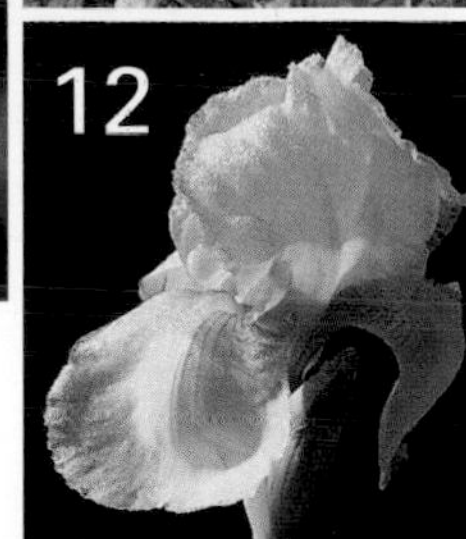

12

## pink and mauve (continued)

### 1 Paeonia lactiflora 'Bowl of Beauty'
Herbaceous peony

This example of an imperial, or anemone-form, peony has goblet-shaped semi-double flowers with pink petals and creamy petal-like strips (petaloids), which replace true stamens. Hardy.
**Height and spread:** 1m (3ft)
**Site:** Sun, partial shade. Fertile and moist but well-drained soil
**Use:** Sunny or lightly shaded border
**Good companions:** *Hydrangea paniculata* 'Unique', *Osmanthus delavayi, Rosa* Mary Rose

### 2 Persicaria bistorta 'Superba'
Bistort

Broad basal leaves make a light green weed-excluding clump, above which branching stems hold up short 'bottlebrushes' of tiny soft pink blooms. Starts flowering in late spring. Hardy.
**Height and spread:** 1m (3ft)
**Site:** Sun, partial shade. Fertile and moist soil
**Use:** Ground cover, moist border, waterside, wild garden
**Good companions:** *Astrantia major* subsp. *involucrata* 'Shaggy', *Hemerocallis* 'Summer Wine', *Rodgersia pinnata* 'Superba'

### 3 Thalictrum aquilegiifolium
Meadow rue

The light green foliage has a ferny delicacy, above which sprays of tiny purplish buds open to fluffy heads of mauve-pink stamens. In the form 'Thundercloud' the misty flower clusters are dark purple. Hardy.
**Height:** 1m (3ft) **Spread:** 45cm (18in)
**Site:** Sun, partial shade, Humus-rich and moist but well-drained soil
**Use:** Sunny or lightly shaded border
**Good companions:** *Aconitum* 'Ivorine', *Fuchsia magellanica* 'Versicolor', *Hosta* 'Halcyon'

### 4 Tiarella wherryi
Foam flower

This forms slow-spreading clumps of hairy maple-like leaves, which usually show bronze tints or flecks on pale green and in winter become coppery. In late spring and early summer there are spikes of tiny starry flowers that are pink-tinted cream. Hardy.
**Height:** 35cm (14in) **Spread:** 30cm (12in)
**Site:** Partial shade, shade. Humus-rich and moist but well-drained soil
**Good companions:** *Erythronium californicum* 'White Beauty', *Trillium grandiflorum, Uvularia grandiflora*

### 5 Verbascum 'Helen Johnson'
Mullein

The over-wintering grey-green and finely downy leaves of this plant are arranged in a rosette. From this erupts a branched spike that carries flowers in an unusual shade of brown-pink. An attractive and easy plant but often not long-lived. Hardy.
**Height:** 75cm (2ft 6in) **Spread:** 30cm (12in)
**Site:** Sun. Well-drained soil. Good on lime
**Use:** Gravel garden, rock garden, sunny border
**Good companions:** *Achillea* 'Taygetea', *Eryngium alpinum, Ruta graveolens* 'Jackman's Blue', *Scabiosa caucasica* 'Moerheim Blue'

### 6 Veronica spicata 'Heidekind'
Speedwell

This useful variation of the blue-flowered mat-forming species produces short spikes of small pink flowers above grey-green leaves over a long flowering season in midsummer. Hardy.
**Height:** 30cm (12in) **Spread:** 45cm (18in)
**Site:** Sun. Moist but well-drained soil
**Use:** Edging, front of sunny border, large rock garden or raised bed
**Good companions:** *Anchusa azurea* 'Loddon Royalist', *Diascia rigescens, Penstemon* 'Evelyn'

## bronze and maroon

### 7 Geum rivale 'Leonard's Variety'
Water avens

From a clump of divided leaves rise branching mahogany stems that bear drooping bell-shaped flowers. The petals are orange-pink and the calyx (the structure at the base of the flower) is maroon. Hardy.
**Height:** 40cm (16in) **Spread:** 50cm (20in)
**Site:** Sun, partial shade. Humus-rich, moist soil
**Use:** Front of sunny or lightly shaded border, waterside
**Good companions:** *Astrantia major* subsp. *involucrata* 'Shaggy', *Caltha palustris* 'Flore Pleno', *Phalaris arundinacea* var. *picta* 'Feesey'

1

4

5

2

6

3

## red and russet

### 8 Aquilegia McKana Group
Columbine

Long-spurred flowers in red, yellow or blue, often bicoloured as shown here, are elegantly poised at different angles above divided foliage. Plants are usually short-lived but populations are maintained by self-seeding. Hardy.
**Height:** 75cm (2ft 6in) **Spread:** 60cm (2ft)
**Site:** Sun, partial shade. Moist and well-drained soil
**Use:** Sunny or lightly shaded border, woodland garden
**Good companions:** *Aconitum* 'Spark's Variety', *Geranium psilostemon, Smilacina racemosa, Viburnum* x *bodnantense* 'Dawn'

### 9 Astilbe x arendsii 'Fanal'
Astilbe

This is a richly coloured astilbe with dark green, prettily serrated divided leaves. Long-lasting plumes of tiny deep red flowers remain attractive after the colour has faded. Does well in full sun only where the soil is reliably moist. Hardy.
**Height:** 60cm (2ft) **Spread:** 45cm (18in)
**Site:** Partial shade, sun. Humus-rich, moist, even boggy soil
**Use:** Bog garden, moist border, waterside
**Good companions:** *Astilbe chinensis* var. *taquetii* 'Superba', *Euphorbia palustris, Hosta* 'Royal Standard', *Rheum palmatum* 'Atrosanguineum'

### 10 Paeonia lactiflora 'Karl Rosenfield'
Herbaceous peony

Double herbaceous peonies may lack the refinement of the singles but they last longer in flower. They all have attractive foliage that is tinted red-brown in spring. This example bears deep wine-red globe-shaped blooms on strong stems and is good for cutting. Hardy.
**General care:** Insert supports before plants are fully developed.
**Height and spread:** 75cm (2ft 6in)
**Site:** Sun, partial shade. Fertile and moist but well-drained soil
**Use:** Sunny or lightly shaded border
**Good companions:** *Aconitum* 'Spark's Variety', *Fuchsia magellanica* 'Versicolor', *Rosa* 'Céleste', *Rosa* 'Louise Odier'

## yellow and orange

### 11 Euphorbia griffithii 'Fireglow'
Milkwood, spurge

A colonising euphorbia with running roots, but where there is room for it the orange-red flower-like bracts that stand above the rich green leaves make welcome patches of colour in sun or shade. Hardy.
**Height:** 75cm (2ft 6in) **Spread:** 1m (3ft)
**Site:** Partial shade, sun. Moist but well-drained soil
**Use:** Sunny or lightly shaded border, woodland garden
**Good companions:** *Epimedium* x *versicolor* 'Sulphureum', *Helleborus argutifolius, Hemerocallis* 'Summer Wine'

### 12 Kniphofia 'Early Buttercup'
Red hot poker, torch lily

Red hot pokers provide some of the most effective vertical accents in borders. This early flowering deciduous hybrid produces spikes of tubular orange-yellow flowers from a clump of narrow leaves. Hardy.
**Height:** 1m (3ft)
**Spread:** 60cm (2ft)
**Site:** Sun. Humus-rich and moist but well-drained soil
**Use:** Sunny border
**Good companions:** *Crocosmia* x *crocosmiiflora* 'Emily McKenzie', *Hemerocallis lilioasphodelus, Miscanthus sinensis* 'Silberfeder'

1 **Achillea 'Taygetea'**
**Yarrow**
Flat, pale yellow flowerheads, which can be up to 10cm (4in) across, top a clump of silver-grey ferny leaves. Flowering often continues through summer. Good for cutting. Hardy.
**Height:** 50cm (20in) **Spread:** 45cm (18in)
**Site:** Sun. Well-drained soil
**Use:** Gravel garden, sunny border
**Good companions:** *Coreopsis verticillata* 'Grandiflora', *Iris* 'Rare Edition', *Origanum laevigatum* 'Herrenhausen'

2 **Anthemis tinctoria 'E.C. Buxton'**
**Golden marguerite, Oxeye chamomile**
Golden marguerites are stiff-stemmed perennials with ferny leaves. Various cultivars produce large quantities of daisy-like flowers in shades of yellow. Throughout summer 'E.C. Buxton' bears lemon-yellow blooms that complement a range of colour schemes. Often short-lived. Hardy.
**General care:** Cut back hard immediately after flowering.
**Height and spread:** 1m (3ft)
**Site:** Sun. Well-drained soil
**Use:** Gravel garden, sunny border
**Good companions:** *Allium cristophii, Artemisia* 'Powis Castle', *Gladiolus communis* subsp. *byzantinus, Stachys byzantina* 'Silver Carpet'

3 **Hakonechloa macra 'Alboaurea'**
The arching ribbon-like leaves of this slowly spreading and clump-forming deciduous grass make a soft mound. Their warm yellow variegation is deepened by shades of tan. Hardy.
**Height and spread:** 45cm (18in)
**Site:** Partial shade, sun. Humus-rich and moist but well-drained soil
**Compost:** Soil-based (John Innes No. 2) with added leaf-mould
**Use:** Container, sunny or lightly shaded border
**Good companions:** *Heuchera micrantha* var. *diversifolia* 'Palace Purple', *Hosta* 'Royal Standard', *Ophiopogon planiscapus* 'Nigrescens'

4 **Hemerocallis lilioasphodelus**
**Daylily**
From a clump of semi-evergreen narrow leaves rise stems carrying star-shaped clear yellow flowers. These are sweetly scented. Hardy.
**Height and spread:** 1m (3ft)
**Site:** Sun, partial shade. Fertile and moist but well-drained soil
**Use:** Sunny or lightly shaded border
**Good companions:** *Geranium* 'Johnson's Blue', *Geranium* x *magnificum, Ranunculus aconitifolius* 'Flore Pleno'

5 **Hosta 'Gold Standard'**
**Plantain lily**
This striking foliage plant forms a clump of conspicuously veined, oval to heart-shaped leaves that are

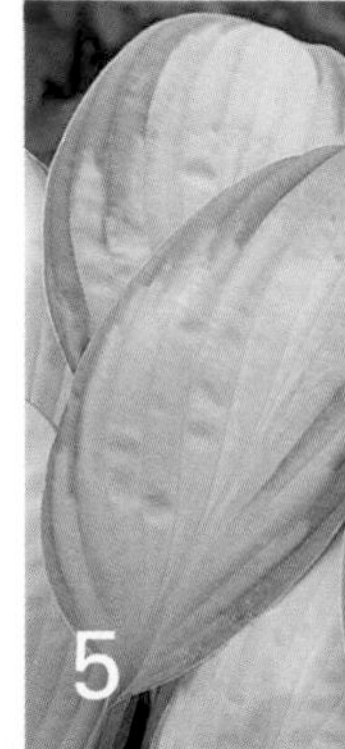
5

3

6

2

4

7

8

11

12

9

10

greenish yellow with an irregular, narrow, dark green margin. There are mauve-blue, funnel-shaped flowers in midsummer. Hardy.
**Height:** 60cm (2ft) **Spread:** 75cm (2ft 6in)
**Site:** Sun, partial shade. Fertile and moist but well-drained soil
**Use:** Ground cover, sunny or lightly shaded border
**Good companions:** *Euphorbia griffithii* 'Fireglow', *Hakonechloa macra* 'Alboaurea', *Miscanthus sinensis* 'Zebrinus', *Tellima grandiflora* 'Purpurteppich'

### 6 Lupinus 'Chandelier'
Lupin

The leaves of the hybrid lupins have long slender leaflets that are covered with fine hairs. The flowers are ranked in dense vertical spikes and often show a contrast of two colours, as in 'Chandelier', which combines pale and rich yellow. 'The Governor' has deep blue and white flowers. Hardy.
**General care:** To encourage the production of secondary spikes, remove the first spikes as soon as the flowers have faded.
**Height:** 1m (3ft) **Spread:** 75cm (2ft 6in)
**Site:** Sun, partial shade. Lime-free, light and well-drained soil
**Use:** Sunny or lightly shaded border
**Good companions:** *Aquilegia* McKana Group, *Aster* x *frikartii* 'Mönch', *Echinacea purpurea*

### 7 Miscanthus sinensis 'Zebrinus'
Zebra grass

Stiff stems make an upright clump from which gracefully arch narrow leaves. These have yellow crossbanding at broken intervals. This striking grass rarely produces flowers in a northern temperate summer. Hardy.
**Height:** 1.2m (4ft) **Spread:** 60cm (2ft)
**Site:** Sun. Moist but well-drained soil
**Use:** Sunny border, waterside
**Good companions:** *Cortaderia selloana* 'Sunningdale Silver', *Miscanthus sinensis* 'Silberfeder', *Phormium* 'Sundowner'

### 8 Thalictrum flavum subsp. glaucum
Yellow meadow rue

The frond-like leaves are blue-grey with hints of purple; excellent for flower arrangements. In midsummer stout stems carrying fluffy heads of pale yellow flowers rise through the foliage. Hardy.
**General care:** Plants usually need staking.
**Height:** 1.5m (5ft) **Spread:** 60cm (2ft)
**Site:** Partial shade, sun. Fertile and moist but well-drained soil
**Use:** Lightly shaded or sunny border, waterside
**Good companions:** *Aconitum* 'Spark's Variety', *Ligularia* 'The Rocket', *Miscanthus sinensis* 'Silberfeder'

### 9 Verbascum Cotswold Group 'Gainsborough'
Mullein

Crinkled grey leaves radiate to form a basal rosette from which rise strong vertical spikes that are set with numerous saucer-shaped flowers of cool lemon-yellow. Not long-lived but an excellent tall upright plant for growing among other sun-lovers. Hardy.
**General care:** To encourage the development of secondary flower spikes cut down old spikes as soon as flowers fade.
**Height:** 1.2m (4ft) **Spread:** 40cm (16in)
**Site:** Sun. Well-drained soil. Good on lime
**Use:** Gravel garden, sunny border
**Good companions:** *Artemisia* 'Powis Castle', *Eryngium* x *tripartitum*, *Verbena bonariensis*

## cream and white

### 10 Aconitum 'Ivorine'
Aconite, monkshood

Cut lobed leaves form a rich green clump from which rise spires of creamy-white hooded flowers in late spring and early summer. Excellent in the garden and for cutting. All parts of the plant are toxic and contact with the foliage may cause a skin reaction. Hardy.
**Height:** 1m (3ft) **Spread:** 45cm (18in)
**Site:** Partial shade, sun. Fertile, humus-rich and moist but well-drained soil
**Use:** Border, woodland garden
**Good companions:** *Astilbe* 'Professor van der Wielen', *Dryopteris wallichiana, Hosta lancifolia, Polygonatum* x *hybridum*

### 11 Astilbe x arendsii 'Irrlicht'
Frothy plumes of white flowers rise above an attractive clump formed from dark green divided leaves. Although this plant starts to bloom in late spring, it reaches its peak in early summer. The plumes remain ornamental after the flowers have faded. Hardy.
**Height and spread:** 50cm (20in)
**Site:** Partial shade, sun. Humus-rich and moist, even boggy soil
**Use:** Bog garden, moist border, waterside
**Good companions:** *Lobelia* 'Queen Victoria', *Persicara bistorta* 'Superba', *Rodgersia pinnata* 'Superba'

### 12 Geranium clarkei x collinum 'Kashmir White'
Cranesbill

This plant spreads underground to produce a ground-covering carpet of lobed and deeply divided leaves. Throughout summer there are white flowers, which are prettily marked with narrow purple veins. Hardy.
**Height:** 45cm (18in) **Spread:** 75cm (2ft 6in)
**Site:** Sun, partial shade. Well-drained soil
**Use:** Ground cover, sunny or lightly shaded border, woodland garden
**Good companions:** *Dicentra* 'Langtrees', *Epimedium* x *youngianum* 'Niveum', *Tiarella cordifolia*

## cream and white (continued)

### 1 Hosta 'Francee'
Plantain lily

Rich green puckered and veined leaves, defined by a crisp white margin, make a substantial clump of foliage. In summer arching stems carry mauve funnel-shaped flowers. Hardy.

**Height:** 60cm (2ft) **Spread:** 1m (3ft)
**Site:** Partial shade, sun. Fertile and moist but well-drained soil
**Compost:** Soil-based (John Innes No. 2) with added leaf-mould, or soil-less
**Use:** Container, lightly shaded or sunny border, waterside, woodland garden
**Good companions**: *Brunnera macrophylla, Dicentra spectabilis, Dryopteris erythrosora, Tiarella wherryi*

### 2 Hosta 'Ginko Craig'
Plantain lily

Variegated foliage plant with white-margined dark green leaves and in summer violet-purple trumpet-shaped flowers. In full shade leaves may be completely white. On young specimens leaves are lance shaped, but may be broader on plants left to build up for several years. Hardy.

**Height:** 25cm (10in) **Spread:** 45cm (18in)
**Site:** Partial shade, shade. Fertile and moist but well-drained soil
**Use:** Shaded border, waterside, woodland garden
**Good companions:** *Aconitum* 'Spark's Variety', *Dicentra spectabilis, Geranium macrorrhizum* 'Ingwersen's Variety'

### 3 Iris pallida 'Argentea Variegata'
Bearded iris

Clump of sword-like leaves that are striped vertically grey-green and white. Scented soft blue flowers emerge crinkled from silvered papery bracts for a brief season in early summer. Hardy.

**Height:** 1m (3ft) **Spread:** 25cm (10in)
**Site:** Sun. Fertile and well-drained soil, preferably neutral
**Use:** Gravel garden, sunny border
**Good companions:** *Artemesia ludoviciana* 'Valerie Finnis', *Lupinus* 'Chandelier', *Verbascum* Cotswold Group 'Gainsborough'

### 4 Leucanthemum x superbum 'Snowcap'
Shasta daisy

The good show of white blooms has made the shasta daisy hybrids popular summer flowers in spite of their undistinguished dark green foliage. Taller examples, such as the double 'Wirral Supreme', are good for cutting, but in the garden the stems, up to 75cm (2ft 6in) long, often need support. The free-flowering single 'Snowcap' is self-reliant. Hardy.

**Height and spread:** 45cm (18in)
**Site:** Sun, partial shade. Moist but well-drained soil
**Use:** Sunny or lightly shaded border
**Good companions:** *Ceratostigma willmottianum, Gladiolus* 'The Bride', *Veronica spicata* 'Heidekind'

### 5 Paeonia lactiflora 'Festiva Maxima'
Herbaceous peony

Stout stems carry scented double flowers, with loosely jumbled petals, above a good clump of leaves. The blooms are white, red tinged at first, and sparingly flecked with crimson. Good for cutting. Hardy.

**General care:** Insert supports before plants are fully developed.
**Height and spread:** 75cm (2ft 6in)
**Site:** Sun, partial shade. Fertile and moist but well-drained soil
**Use:** Sunny or lightly shaded border
**Good companions:** *Lilium regale, Paeonia lactiflora* 'Bowl of Beauty', *Rosa* Mary Rose

1

2

### 6 Papaver orientale 'Black and White'
Oriental poppy

Elegantly wavy petals make a white cup that is stained crimson-black at the base and cradles a ring of black stamens. Best sited behind other plants to hide the hairy leaves when flowering is over. Hardy.

**Height:** 75cm (2ft 6in) **Spread:** 60cm (2ft)
**Site:** Sun. Well-drained soil
**Use:** Gravel garden, sunny border
**Good companions:** *Coreopsis verticillata* 'Grandiflora', *Echinops ritro* 'Veitch's Blue', *Eryngium alpinum*

### 7 Phalaris arundinacea var. picta 'Feesey'
Gardener's garters

This is a much less invasive plant than the evergreen variegated species. It has ribbon-like leaves that are more white than green and pale green flower spikes with a purplish tinge. Hardy.

**General care:** Cut down old stems in late spring.
**Height and spread:** 1m (3ft)
**Site:** Sun, partial shade. Reasonably moist but well-drained soil
**Use:** Ground cover, sunny or lightly shaded border, water side
**Good companions:** *Hemerocallis* 'Summer Wine', *Monarda* 'Prärienacht', *Macleaya cordata* 'Flamingo', *Phormium* 'Sundowner'

3

4

### 8 Sisyrinchium striatum 'Aunt May'

Blade-like grey-green leaves, striped lengthwise with creamy yellow, make an iris-like clump out of which zig-zag spikes of cream flowers. Hardy.

**Height:** 50cm (20in)
**Spread:** 25cm (10in)
**Site:** Sun. Well-drained soil
**Use:** Gravel garden, sunny border
**Good companions:** *Euphorbia polychroma, Knautia macedonica, Sedum spectabile* 'Brilliant', *Veronica austriaca* subsp. *teucrium* 'Kapitän'

9 **Trillium grandiflorum**
Wake robin
The leaves and the parts of the flower are arranged in threes. The veined, pristine white flowers are backed by green petal-like sepals and often take on a pink tint as they age. 'Flore Pleno' is a beautifully proportioned double. Hardy.
**Height:** 40cm (16in) **Spread:** 30cm (12in)
**Site:** Partial shade, shade. Fertile, humus-rich and moist but well-drained soil, preferably lime-free
**Use:** Shady border, woodland garden
**Good companions:** *Buddleja davidii* 'Black Knight', *Verbascum* 'Helen Johnson'

10 **Viola cornuta Alba Group**
Horned violet, Viola
White flowers are borne in profusion in spring and summer and often again in late summer if the plant is clipped back after the first display. Useful for lighting up the base of shrubs. Blue and purple forms are also worth growing. Hardy.
**Height:** 20cm (8in) **Spread:** 45cm (18in)
**Site:** Sun, partial shade. Fertile and moist but well-drained soil
**Use:** Sunny or lightly shaded border
**Good companions:** *Geranium* 'Johnson's Blue', *Rosa glauca*, *Spiraea japonica* 'Anthony Waterer'

## silver and grey

11 **Artemisia ludoviciana 'Valerie Finnis'**
Western mugwort
Foliage plant with silvery-grey cut leaves arranged in flower-like rosettes. Useful for teaming with many summer flowers. Yellow-brown flowerheads appear in the second half of summer. Hardy.
**Height and spread:** 60cm (2ft)
**Site:** Sun. Well-drained soil
**Use:** Gravel garden, sunny border
**Good companions:** *Allium* 'Globemaster', *Gladiolus communis* subsp. *byzantinus*, *Lavandula* x *intermedia* Dutch Group, *Stachys byzantina* 'Silver Carpet'

12 **Artemisia 'Powis Castle'**
Mugwort, Sagebrush, Wormwood
Evergreen shrubby foliage plant. The finely dissected grey foliage makes a dense mound and in a hot dry summer creates the effect of shimmering silver filigree. Not fully hardy.
**Height:** 75cm (2ft 6in) **Spread:** 1.2m (4ft)
**Site:** Sun. Well-drained soil
**Use:** Gravel garden, sunny border
**Good companions:** *Buddleja davidii* 'Black Knight', *Verbascum* 'Helen Johnson'

## silver and grey (continued)

### 1 Hosta sieboldiana var. elegans
Plantain lily

One of the most distinguished herbaceous foliage plants, this has large, almost heart-shaped blue-green leaves, up to 30cm (12in) long. These are thick and waxy, with a puckered and veined surface that creates a rich pattern of shadows when lit from the side. Pale mauve trumpet-shaped flowers appear in early summer. Hardy.
**Height:** 1m (3ft) **Spread:** 1.2m (4ft)
**Site:** Sun, partial shade. Fertile and moist but well-drained soil
**Compost:** Soil-based (John Innes No. 2) with added leaf-mould, or soil-less
**Use:** Container, ground cover, sunny or lightly shaded border, waterside
**Good companions:** *Brunnera macrophylla, Digitalis purpurea, Viola cornuta* Alba Group

### 2 Stachys byzantina 'Silver Carpet'
Lambs' ears, Lambs' lugs, Lambs' tails, Lambs' tongues

Common names for the species refer to the shape and thickness of the leaves and their woolly texture. This non-flowering form makes a dense carpet of grey-green leaves. Hardy.
**Height:** 25cm (10in) **Spread:** 60cm (2ft)
**Soil:** Sun. Well-drained soil
**Use:** Gravel garden, ground cover, front of sunny border
**Good companions:** *Gypsophila* 'Rosenschleier', *Nepeta* 'Six Hills Giant', *Origanum laevigatum* 'Herrenhausen'

## green

### 3 Alchemilla mollis
Lady's mantle

Foliage plant with light green rounded leaves that are softly hairy and have a wavy and serrated outline. Airy sprays of tiny greenish yellow flowers froth above and around the clump from early and into late summer. Self-seeds freely. Hardy.
**Height:** 50cm (20in) **Spread:** 75cm (2ft 6in)
**Site:** Sun, partial shade. Well-drained soil
**Use:** Ground cover, sunny or shaded border
**Good companions:** *Cornus kousa* var. *chinensis, Hydrangea paniculata* 'Unique', *Paeonia delavayi* var. *ludlowii*

### 4 Asplenium scolopendrium
Hart's tongue fern

Bright evergreen fern with glossy, leathery fronds that are strap shaped with a wavy margin. In the Crispum Group the frond margins are more strongly crimped and waved. Hardy.
**Height and spread:** 60cm (2ft)
**Site:** Partial shade. Humus-rich and moist but well-drained soil
**Use:** Shady border, woodland garden
**Good companions:** *Galanthus nivalis, Helleborus orientalis, Prunus* x *subhirtella* 'Autumnalis'

### 5 Astrantia major subsp. involucrata 'Shaggy'
Hattie's pincushion, Masterwort

This has deeply cut fingered leaves and each 'pincushion' is surrounded by long bracts that resemble green-tipped petals of pink-flushed flowers. Hardy.
**Height:** 60cm (2ft) **Spread:** 45cm (18in)
**Site:** Sun, partial shade. Humus-rich, moist soil
**Use:** Moist border, waterside, woodland garden
**Good companions:** *Cardamine pratensis* 'Flore Pleno', *Dicentra spectabilis, Dryopteris affinis*

### 6 Hosta 'Royal Standard'
Plantain lily

This large hosta is grown mainly for its glossy mid-green leaves. These are of elongated heart shape and deeply veined. In summer the clump is topped by scented white flowers. Hardy.
**Height:** 1m (3ft) **Spread:** 1.2m (4ft)
**Site:** Partial shade, sun. Fertile and moist but well-drained soil
**Compost:** Soil-based (John Innes No. 2) with added leaf-mould, or soil-less
**Use:** Container, ground cover, sunny or lightly shaded border, waterside
**Good companions:** *Astilbe* 'Bronce Elegans', *Astilbe* x *arendsii* 'Irrlicht', *Hemerocallis* 'Pardon Me'

1

3

2

4

5

6

# pelargoniums

These tender evergreen perennials are grown as bedding and container plants for their colourful flowers and foliage. They need a well-drained soil or soil-based (John Innes No. 2) or soil-less compost, and must be overwintered under glass, at a minimum temperature of 2°C (36°F).

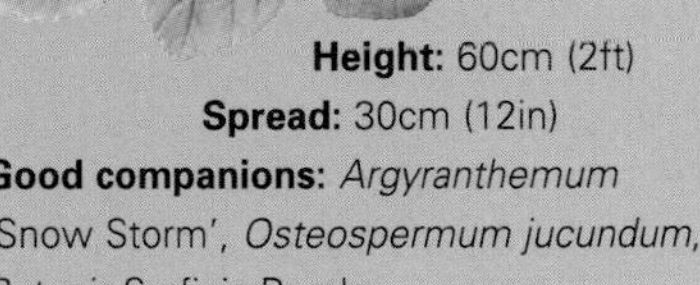

1

2

3

4

5

6

7

8

1 **Pelargonium 'Chocolate Peppermint'**
Scented-leaved pelargonium with chocolate-marked dark green leaves. Peppermint scented when bruised. Small mauve flowers in summer.
**Height:** 45cm (18in) **Spread:** 75cm (2ft 6in)
**Good companions:** *Helichrysum petiolare, Tropaeolum* Alaska Series, *Verbena* 'Peaches and Cream'

2 **Pelargonium 'Bird Dancer'**
Stellar pelargonium with aromatic leaves and spindly flowers composed of three pale pink bottom petals and two salmon-pink top petals.
**Height:** 20cm (8in) **Spread:** 15cm (6in)
**Good companions:** *Helichrysum petiolare, Lobelia erinus* 'Cobalt Blue', *Pelargonium* 'Copthorne'

3 **Pelargonium 'Caroline Schmidt'**
Erect, bushy fancy-leaved zonal pelargonium with bright red double flowers and silvery-white-edged rounded leaves.
**Height:** 30cm (12in) **Spread:** 20cm (8in)
**Good companions:** *Antirrhinum* 'Tahiti', *Brachyscome iberidifolia* Splendour Series, *Tropaeolum* 'Alaska'

4 **Pelargonium 'Copthorne'**
Shrubby scented-leaved pelargonium that releases a cedar-like spicy scent when bruised. The pale mauve flowers are heavily marked on the upper petals.
**Height:** 50cm (20in) **Spread:** 25cm (10in)
**Good companions:** *Fuchsia* 'La Campanella', *Lobelia erinus* Cascade Series, *Verbena* 'Imagination'

5 **Pelargonium 'Bolero'**
Bushy Unique pelargonium with aromatic grey-green leaves and darkly marked salmon-pink trumpet-shaped flowers.
**Height:** 60cm (2ft)
**Spread:** 30cm (12in)
**Good companions:** *Argyranthemum* 'Snow Storm', *Osteospermum jucundum, Petunia* Surfinia Purple

6 **Pelargonium 'L'Elégante'**
Trailing ivy-leaved pelargonium, much used as a foliage plant for containers. The cream variegation of the leaves is often flushed purplish pink if the plant is kept dry. Clusters of single white flowers are lightly tinted mauve.
**Height:** 20cm (8in) **Spread:** 30cm (12in)
**Good companions:** *Felicia amelloides* 'Santa Anita', *Scaevola aemula* 'Blue Wonder', *Verbena* 'Silver Anne'

7 **Pelargonium 'Paton's Unique'**
Vigorous, shrubby pelargonium with strongly aromatic lobed leaves. The magenta-pink funnel-shaped flowers have purple veins and a white throat.
**Height:** 20cm (8in) **Spread:** 30cm (12in)
**Good companions:** *Convulvulus sabatius, Diascia barberae* 'Ruby Field', *Pelargonium* 'L'Elégante'

8 **Pelargonium 'Captain Starlight'**
Shrubby Angel pelargonium with small bicoloured single flowers. The upper petals are purple and the lower ones mauve.
**Height:** 35cm (14in) **Spread:** 20cm (8in)
**Good companions:** *Fuchsia* 'La Campanella', *Lobelia erinus* Cascade Series, *Pelargonium* 'L'Elégante'

# annuals & biennials

Since annuals and biennials quickly reach flowering maturity, they are the ideal plants for filling beds and containers with colourful summer displays.

## purple, blue and violet

### 1 Centaurea cyanus
Blue-bottle, Cornflower

The fringed flowerheads of this annual are usually an intense violet-blue, but white, pink and red cultivars are also available. Tall cultivars are excellent for cutting. Hardy.

**General care:** Sow seed *in situ* in early autumn or early spring.

**Height:** 1m (3ft) **Spread:** 20cm (8in)

**Soil:** Sun. Well-drained soil

**Use:** Sunny bed or border, wildflower garden

**Good companions:** *Delphinium grandiflorum* 'Blue Butterfly', *Papaver rhoeas* 'Mother of Pearl'

### 2 Consolida ajacis Giant Imperial Series
Larkspur

An erect annual with finely dissected leaves and dense spikes of single or double flowers in blue, purple, pink or white. Excellent for cutting. Hardy.

**General care:** Sow seed *in situ* in early autumn or in mid to late spring.

**Height:** 1m (3ft) **Spread:** 35cm (14in)

**Site:** Sun. Well-drained soil

**Use:** Sunny bed or border

**Good companions:** *Papaver rhoeas* 'Mother of Pearl', *Salvia viridis* 'Oxford Blue'

### 3 Delphinium grandiflorum 'Blue Butterfly'

Short-lived perennial usually grown as an annual. The blue funnel-shaped flowers are spurred and carried above a base of fingered leaves. Hardy.

**General care:** Sow seed under glass at 13°C (55°F) in late winter. Plant out in late spring or early summer.

**Height:** 50cm (20in) **Spread:** 30cm (12in)

**Site:** Sun. Well-drained soil

**Use:** Sunny bed or border

**Good companions:** *Gladiolus* 'The Bride', *Nigella damascena* 'Miss Jekyll', *Tagetes* 'Lemon Gem'

### 4 Nigella damascena 'Miss Jekyll'
Devil-in-a-bush, Love-in-a-mist

Bushy annual with feathery foliage and sky-blue semi-double flowers within a ruff of thread-like bracts, over a long summer season. Hardy.

**General care:** Sow seed *in situ* in early autumn or early spring.

**Height:** 45cm (18in) **Spread:** 25cm (10in)

**Site:** Sun. Well-drained soil

**Use:** Sunny bed or border

**Good companions:** *Antirrhinum* Sonnet Series, *Eschscholzia californica*, *Papaver nudicaule*

### 5 Verbena 'Imagination'

Sprawling hybrid verbena raised annually from seed, with heads of small violet flowers above divided leaves throughout summer. Half hardy.

**General care:** Sow seed under glass at 18-21°C (64-70°F) in late winter to early spring. Plant out in early summer.

**Height:** 45cm (18in) **Spread:** 50cm (20in)

**Site:** Sun. Moist but well-drained soil

**Compost:** Soil-based (John Innes No. 2) or soil-less

**Use:** Container, sunny bed

**Good companions:** *Fuchsia* 'La Campanella', *Petunia* 'Surfinia Purple', *Viola* x *wittrockiana* 'Jolly Joker'

### 6 Viola x wittrockiana 'Baby Lucia'
Pansy, Viola

Short-lived evergreen perennial grown as an annual for its generous display of small, yellow-eyed blue flowers in spring and summer. Hardy.

**General care:** Sow seed under glass in late winter or early spring, or outdoors in mid-spring. To prolong flowering deadhead regularly.

**Height:** 15cm (6in) **Spread:** 20cm (8in)

**Site:** Sun, partial shade. Humus-rich and moist but well-drained soil

**Compost:** Soil-based (John Innes No. 2) or soil-less

**Use:** Container, formal bedding, front of border

**Good companions:** *Nicotiana* 'Lime Green', *Tropaeolum* 'Alaska', *Tulipa* 'Spring Green'

1

2

3

4

## pink and mauve

### 7 Ageratum houstonianum
Floss flower

Most cultivars of this annual are compact plants with downy, heart-shaped leaves and clusters of fluffy pompon flowerheads in blue, mauve, pink or white. Flowers until the first frosts. Half hardy.

**General care:** Sow seed under glass, at 14–16°C (57–61°F), in early to mid-spring. Plant out in early summer.

**Height:** 15cm (6in) **Spread:** 20cm (8in)

**Site:** Sun, partial shade. Moist but well-drained soil

**Compost:** Soil-based (John Innes No. 2) or soil-less

**Use:** Container, edging, formal bedding, front of bed or border

**Good companions:** *Verbena* 'Peaches and Cream', *Viola* x *wittrockiana* 'Baby Lucia'

### 8 Clarkia amoena Satin Series
Godetia, Satin flower

Dwarf annual with numerous clusters of sheeny four-petalled flowers in shades of pink and red, often with contrasting colours. Hardy.

**General care:** Sow seed *in situ* in early autumn or early spring.
**Height:** 20cm (8in) **Spread:** 30cm (12in)
**Site:** Sun. Moist but well-drained soil
**Use:** Sunny bed or border
**Good companions:** *Ageratum houstonianum*, *Cleome hassleriana* 'Rose Queen', *Nigella damascena* 'Miss Jekyll Sky Blue'

### 9 Digitalis purpurea
Foxglove

Biennial or short-lived perennial with spires of pink, purple or white flowers, spotted inside. Self-seeds to excess but suits wild areas. Hardy.
**General care:** Sow seed *in situ* from late spring to early summer.
**Height:** 1.5m (5ft) **Spread:** 50cm (20in)
**Site:** Partial shade, sun. Moist but well-drained soil
**Use:** Wild garden, woodland garden
**Good companions:** *Aquilegia* 'Hensol Harebell', *Lilium martagon*, *Myosotis sylvatica* 'Royal Blue'

### 10 Lathyrus odoratus 'Duke of York'
Sweet pea

Sweetly scented annual tendril climber. Old-fashioned cultivars, such as 'Duke of York' and 'Painted Lady', have small pea flowers in blue, pink or red. Modern cultivars have larger flowers with ruffled petals in many colours. Hardy.
**General care:** Sow seed under glass in autumn or early spring and plant out in spring. Alternatively, sow *in situ* in mid-spring. Deadhead regularly.
**Height:** 2m (6ft) **Spread:** 60cm (2ft)
**Site:** Sun. Humus-rich, fertile and well-drained soil
**Use:** Screen, tripod climber
**Good companions:** *Campanula lactiflora*, *Lilium regale*, *Rosa* 'Céleste'

### 11 Lobelia erinus Cascade Series
Lobelia

This bushy or trailing perennial is grown as an annual. All summer the dark green, sometimes bronzed leaves are obscured by small flowers. Cascade Series is trailing and has pink, purple, blue, red or white flowers. Half hardy.
**General care:** Sow seed under glass at 16–18°C (61–64°F) in late winter. Plant out in early summer.
**Height:** 15cm (6in) **Spread:** 20cm (8in)
**Site:** Sun, partial shade. Fertile and moist but well-drained soil
**Compost:** Soil-based (John Innes No. 2) or soil-less
**Use:** Container, raised bed
**Good companions:** *Fuchsia* 'Leonora', *Petunia* Surfinia Purple, *Verbena* 'Silver Anne'

### 12 Matthiola incana Ten Week Series
Gillyflower, stock

Ten Week stocks are grown as annuals for their richly scented blooms. Tall and dwarf cultivars bear single or double flowers in pink, mauve, purple or red. Not fully hardy.
**General care:** Sow seed under glass at 13–15°C (55–59°F) from late winter to early spring. Plant out in late spring.
**Height:** 45cm (18in) **Spread:** 30cm (12in)
**Site:** Sun. Moist but well-drained soil, preferably slightly limy
**Compost:** Soil-based (John Innes No. 2)
**Use:** Container, sunny bed or border
**Good companions:** *Amaranthus caudatus*, *Centaurea cyanus*, *Cosmos bipinnatus* Sensation Series

8

10

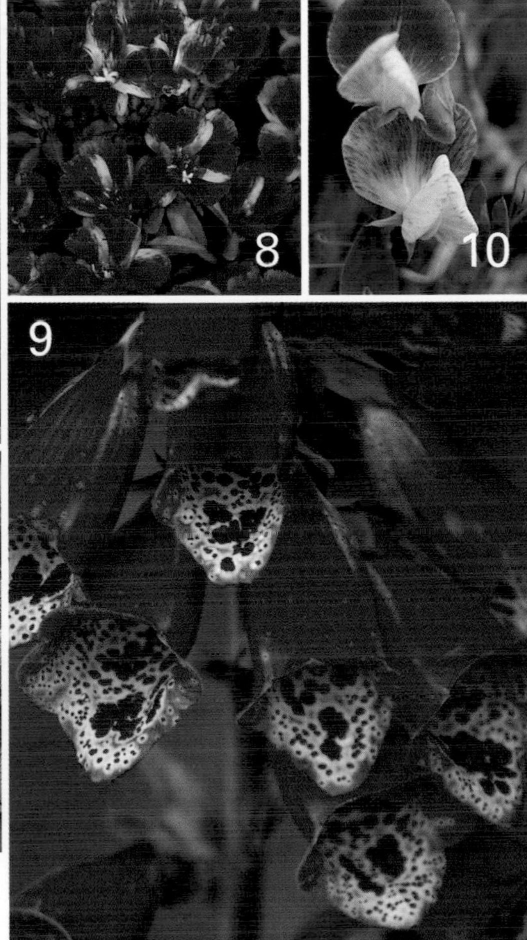

6

## pink and mauve (continued)

### 1 Papaver somniferum
Opium poppy

Erect annual with tall stems, deeply lobed grey-green leaves and in summer pink, mauve, red or white bowl-shaped flowers, which are up to 10cm (4in) across and followed by ornamental flat-topped seed pods. Hardy.

**General care:** Sow seed *in situ* in early to mid-spring. To prevent excessive self-seeding cut seed pods while they are still blue-green.
**Height:** 1.2m (4ft) **Spread:** 30cm (12in)
**Site:** Sun. Well-drained soil
**Use:** Sunny bed or border
**Good companions:** *Papaver rhoeas* 'Mother of Pearl', *Perovska atriplicifolia* 'Blue Spire', *Verbena bonariensis*

### 2 Petunia Fantasy Series

Hybrid petunias are bushy or trailing perennials grown as annuals. They produce single or double trumpet-shaped flowers through summer. Some are sweetly scented. Fantasy Series is compact and bears small pink to red flowers. Half hardy.

**General care:** Sow seed under glass at 15°C (59°F) in early spring.
**Height:** 15cm (6in) **Spread:** 20cm (8in)
**Site:** Sun. Well-drained soil
**Compost:** Soil-based (John Innes No. 1) or soil-less, both with added sharp sand
**Use:** Container, edging, formal bedding, front of sunny border
**Good companions:** *Gladiolus* 'The Bride', *Lavatera trimestris* 'Mont Blanc', *Nigella damascena* 'Miss Jekyll Sky Blue'

## red and russet

### 3 Alcea rosea 'Nigra'
Hollyhock

This short-lived perennial is best grown as an annual or biennial to minimise the spread of hollyhock rust. It has rough hairy leaves and a tough stem that shoots up to bear single funnel-shaped flowers. These are dark maroon with a yellow throat. Hardy.

**General care:** To grow as a biennial, sow seed in a nursery bed in early to midsummer. To grow as an annual, sow seed under glass at 13°C (55°F) in late winter. Plant out in late spring.
**Height:** 2.5m (8ft) **Spread:** 50cm (20in)
**Site:** Sun. Fertile and moist but well-drained soil
**Use:** Sunny bed or border
**Good companions:** *Clematis* 'Royal Velours', *Lilium regale, Rosa* 'Madame Alfred Carrière', *Tulipa* 'Queen of Night'

### 4 Antirrhinum Sonnet Series
Snapdragon

These short-lived shrubby perennials are grown as annuals in dwarf, intermediate or tall cultivars. The common name derives from the two-lipped flowers, which are carried on spikes. Sonnet Series is intermediate and bears red, pink, yellow or white flowers. It begins its long flowering season early. Half hardy.

**General care:** Sow seed under glass, at 16–18°C (61–64°F), in late winter or early spring. Plant out in late spring or early summer.
**Height:** 40cm (16in) **Spread:** 30cm (12in)
**Site:** Sun. Fertile and well-drained soil
**Compost:** Soil-based (John Innes No. 2) or soil-less
**Use:** Container, formal bedding, front of sunny border
**Good companions:** *Artemisia ludoviciana* 'Valerie Finnis', *Eryngium* x *tripartitum, Perovskia* 'Blue Spire'

### 5 Dianthus barbatus 'Roundabout'
Sweet william

Sweet williams are short-lived perennials grown as biennials for their flat-headed clusters of scented single or double flowers. These are red, maroon or white and often bicoloured and prettily marked. 'Roundabout' is compact and includes many bicolours. The taller kinds are particularly good for cutting. Hardy.

**General care:** Sow seed under glass at 13°C (55°F) in late winter or early spring. Plant out in late spring or early summer.
**Height:** 20cm (8in) **Spread:** 25cm (10in)
**Site:** Sun. Well-drained. Good on lime
**Use:** Sunny bed or border
**Good companions:** *Antirrhinum* Sonnet Series, *Delphinium grandiflorum* 'Blue Butterfly', *Tulipa* 'Mount Tacoma'

### 6 Tropaeolum majus 'Empress of India'
Nasturtium

Compact version of what is often a vigorous scrambling annual. The wavy-edged rounded leaves are blue-green and the scented spurred flowers are velvety scarlet. They are borne

throughout summer if plants are regularly deadheaded. Half hardy.
**General care:** Sow seed under glass at 13–16°C (55–66°F) in late winter or early spring. Plant out in late spring or early summer. To prolong flowering deadhead regularly.
**Height:** 30cm (12in) **Spread:** 45cm (18in)
**Site:** Sun. Moist but well drained soil
**Compost:** Soil-based (John Innes No. 2) or soil-less, both with added grit
**Use:** Container, formal bedding, front of sunny border
**Good companions:** *Amaranthus caudatus, Molucella laevis, Nicotiana* 'Lime Green'

## yellow and orange

### 7 Eschscholzia californica
California poppy
Annual with finely cut blue-green leaves and silky saucer-shaped poppies in yellow, cream, pink or scarlet. The flowering season lasts all summer but individual plants stop blooming when cylindrical seedpods develop. Good for cutting. Hardy.
**General care:** Sow seed *in situ* in early autumn or mid-spring.
**Height:** 25cm (10in) **Spread:** 20cm (8in)
**Site:** Sun. Well-drained, preferably poor soil
**Use:** Gravel garden, sunny bed or border
**Good companions:** *Allium cristophii, Artemisia* 'Powis Castle', *Calendula officinalis* 'Fiesta Gitana'

### 8 Papaver nudicaule
Arctic poppy, Icelandic poppy
Hairy perennial grown as a biennial for its exquisite flowers in yellow, orange, pink or white. 'Summer Breeze' has a long flowering season. Hardy.
**General care:** Sow seed *in situ* in late spring or early summer.
**Height:** 40cm (16in) **Spread:** 15cm (6in)
**Site:** Sun. Well-drained soil
**Use:** Sunny bed or border
**Good companions:** *Anthemis tinctoria* 'E.C. Buxton', *Lupinus* 'Chandelier', *Rudbeckia fulgida* var. *sullivantii* 'Goldsturm'

### 9 Viola x wittrockiana 'Jolly Joker'
Pansy, Viola
Short-lived evergreen perennial grown as an annual. Medium flowers with orange face and rich purple edging, whiskers and upper petals. Hardy.
**General care:** Sow seed under glass in late winter or early spring or outdoors in mid-spring.
**Height:** 20cm (8in) **Spread:** 25cm (10in)
**Site:** Sun or partial shade. Humus-rich and moist but well-drained soil
**Compost:** Soil-based (John Innes No.2) or soil-less
**Use:** Container, edging, formal bedding, front of border
**Good companions:** *Brachyscome iberidifolia* 'Purple Splendour', *Lobelia erinus* ascade Series, *Verbena* 'Imagination'

## silver and grey

### 10 Helichrysum petiolare
This sprawling evergreen shrub with woolly greyish leaves is usually grown as an annual for containers. Variegated cultivars and the yellow-green form 'Limelight' extend the range of foliage effects. Half hardy.
**General care:** In the growing season pinch back long stems to encourage bushy growth.
**Height:** 60cm (2ft) **Spread:** 1.5m (5ft)
**Site:** Sun. Well-drained soil
**Compost:** Soil-based (John Innes No. 2) or soil-less
**Use:** Container, sunny bed or border
**Good companions:** *Argyranthemum* 'Vancouver', *Osteospermum jucundum, Petunia* 'Surfinia Purple', *Scaevola aemula* 'Blue Wonder'

### 11 Papaver rhoeas 'Mother of Pearl'
Corn poppy, Field poppy, Flanders poppy
The common red annual has been bred for colour variations. 'Mother of Pearl' is in pastel shades of dove-grey, mauve-blue and soft pink. Hardy.
**General care:** Sow seed *in situ* in early autumn or early to mid-spring.
**Height:** 1m (3ft) **Spread:** 60cm (2ft)
**Site:** Sun. Well-drained soil
**Use:** Sunny bed or border, wildflower garden
**Good companions:** *Consolida ajacis* Imperial Series, *Convolvulus cneorum, Diascia barberae* 'Ruby Field'

## green

### 12 Nicotiana 'Lime Green'
Tobacco plant
Upright, sticky annual grown for the clusters of yellow-green tubular flowers that are produced all summer. All parts are toxic. Half hardy.
**General care:** Sow seed under glass at 18°C (64°F) in late winter or early spring. Plant out in early summer.
**Height:** 60cm (2ft) **Spread:** 25cm (10in)
**Site:** Sun, partial shade. Moist, well-drained soil
**Use:** Formal bedding, border
**Good companions:** *Impatiens walleriana* Tempo Series, *Molucella laevis, Tropaeolum* 'Alaska'

# bulbs

Bulbs are perennials with underground food storage organs that are described technically as true bulbs, corms, tubers or rhizomes. The small bulbs of spring are followed by a progression of stately bulbs throughout summer.

## purple, blue and violet

### 1 Allium cristophii

**Ornamental onion**

Strap-shaped, rather hairy leaves surround a stout stem, which supports a head, up to 20cm (8in) across, of purple-pink starry flowers. These glint with a metallic sheen and remain ornamental when dried. Hardy.

**General care:** Plant in autumn with the top of the bulb about 10cm (4in) deep.
**Height:** 45cm (18in) **Spread:** 20cm (8in)
**Site:** Sun. Well-drained soil
**Use:** Gravel garden, sunny border
**Good companions:** *Gladiolus communis* subsp. *byzantinus, Santolina chamaecyparissus, Verbena bonariensis*

### 2 Allium 'Globemaster'

**Ornamental onion**

A sturdy stem rises from grey-green strap-like leaves and supports a spherical head, up to 20cm (8in) across, of violet-blue starry flowers. The heads remain attractive when dried. Hardy.

**General care:** Plant in autumn with the top of the bulb about 10cm (4in) deep.
**Height:** 75cm (2ft 6in) **Spread:** 20cm (8in)
**Site:** Sun. Well-drained soil
**Use:** Gravel garden, sunny border
**Good companions:** *Buddleja davidii* 'Black Knight', *Eryngium* x *tripartitum, Stipa gigantea*

### 3 Allium hollandicum 'Purple Sensation'

**Ornamental onion**

The strap-like leaves begin to wither in late spring when tall stems rise to support spherical heads, about 10cm (4in) across, packed with rich purple-pink starry flowers. Attractive when dried. Hardy.

**General care:** Plant in autumn with the top of the bulb about 10cm (4in) deep.
**Height:** 1m (3ft) **Spread:** 15cm (6in)
**Site:** Sun. Well-drained soil
**Use:** Gravel garden, sunny border
**Good companions:** *Artemisia* 'Powis Castle', *Buddleja* 'Lochinch', *Euphorbia characias* subsp. *wulfenii*

### 4 Camassia leichtlinii 'Electra'

The straight flowering stem rises above linear basal leaves and carries numerous purple-blue starry flowers. Does well in damp meadow-like conditions. Not fully hardy.

**General care:** Plant in autumn with the top of the bulb about 10cm (4in) deep.
**Height:** 1.2m (4ft) **Spread:** 20cm (8in)
**Site:** Sun, partial shade. Humus-rich and moist but well-drained soil
**Use:** Moist border, wild garden
**Good companions:** *Cardamine pratensis* 'Flore Pleno', *Fritillaria meleagris, Iris sibirica* 'Ego'

### 5 Scilla peruviana

**Cuban lily, Squill**

In late spring and early summer this bulb produces conical heads that are densely packed

8

9

10

11

12

with up to 100 blue starry flowers. It is nearly evergreen, but as the strap like leaves become untidy in late summer, it is best to plant to hide them. Hardy.
**General care:** Plant in early autumn with the top of the bulb just covered.
**Height:** 30cm (12in) **Spread:** 25cm (10in)
**Site:** Sun. Moist but well-drained soil
**Use:** Sunny border
**Good companions:** *Cosmos bipinnatus* Sensation Series, *Lavatera trimestris* 'Mont Blanc', *Lupinus* 'Chandelier'

## pink and mauve

### 6 Arisaema candidissimum

The true flowers are insignificant but arranged around the base of a white to greenish yellow pencil-like structure, the spadix. This is surrounded by a hooded flower-like bract, or spathe, that is white, broadly striped with pink, and suffused with green. The sweet scent is a surprise. Three-lobed leaves expand after the spathe develops. Not fully hardy.
**General care:** Plant in mid-autumn with the top of the tuber about 15cm (6in) deep.
**Height:** 30cm (12in) **Spread:** 15cm (6in)
**Site:** Sun, partial shade. Lime-free, humus-rich and moist but well-drained soil
**Use:** Peat bed, sunny or lightly shaded border
**Good companions:** *Erythronium californicum* 'White Beauty', *Trillium erectum, Uvularia grandiflora*

### 7 Gladiolus communis subsp. byzantinus

Gladiolus

This southern European species produces a fan of narrow leaves and spikes carrying two ranks of about 20 funnel-shaped flowers in piercing magenta. Unlike the South African species and hybrids, it does not need to be lifted annually and often spreads freely. Hardy.
**General care:** Plant in autumn with the top of the corm about 10cm (4in) deep.
**Height:** 1m (3ft) **Spread:** 8cm (3in)
**Site:** Sun. Well-drained soil
**Use:** Gravel garden, sunny border
**Good companions:** *Artemisia ludoviciana* 'Valerie Finnis', *Ruta graveolens* 'Jackman's Blue'

## red and russet

### 8 Tulipa sprengeri

Species tulip

The last of the tulips to flower, this extends their season into summer. The narrow glossy leaves develop before the bright scarlet flowers open. These have pointed petals and are about 10cm (4in) across. Self-seeds to form colonies in a wide range of conditions. Hardy.
**General care:** Plant in late autumn with the top of the bulb about 15cm (6in) deep.
**Height:** 50cm (20in) **Spread:** 15cm (6in)
**Site:** Sun, partial shade. Humus-rich and well-drained soil
**Use:** Sunny or lightly shaded border, wild garden, woodland garden
**Good companions:** *Anemone blanda, Hyacinthoides non-scripta, Lilium martagon* var. *album*

## cream and white

### 9 Gladiolus 'The Bride'

Miniature gladiolus

Slender hybrid gladiolus with blade-like leaves and spikes of neat white flowers. Half hardy.
**General care:** Plant in spring on a layer of coarse sand with the top of the corm about 10cm (4in) deep. Lift in autumn.
**Height:** 60cm (2ft) **Spread:** 8cm (3in)
**Site:** Sun. Well-drained soil
**Use:** Sunny bed or border
**Good companions:** *Paeonia lactiflora* 'Bowl of Beauty', *Nigella damascena* 'Miss Jekyll', *Veronica spicata* 'Heidekind'

### 10 Lilium candidum

Madonna lily

A stiff flowering stem rises from a rosette of overwintering leaves and carries up to 15 white trumpet-shaped blooms. Richly scented. Hardy.
**General care:** Plant in mid-autumn with the top of the bulb just covered.
**Height:** 1.5m (5ft) **Spread:** 25cm (10in)
**Site:** Sun. Well-drained soil, preferably limy
**Use:** Sunny border
**Good companions:** *Campanula persicifolia, Erysimum* 'Bowles' Mauve', *Papaver orientale* 'Black and White'

### 11 Lilium martagon var. album

Common turkscap lily

Upright stems carry up to 50 white nodding flowers with rolled back segments. The species has purplish pink flowers. Will build up colonies in a wide range of conditions. Hardy.
**General care:** Plant between mid-autumn and early spring with the top of the bulb about 20cm (8in) deep – the roots develop above the bulb.
**Height:** 1.5m (5ft) **Spread:** 20cm (8in)
**Soil:** Sun, partial shade. Well-drained soil. Good on lime
**Use:** Sunny or lightly shaded border, woodland garden
**Good companions:** *Geranium phaeum, Helleborus orientalis, Lunaria annua*

### 12 Lilium regale

Regal lily

Wiry stems carry white funnel-shaped flowers with purple staining on the outside and golden anthers. Scented and good for cutting. Hardy.
**General care:** Plant between mid-autumn and early spring with the top of the bulb about 20cm (8in) deep – the roots develop above the bulb.
**Height:** 1.5m (5ft) **Spread:** 30cm (12in)
**Site:** Sun. Humus-rich, fertile, well-drained soil
**Compost:** Soil-based (John Innes No. 2) with added leaf-mould and grit
**Use:** Container, sunny border
**Companions:** *Campanula lactiflora, Geranium* x *magnificum, Rosa* 'Golden Wings', *Rosa* 'Nevada'

# climbers

Trained on architectural supports or other plants, climbers assert the vertical dimension of the garden. They twine, cling with aerial roots or clasp with tendrils. Plant in the dormant season.

## purple, blue and violet

### 1 Passiflora caerulea
Blue passion flower

This tendril climber has pliant stems and more or less evergreen fingered leaves. Throughout summer there are showy flowers, with a ring (corona) of blue filaments radiating over white segments. Edible fruits, orange when ripe, follow. Not fully hardy.

**General care:** In late winter or early spring cut a proportion of stems hard back.
**Height:** 10m (33ft)
**Spread:** 5m (15ft)
**Site:** Sun, partial shade. Well-drained soil
**Use:** Pergola, screen, wall
**Good companions:** *Clematis* 'Bill MacKenzie', *Rosa* Golden Showers, *Solanum crispum* 'Glasnevin'

### 2 Wisteria floribunda 'Multijuga'
Japanese wisteria

Vigorous twining climber with elegant deciduous foliage, the leaves composed of numerous leaflets. The fragrant, mauve-blue pea flowers of 'Multijuga' trail in drooping sprays up to 1m (3ft) long. Hardy.

**General care:** Prune in late summer and winter.
**Height:** 10m (33ft) **Spread:** 6m (20ft)
**Site:** Sun, partial shade. Moist but well-drained soil, preferably lime-free
**Use:** Pergola, trained standard, tree climber, wall
**Good companions:** *Clematis montana* var. *rubens* 'Elizabeth', *Hedera colchica* 'Dentata Variegata', *Rosa* 'Paul's Himalayan Musk'

### 3 Wisteria x formosa 'Yae-kokuryû'
Wisteria

Vigorous, twining deciduous climber with attractive large leaves divided into numerous leaflets. In late spring and early summer it bears trailing sprays of violet-purple pea flowers. Hardy.

**General care:** Prune in late summer and again in winter.
**Height:** 10m (33ft)
**Spread:** 6m (20ft)
**Site:** Sun, partial shade. Moist but well-drained soil, preferably lime-free
**Use:** Pergola, trained standard, tree climber, wall
**Good companions:** *Lonicera* x *tellmanniana*, *Rosa banksiae* 'Lutea', *Vitis vinifera* 'Purpurea'

## pink and mauve

### 4 Actinidia kolomikta
Deciduous twining climber with insignificant flowers but dramatic foliage when grown in full sun. The dark green heart-shaped leaves become tipped with pink and white, some whole leaves starting white and gradually becoming tinged with pink. Hardy.

**General care:** Little pruning required but when necessary cut back in late winter.
**Height and spread:** 4m (12ft)
**Site:** Sun, partial shade. Humus-rich and moist but well-drained soil
**Use:** Sheltered wall
**Good companions:** *Jasminum officinale*, *Rosa* 'Aimée Vibert', *Rosa* 'Parade'

## red and russet

### 5 Schisandra rubriflora
Deciduous twining climber with reddish shoots, dark green leaves and deep red flowers – male and female on separate plants. Female plants may produce skeins of small, inedible red fruits if grown near a male plant. Hardy.

**General care:** Prune back sideshoots to three or four buds in late winter or early spring.
**Height:** 10m (33ft) **Spread:** 5m (15ft)
**Site:** Sun, partial shade. Moist but well-drained soil, preferably lime-free
**Use:** Pergola, wall
**Good companions:** *Lonicera* x *tellmanniana*, *Rosa* 'Bobbie James', *Vitis coignetiae*

### 6 Vitis vinifera 'Purpurea'
Grape vine, Vine

Vines are deciduous tendril climbers. This cultivar is grown for its foliage and has white downy young leaves that turn claret-red. The purple grapes taste unpleasant. Hardy.

**General care:** Prune in midwinter.
**Height:** 8m (25ft) **Spread:** 5m (15ft)
**Site:** Sun, partial shade, Fertile and well-drained soil, preferably limy
**Use:** Arbour, pergola, wall
**Good companions:** *Clematis montana* var. *rubens* 'Elizabeth', *Lonicera periclymenum* 'Serotina', *Rosa* 'Bobbie James'

## yellow and orange

### 7 Lonicera periclymenum 'Belgica'

Early Dutch honeysuckle

Deciduous twining climber with purplish stems and in late spring and early summer purple-and-yellow flowers. Powerfully scented. Hardy.

**General care:** Prune after flowering, clearing out old stems every two or three years.

**Height:** 5m (15ft) **Spread:** 2.5m (8ft)

**Site:** Partial shade, sun. Humus-rich and moist but well-drained soil

**Use:** Arbour, arch, pergola, tripod, wall

**Good companions:** *Clematis* 'The Vagabond', *Jasminum nudiflorum, Lonicera periclymenum* 'Serotina'

### 8 Lonicera x tellmanniana

Honeysuckle

Deciduous twining climber. The uppermost pair of leaves on each stem is arranged like a cup below a whorl of bronze-yellow two-lipped flowers, from late spring to midsummer. Unscented. Hardy.

**General care:** Plant with the base in shade. Prune after flowering, clearing out old stems every two or three years.

**Height:** 5m (15ft) **Spread:** 2.5m (8ft)

**Site:** Partial shade, sun. Humus-rich and moist but well-drained soil

**Use:** Arbour, arch, pergola, tripod, wall

**Good companions:** *Clematis* 'Royal Velours', *Rosa banksiae* 'Lutea', *Wisteria* x *formosa* 'Yae-kokuryû'

## cream and white

### 9 Hydrangea anomala subsp. petiolaris

Climbing hydrangea

This deciduous climber clings by means of aerial roots. Clusters of tiny, creamy-green fertile flowers surrounded by larger white sterile flowers contrast well with the dark green leaves. Attractive red-brown stems in winter. Hardy.

**General care:** Prune only if necessary to restrict growth immediately after flowering.

**Height:** 10m (33ft) **Spread:** 6m (20ft)

**Site:** Partial shade, sun. Fertile and moist but well-drained soil

**Use:** Screen, wall

**Good companions:** *Clematis* 'Royal Velours', *Cotoneaster horizontalis, Rosa* 'Madame Alfred Carrière'

### 10 Jasminum officinale

Jasmine

Deciduous twining climber with dark green divided leaves and sweetly scented, white star-shaped flowers through summer. Not fully hardy.

**General care:** Thin out overgrown plants after flowering.

**Height:** 10m (33ft) **Spread:** 5m (15ft)

**Site:** Sun, partial shade. Moist but well-drained soil

**Use:** Arbour, pergola, wall

**Good companions:** *Clematis* 'Comtesse de Bouchaud', *Osmanthus delavayi, Rosa* 'Madame Grégoire Staechelin'

## green

### 11 Humulus lupulus 'Aureus'

Hop

Vigorous twining perennial climber with deeply lobed, bristly leaves. 'Aureus' has yellow-green leaves. For best colour grow in full sun. Hardy.

**General care:** Check tendency to spread too far.

**Height:** 6m (20ft) **Spread:** 4m (12ft)

**Site:** Sun, partial shade. Moist but well-drained soil

**Use:** Arbour, screen, tripod, wall

**Good companions:** *Aconitum* 'Ivorine', *Clematis* 'Perle d'Azur', *Geranium* 'Johnson's Blue'

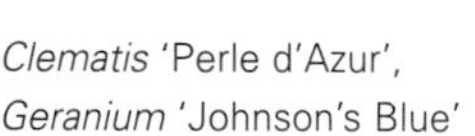

### 12 Parthenocissus henryana

Chinese Virginia creeper

Deciduous tree climber with suckers. The velvety-green, sometimes bronzed leaves have silvery veins and turn red in autumn. Not fully hardy.

**General care:** Prune after flowering, clearing out old stems every two or three years.

**Height:** 10m (33ft) **Spread:** 6m (20ft)

**Site:** Partial shade, sun. Fertile, well-drained soil

**Use:** Sheltered wall, ground cover

**Good companions:** *Clematis montana* var. *rubens* 'Elizabeth', *Euonymus fortunei* 'Silver Queen', *Hedera colchica* 'Dentata Variegata'

# clematis

Many large-flowered clematis hybrids bloom over a long season and are useful for growing over shrubs, tripods and walls. Plant them in autumn or spring, with the roots in shade, in humus-rich, well-drained soil; clematis do well on lime. For containers use a soil-based compost (John Innes No. 3). Prune in late spring or early autumn, cutting back to a pair of strong buds. All the clematis featured here are hardy and deciduous.

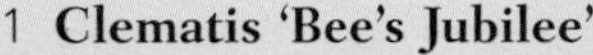

### 1 Clematis 'Bee's Jubilee'

Dark pink bars along the centre of each petal-like sepal give the mauve-pink single flowers, up to 20cm (8in) across, a starry appearance. Flowers again in early autumn. Ornamental seed heads follow the flowers.
**Height:** 2.5m (8ft) **Spread:** 1m (3ft)
**Good companions:** *Anemone* x *hybrida* 'Whirlwind', *Clematis macropetala, Rosa* 'Parade'

### 2 Clematis 'Gillian Blades'

Single white flowers, up to 20cm (8in) across, with overlapping petal-like sepals that have mauve-tinted crimped margins and soft yellow anthers. Flowers from late spring to early summer and again in early autumn.
**Height:** 2.5m (8ft) **Spread:** 1m (3ft)
**Good companions:** *Anemone* x *hybrida* 'Whirlwind', *Clematis* 'Perle d'Azur', *Rosa* 'Parade'

### 3 Clematis 'Perle d'Azur'

Sky-blue flowers, up to 15cm (6in) across and with pale yellow anthers, are produced over a long summer season. The tips of the petal-like sepals are turned back.
**Height:** 3m (10ft) **Spread:** 1m (3ft)
**Good companions:** *Campanula lactiflora* 'Prichard's Variety', *Lathyrus odoratus* 'Noel Sutton', *Rosa* 'Gloire de Dijon', *Rosa* 'Madame Grégoire Staechelin'

1

### 4 Clematis 'Niobe'

This versatile hybrid produces deep red single flowers up to 20cm (8in) across. The broad petal-like sepals are ridged lengthwise and the anthers are yellow.
**Height:** 2.5m (8ft) **Spread:** 1m (3ft)
**Good companions:** *Clematis* 'Gillian Blades', *Syringa vulgaris* 'Madame Lemoine', *Rosa* 'Parade'

### 5 Clematis 'Jackmanii'

From early summer to autumn this hybrid bears violet-purple single flowers, about 10cm (4in) across. They open flat and are of velvety texture.
**Height:** 3m (10ft) **Spread:** 1m (3ft)
**Good companions:** *Clematis* 'Helsingborg', *Clematis* 'Bill MacKenzie', *Rosa* 'Maigold'

### 6 Clematis 'The Vagabond'

Short-growing climber suitable for a small garden. Each petal-like sepal of the rich maroon-purple flowers has a central reddish bar. The anthers are creamy yellow. Flowers again in late summer and autumn.
**Height:** 2m (6ft) **Spread:** 1m (3ft)
**Good companions:** *Clematis alpina* subsp. *sibirica* 'White Moth', *Rosa* 'Aimée Vibert', *Solanum crispum* 'Glasnevin'

### 7 Clematis Blue Moon

Flowers are 15cm (6in) or more across. The central bars of the petal-like sepals are at first greenish white and then more silvery, but the ruffled margins are pale mauve-blue. Maroon anthers make a dark, eye-catching centre. Flowers from late spring to early summer and again in early autumn.
**Height:** 3m (10ft) **Spread:** 1m (3ft)
**Good companions:** *Aquilegia vulgaris* 'Nivea', *Digitalis purpurea, Lunaria annua, Rosa* 'Madame Alfred Carrière'

### 8 Clematis 'Lasurstern'

Bears blue flowers, often more than 15cm (6in) across, that consist of 7–8 wavy-margined finely tapered petal-like sepals. There is a crop of smaller flowers in early autumn.
**Height:** 3m (10ft) **Spread:** 1m (3ft)
**Good companions:** *Clematis montana* var. *rubens* 'Elizabeth', *Rosa* 'Parade', *Wisteria floribunda* 'Multijuga'

2

3

4
5
6
7
8

# climbing roses

Ramblers and some climbing roses flower in one spectacular flush in early summer. Others bloom nearly continuously or in several flushes from early summer to autumn. Both are invaluable for arbours, arches, pillars and walls. Plant in autumn or spring in fertile and moist but well-drained soil. All roses featured here are deciduous and hardy.

2

3

### 1 Rosa 'Bobbie James'

Vigorous rambler with glossy, light green foliage and large trusses of strongly fragrant, creamy-white semi-double flowers. At home scrambling up a sturdy tree.

**Height:** 8m (25ft) **Spread:** 6m (20ft)

**Good companions:** *Solanum laxum* 'Album', *Vitis coignetiae, Vitis vinifera* 'Purpurea'

### 2 Rosa Compassion

Climbing Hybrid Tea rose with dark green foliage. Throughout summer apricot-pink blooms, with yellow and copper tints, open from high-centred buds.

**Height:** 3m (10ft) **Spread:** 2.5m (8ft)

**Good companions:** *Clematis alpina* 'Frances Rivis', *Clematis* 'Lasurstern', *Solanum laxum* 'Album'

### 3 Rosa 'Madame Alfred Carrière'

Vigorous old climber with light green leaves and several flushes of fragrant, creamy-pink double flowers that fade to white. Good for siting on a north-facing wall.

**Height:** 5m (15ft) **Spread:** 3m (10ft)

**Good companions:** *Clematis* 'Perle d'Azur', *Clematis* 'Royal Velours', *Geranium psilostemon*

### 4 Rosa 'Madame Grégoire Staechelin'

Vigorous climbing Hybrid Tea rose with a short season of exceptional double flowers that are pink flushed with red and strongly scented. Large red hips follow. Good for a north-facing wall.

**Height:** 5m (15ft) **Spread:** 3m (10ft)

**Good companions:** *Clematis* 'The Vagabond', *Lonicera japonica* 'Halliana', *Rosa* 'Madame Alfred Carrière'

### 5 Rosa 'Veilchenblau'

This vigorous rambler has almost thornless stems and crowded clusters of fragrant semi-double flowers. Mauve buds open to white-centred violet-purple flowers. Their colour intensifies before fading to slate-grey.

**Height and spread:** 4m (12ft)

**Good companions:** *Jasminum officinale, Lonicera periclymenum* 'Serotina', *Rosa* 'Aimée Vibert'

### 6 Rosa 'Paul's Himalayan Musk'

Rampant rambler best trained into a large tree. The small mauve-pink double flowers are borne profusely in a single magnificent burst, often in trailing sprays.

**Height:** 10m (33ft) **Spread:** 5m (15ft)

**Good companions:** *Schisandra rubriflora, Vitis coignetiae, Wisteria floribunda* 'Multijuga'

### 7 Rosa 'Parade'

Modern climber with glossy leaves and deep pink scented flowers, which open almost flat in several flushes from early summer to early autumn.

**Height and spread:** 3m (10ft)

**Good companions:** *Ceanothus* x *delileanus* 'Topaze', *Clematis* 'Alba Luxurians', *Rosa* Mary Rose

4

5

1

6

7

# shrubs & trees

Trees and shrubs have durable frameworks of woody branches. They bring structure to the garden and their foliage creates shade in summer, while the flowers of many provide long-lasting displays. Plant in the dormant season, preferably in autumn or early spring.

## purple, blue and violet

### 1 Buddleja alternifolia

Deciduous shrub or small tree with slender arching branches and alternate lance-shaped leaves. The fragrant mauve-purple flowers encrust the previous year's growths. Hardy.
**General care:** Immediately after flowering cut back all shoots that have flowered.
**Height and spread:** 4m (12ft)
**Site:** Sun. Fertile and well-drained soil
**Use:** Specimen standard, sunny border
**Good companions:** *Buddleja davidii* 'Black Knight', *Hibiscus syriacus* 'Oiseau Bleu', *Rosa* 'Golden Wings'

1

2

3

### 2 Ceanothus 'Italian Skies'

California lilac
Evergreen shrub with a dense framework of branches and dark leaves. In late spring and early summer these are almost hidden by rounded heads of deep blue flowers. Not fully hardy.
**Height:** 1.5m (5ft) **Spread:** 3m (10ft)
**Site:** Sun. Well-drained soil
**Use:** Sunny sheltered border, wall shrub
**Good companions:** *Actinidia kolomikta, Garrya elliptica, Solanum laxum* 'Album'

### 3 Hebe 'Youngii'

Compact evergreen shrub with red-edged leaves. Starry flowers, at first violet-blue but later fading to white, are clustered in small spikes. Hardy.
**Height:** 30cm (12in) **Spread:** 75cm (2ft 6in)
**Site:** Sun. Moist but well-drained soil
**Use:** Sunny border, rock garden, ground cover
**Good companions:** *Diascia rigescens, Monarda* 'Prärienacht', *Sisyrinchium striatum* 'Aunt May'

### 4 Ruta graveolens 'Jackman's Blue'

Rue
Common rue is a strongly aromatic evergreen shrubby herb, but this form is grown as a foliage plant. The divided leaves make a dense blue-green mound. In summer there are clusters of small yellow flowers. Hardy.
**General care:** Trim plants in early spring.

4

5

**Height:** 60cm (2ft) **Spread:** 75cm (2ft 6in)
**Site:** Sun. Well-drained soil
**Use:** Gravel garden, herb garden, sunny border
**Good companions:** *Potentilla fruticosa* 'Tangerine', *Rosa* 'Golden Wings', *Verbascum* 'Helen Johnson'

## pink and mauve

### 5 Abelia schumannii

Bushy deciduous shrub with dark green leaves that are coloured bronze when young. Throughout summer and into autumn lightly scented funnel-shaped flowers are produced prolifically. These are reddish pink on the outside with an orange blotch on the pale inside. Not fully hardy.
**Height and spread:** 2m (6ft)
**Site:** Sun. Well-drained soil
**Use:** Sunny border
**Good companions:** *Caryopteris × clandonensis* 'Heavenly Blue', *Perovskia* 'Blue Spire', *Thalictrum flavum* subsp. *glaucum*

### 6 Cistus 'Silver Pink'

Rock rose, Sun rose
Compact, mound-forming evergreen shrub that bears clusters of silver-pink saucer-shaped flowers. Individual blooms are short-lived but there is a continuous supply over many weeks. Not fully hardy.
**Height:** 75cm (2ft 6in) **Spread:** 1m (3ft)
**Site:** Sun. Well-drained soil
**Use:** Gravel garden, sunny border
**Good companions:** *Allium hollandicum* 'Purple Sensation', *Cistus ladanifer*

6

## pink and mauve (continued)

### 1 Cornus kousa var. chinensis 'Satomi'
Flowering dogwood
*Cornus kousa* itself is a handsome tree or shrub, with tiered branches and conspicuous white petal-like bracts surrounding clusters of tiny flowers. This more upright and richly coloured form has long-lasting bright pink bracts. In autumn the foliage turns red-purple. Hardy.
**Height:** 6m (20ft) **Spread:** 5m (15ft)
**Site:** Sun, partial shade. Humus-rich and moist but well-drained soil, preferably lime-free
**Use:** Specimen shrub, woodland garden
**Good companions:** *Hydrangea macrophylla* 'Blue Wave', *Hydrangea paniculata* 'Unique', *Magnolia* x *kewensis* 'Wada's Memory'

### 2 Deutzia x rosea
Most of the deutzias are undemanding deciduous shrubs that bear a profusion of white, pink or purple blooms. During the first half of summer this compact hybrid produces clusters of pink to red-flushed star-shaped flowers. Hardy.
**General care:** Prune immediately after flowering, cutting back to the base all stems that have flowered.
**Height and spread:** 1.2m (4ft)
**Site:** Sun, partial shade. Well-drained soil
**Use:** Sunny or lightly shaded border, woodland garden
**Good companions:** *Ceratostigma willmottianum*, *Choisya ternata*, *Exochorda* x *macrantha* 'The Bride'

### 3 Kalmia latifolia 'Ostbo Red'
Calico bush
Dense evergreen shrub with glossy leaves. Most of the calico bushes bear clusters of pink flowers, which are very attractive as curiously pleated buds. Those of 'Ostbo Red' are bright red but open to pale pink bowl-shaped blooms. Hardy.
**Height and spread:** 3m (10ft)
**Site:** Partial shade. Lime-free, humus-rich and moist but well-drained soil
**Use:** Shady border, woodland garden
**Good companions:** *Camellia* x *williamsii* 'Donation', *Enkianthus campanulatus*, *Rhododendron* 'Bow Bells', *Rhododendron* 'Loderi King George'

### 4 Kolkwitzia amabalis 'Pink Cloud'
Beauty bush
During late spring and early summer masses of pink bell-shaped flowers, with yellow-flushed throats, cover the arching stems of this twiggy deciduous shrub. Hardy.
**General care:** Prune immediately after flowering.
**Height:** 4m (12ft) **Spread:** 3m (10ft)
**Site:** Sun. Well-drained soil
**Use:** Specimen shrub, sunny border
**Good companions:** *Geranium macrorrhizum* 'Ingwersen's Variety', *Geranium wallichianum* 'Buxton's Variety', *Rosa* 'Nevada'

### 5 Rhododendron 'Vanessa Pastel'
This compact evergreen hybrid produces trusses of creamy-pink funnel-shaped flowers at the end of the rhododendron season. The crimson eye contrasts with the soft colours of the flowers as does the deeper pink of the buds. Hardy.
**Height and spread:** 2m (6ft)
**Site:** Partial shade. Lime-free, humus-rich and moist but well-drained soil
**Use:** Lightly shaded border, woodland garden
**Good companions:** *Enkianthus campanulatus*, *Eucryphia* x *nymansensis* 'Nymansay', *Meconopsis betonicifolia*

### 6 Weigela 'Victoria'
The hybrid weigelas are showy deciduous shrubs that produce bell-shaped flowers in profusion from late spring to early summer. The colour range includes shades of pink to crimson and sometimes white. 'Victoria' has red-pink flowers

and purplish leaves. Hardy.
**General care:** Prune after flowering.
**Height and spread:** 2m (6ft)
**Site:** Sun, partial shade. Well-drained soil
**Use:** Sunny or lightly shaded border
**Good companions:** *Deutzia* x *rosea*, *Forsythia* x *intermedia* 'Lynwood', *Iris* 'Florentina', *Kolkwitzia amabilis* 'Pink Cloud'

## red and russet

### 7 Fuchsia 'Lady Thumb'
Hybrid fuchsia
The small semi-double flowers of this upright fuchsia have a red-veined white skirt (corolla) below the light crimson tube and spreading sepals. The flowering season lasts from early summer until autumn. Not fully hardy.
**General care:** Cut back to a low framework in early spring.
**Height:** 30cm (12in) **Spread:** 45cm (18in)
**Site:** Sun, partial shade. Fertile and moist but well-drained soil
**Compost:** Soil-based (John Innes No. 3) or soil-less
**Use:** Container, sunny or lightly shaded border
**Good companions:** *Brachyscome iberidifolia* 'Purple Splendour', *Helichrysum petiolare*, *Lobelia erinus* Cascade Series, *Verbena* 'Silver Anne'

7

8

### 8 Rhododendron 'Britannia'
Evergreen shrub that makes a somewhat flattened rounded bush with pale green leaves. It bears dense trusses of radiant scarlet bell-shaped flowers. Hardy.
**Height:** 1.5m (5ft)
**Spread:** 2.4m (8ft)
**Site:** Partial shade. Lime-free, humus-rich and moist but well-drained soil
**Use:** Lightly shaded border, woodland garden
**Good companions:** *Camellia japonica* 'Bob Hope', *Magnolia denudata*, *Pieris* 'Forest Flame'

9

10

## yellow and orange

### 9 Gleditsia triacanthos 'Sunburst'
Honey locust
Deciduous tree, which, unlike other honey locusts, is thornless and does not produce seedpods. It is grown for its bright yellow young foliage, which becomes light green as summer progresses and turns yellow again in autumn. Hardy.
**Height:** 12m (40ft) **Spread:** 9m (30ft)
**Site:** Sun. Well-drained soil
**Use:** Canopy in mixed planting, specimen tree
**Good companions:** *Arbutus unedo*, *Crataegus persimilis* 'Prunifolia', *Genista aetnensis*

### 10 Potentilla fruticosa 'Tangerine'
Cinquefoil
The numerous cultivars of *Potentilla fruticosa* are mainly compact deciduous shrubs that flower from late spring until autumn in yellow, cream, white, pink or red. 'Tangerine' is a spreading plant with orange-yellow blooms. Hardy.
**Height:** 1m (3ft) **Spread:** 1.5m (5ft)
**Site:** Sun. Well-drained soil
**Use:** Gravel garden, sunny bed, large rock garden
**Good companions:** *Buddleja* 'Lochinch', *Caryopteris* x *clandonensis* 'Heavenly Blue', *Lavandula* x *intermedia* Dutch Group, *Origanum laevigatum* 'Herrenhausen'

11

### 11 Rhododendron luteum
Deciduous azalea
This open deciduous shrub has slightly hairy lance-shaped leaves that turn rich shades of red in autumn. In late spring and early summer clusters of yellow trumpet-shaped flowers exhale a strong, sweet scent. Easy to grow and more tolerant of dry conditions than most azaleas. Hardy.
**Height and spread:** 4m (12ft)
**Site:** Sun, partial shade. Lime-free, humus-rich and moist but well-drained soil
**Use:** Sunny or lightly shaded border, woodland garden
**Good companions:** *Fothergilla major* Monticola Group, *Halesia carolina*, *Hamamelis* x *intermedia* 'Diane', *Magnolia* 'Elizabeth'

12

### 12 Robinia pseudoacacia 'Frisia'
Black locust, False acacia, Locust
Rugged, medium-sized deciduous tree with spiny twigs. The leaves, about 30cm (12in) long and composed of numerous leaflets, are at first rich yellow then become yellow-green during summer and finally orange-yellow in autumn. Hardy.
**Height:** 15m (50ft) **Spread:** 8m (25ft)
**Site:** Sun. Well-drained soil
**Use:** Canopy in mixed planting, specimen tree
**Good companions:** *Buddleja davidii* 'Black Knight', *Cotinus* 'Grace', *Cryptomeria japonica* Elegans Group

## cream and white

### 1 Cistus ladanifer
Common gum cistus, Laudanum
Erect evergreen shrub with sticky, aromatic lance-shaped leaves. The white flowers are yellow at the centre and usually have a crimson-chocolate blotch at the base of each crumpled petal. Although individual flowers are short-lived, the display is long lasting. Not fully hardy.
**Height:** 2m (6ft) **Spread:** 1.5m (5ft)
**Site:** Sun. Well-drained soil
**Use:** Gravel garden, sunny border
**Good companions:** *Allium cristophii, Lavandula* x *intermedia* Dutch Group, *Lavatera* 'Barnsley'

### 2 Cornus alba 'Elegantissima'
Red-barked dogwood
Several cultivars of the deciduous species are grown to brighten the winter garden with their colourful stems. 'Elegantissima' has attractive red twigs but is grown chiefly for its foliage of grey-green leaves with an irregular white margin. There are white flowers in late spring and early summer. Hardy.
**General care:** Cut back to a framework of stems in early spring.
**Height:** 2.5m (8ft) **Spread:** 3m (10ft)
**Site:** Sun, partial shade. Moist but well-drained soil
**Use:** Sunny or lightly shaded border
**Good companions:** *Clematis* 'Royal Velours', *Thalictrum aquilegiifolium* 'Thundercloud', *Viola cornuta* Alba Group

### 3 Cornus controversa 'Variegata'
Cornel, dogwood
Small deciduous tree with tiered branches and white-variegated foliage. In early summer there are clusters of creamy-white flowers, which are followed by inedible blue-black fruits. Hardy.
**Height:** 7.5m (25ft) **Spread:** 6m (20ft)
**Site:** Sun. Moist but well-drained soil, preferably lime-free
**Use:** Canopy in mixed planting, specimen tree, woodland garden
**Good companions:** *Anemone nemorosa* 'Royal Blue', *Erythronium dens-canis, Narcissus* 'Jack Snipe', *Tulipa sprengeri*

### 4 Magnolia sieboldii
This spreading deciduous shrub has grey-green leaves that are hairy on the underside. In late spring and intermittently throughout summer nodding egg-shaped buds open to fragrant, outward-facing white flowers, 10cm (4in) across, with orange-crimson anthers. Hardy.
**General care:** Carry out any minimal pruning required in early spring. Avoid heavy pruning.
**Height:** 6m (20ft) **Spread:** 9m (30ft)
**Site:** Sun, partial shade. Humus-rich and moist but well-drained soil
**Use:** Specimen shrub, woodland garden
**Good companions:** *Cornus kousa* var. *chinensis, Hamamelis* x *intermedia* 'Arnold Promise', *Hydrangea paniculata* 'Unique'

### 5 Philadelphus 'Belle Etoile'
Mock orange
The hybrid mock oranges are deciduous shrubs with white, sometimes tinted, flowers that are usually strongly scented. The largest, such as the white double 'Virginal,' are 3m (10ft) high. The creamy double 'Manteau d'Hermine' is spreading but only 75cm (2ft 6in) high. This example of medium height has single flowers stained purple at the centre. Hardy.
**General care:** Prune immediately after flowering
**Height:** 2.5m (8ft)
**Spread:** 2m (6ft)
**Site:** Sun, partial shade. Well-drained soil
**Use:** Sunny or lightly shaded border
**Good companions:** *Cornus alba* 'Elegantissima', *Fatsia japonica, Geranium psilostemon*

### 6 Rhododendron 'Loder's White'
This large-leaved evergreen shrub forms a green dome that in summer is studded with cone-shaped trusses of funnel-shaped flowers. These open white from mauve-pink buds and are sparsely flecked with crimson. Hardy.
**Height and spread:** 3m (10ft)
**Site:** Sun, partial shade. Lime-free, humus-rich and moist but well-drained soil
**Use:** Sunny or lightly shaded border, woodland garden
**Good companions:** *Cornus kousa* var. *chinensis* 'Satomi', *Hydrangea macrophylla* 'Blue Wave', *Kalmia latifolia* 'Ostbo Red'

### 7 Styrax japonicus
Japanese snowbell
Deciduous large shrub or small tree with drooping growth and glossy foliage that colours subtly in autumn. White snowdrop-like flowers dangle from the underside of the slender stems. Hardy.
**Height:** 10m (33ft) **Spread:** 7.5m (25ft)
**Site:** Sun. Lime-free, humus-rich and moist but well-drained soil
**Use:** Canopy in mixed planting, specimen shrub or tree, woodland garden
**Good companions:** *Acer japonicum* 'Vitifolium', *Hydrangea aspera* Villosa Group, *Hydrangea paniculata* 'Unique'

## silver and grey

### 8 Artemisia arborescens
This rounded evergreen shrub is grown for the silvery filigree of its aromatic cut leaves. There are small yellow flowerheads in late summer and autumn. Hardy.
**General care:** Keep compact by cutting back in early to mid-spring.
**Height:** 1m (3ft) **Spread:** 1.5m (5ft)
**Site:** Sun. Well-drained soil
**Use:** Gravel garden, sunny border
**Good companions:** *Gladiolus communis* subsp. *byzantinus, Lavandula* x *intermedia* Dutch Group, *Verbascum* 'Helen Johnson'

## green

### 9 Melianthus major
Honey bush
Hollow-stemmed evergreen shrub grown mainly

4

7

9

8

10

5

6

for its grey or blue-green foliage. The deeply divided leaves are up to 50cm (20in) long. Maroon flowers may appear in early summer. Half hardy, but sprouts from the base if hit by frosts.
**Height:** 2.5m (8ft) **Spread:** 3m (10ft)
**Site:** Sun. Well-drained soil
**Compost:** Soil-based (John Innes No. 2)
**Use:** Container, sunny border
**Good companions:** *Argyranthemum* 'Vancouver', *Helichrysum petiolare, Pelargonium* 'Chocolate Peppermint'

### 10 Betula pendula 'Youngii'
Young's weeping birch

The common birch is a graceful deciduous tree with white bark and diamond-shaped leaves that move freely on slender stems. 'Youngii' makes a small, dome-shaped weeping tree with mid-green leaves that turn yellow in autumn. Hardy.
**Height:** 7.5m (25ft) **Spread:** 6m (20ft)
**Site:** Sun, partial shade. Moist but well-drained soil
**Use:** Canopy in mixed planting, specimen tree
**Good companions:** *Helleborus foetidus, Iris foetidissima, Narcissus* 'Peeping Tom', *Pachysandra terminalis*

### 11 Fargesia murielae
Umbrella bamboo

Clump-forming evergreen bamboo with a column of arching yellow-green canes and showers of bright green leaves. Expands slowly. Hardy.

11

12

**Height:** 4m (12ft) **Spread:** 2m (6ft)
**Site:** Sun, partial shade. Moist, well-drained soil
**Compost:** Soil-based (John Innes No. 3) with added leaf-mould
**Use:** Container, hedge, screen, specimen clump, waterside, woodland garden
**Good companions:** *Acer palmatum* 'Bloodgood', *Asplenium scolopendrium, Dryopteris wallichianum, Fatsia japonica*

### 12 Trachycarpus fortunei
Chusan palm

Slow-growing evergreen palm with an impressive head of pleated fan-shaped leaves. Mature specimens produce large clusters of creamy-yellow flowers in early summer, sometimes followed by inedible blue-black fruits. Requires a sheltered position. Not fully hardy.
**Height:** 10m (33ft) **Spread:** 3m (10ft)
**Site:** Sun, partial shade. Fertile, well-drained soil
**Use:** Specimen tree, sunny border
**Good companions:** *Choisya ternata, Fatsia japonica, Phormium* 'Sundowner'

# shrub roses

The non-climbing roses are a very mixed group of shrubs, but all flower generously – some in one magnificent flush while others repeat over a long season that may extend into autumn. Plant in autumn or spring in fertile and moist but well-drained soil, in full sun. All roses featured here are deciduous and hardy.

1

### 1 Rosa 'Céleste'

Alba rose with grey-green foliage and soft pink semi-double blooms. Flowers once only but the fragrant flowers are of exquisite quality.
**Height:** 2m (6ft) **Spread:** 1.2m (4ft)
**Good companions:** *Campanula persicifolia, Lilium regale, Viola cornuta* Alba Group

### 2 Rosa Mary Rose

English shrub rose with dull mat foliage but fragrant, pink, loose-petalled double flowers that are borne almost continuously over a long season.
**Height and spread:** 1.2m (4ft)
**Good companions:** *Delphinium* Belladonna Group 'Cliveden Beauty', *Geranium* 'Johnson's Blue', *Penstemon* 'Evelyn'

### 3 Rosa Bonica

This spreading ground-covering shrub rose has rich green glossy foliage and bears sprays of double pink flowers throughout summer and into autumn.
**Height:** 1m (3ft) **Spread:** 2m (6ft)
**Good companions:** *Dianthus* 'Gran's Favourite', *Stachys byzantina* 'Silver Carpet', *Veronica spicata* 'Heidekind'

### 4 Rosa 'Reine des Violettes'

Hybrid perpetual rose with grey-green leaves and velvety violet-purple double flowers that open flat. Good scent.
**Height:** 1.5m (5ft) **Spread:** 1m (3ft)
**Good companions:** *Nepeta* 'Six Hills Giant', *Rosa* 'Céleste', *Rosa* 'Louise Odier'

### 5 Rosa Alexander

Vigorous hybrid tea rose with glossy dark green foliage and conical buds. The bright vermilion blooms have scalloped petals and repeat well in several flushes during summer and early autumn. Long stemmed and good for cutting.
**Height:** 2m (6ft) **Spread:** 75cm (2ft 6in)
**Good companions:** *Diascia barberae* 'Ruby Field', *Geranium* x *magnificum, Nepeta* 'Six Hills Giant'

### 6 Rosa 'Complicata'

Gallica rose with single bright pink flowers, paler in the centre and up to 10cm (4in) across, borne along the full length of arching stems. Lightly scented.
**Height:** 1.5m (5ft)
**Spread:** 2.5m (8ft)
**Good companions:** *Campanula persicifolia, Dianthus* 'Gran's Favourite', *Viola cornuta* Alba Group

### 7 Rosa 'Nevada'

Large arching shrub rose, with almost thornless red stems and lightly scented, creamy white, flat semi-double blooms. These appear from late spring to early summer, when they peak, and again in autumn.
**Height and spread:** 2.5m (8ft)
**Good companions:** *Campanula lactiflora, Galtonia candicans, Paeonia mlokosewitschii, Tulipa* 'Spring Green'

### 8 Rosa 'Golden Wings'

This vigorous thorny shrub rose flowers with few pauses throughout summer and into autumn. The single or semi-double yellow blooms have a sweet fresh scent.
**Height :** 2m (6ft) **Spread:** 75cm (2ft 6in)
**Good companions:** *Crocosmia* 'Lucifer', *Geranium* x *magnificum, Veronica austriaca* subsp. *teucrium* 'Kapitän'

### 9 Rosa Mountbatten

Vigorous, tall floribunda rose that flowers freely in summer and again in autumn. The conical buds open to bright yellow double flowers that are well scented.
**Height:** 2m (6ft) **Spread:** 75cm (2ft 6in)
**Good companions:** *Alchemilla mollis, Buxus sempervirens* 'Suffruticosa', *Lavandula angustifolia* 'Hidcote', *Viola* 'Baby Lucia'

# alpines

Most of these small perennials and shrubs will thrive in any sunny, well-drained conditions, not just in rock gardens. Many are at their flowering peak in early summer. Plant in mild weather between autumn and early spring.

1

2

## purple, blue and violet

### 1 Campanula cochleariifolia

Fairies' thimbles

This easily grown dwarf perennial colonises ground with thin running roots, creating mats of shiny green leaves, over which dangle small blue or white bells. Hardy.

**Height:** 8cm (3in) **Spread:** 45cm (18in) or more

**Site:** Sun, partial shade. Moist, well-drained soil

**Use:** Paving, raised bed, rock garden, wall

**Good companions:** *Armeria maritima* 'Düsseldorfer Stolz', *Geranium cinereum* 'Ballerina', *Hebe cupressoides* 'Boughton Dome'

### 2 Lithodora diffusa 'Heavenly Blue'

This shrubby evergreen forms wide mats of dark, slightly hairy leaves. In late spring and early summer the trailing stems are sheeted with flowers of intense blue. Hardy.

**Height:** 15cm (6in) **Spread:** 75cm (2ft 6in) or more

**Site:** Sun. Lime-free and humus-rich but well-drained soil

**Use:** Bank, raised bed, rock garden, ground cover

**Good companions:** *Calluna vulgaris* 'Darkness', *Gaultheria mucronata* 'Bell's Seedling', *Sorbus reducta*

## pink and mauve

### 3 Armeria maritima 'Düsseldorfer Stolz'

Sea thrift

The grass-like leaves of sea thrift, an evergreen perennial, are packed together to form a close hummock, above which small starry flowers are carried in late spring and summer. 'Düsseldorfer Stolz' bears red-pink flowers, but other forms are usually softer pink or occasionally white. Hardy.

**Height:** 20cm (8in) **Spread:** 30cm (12in)

**Site:** Sun. Well-drained soil

**Compost:** Soil-based (John Innes No. 1) with added grit

**Use:** Paving, raised bed, rock garden, trough, ground cover

**Good companions:** *Artemisia schmidtiana* 'Nana', *Convolvulus sabatius, Geranium cinereum* 'Ballerina'

### 4 Dianthus alpinus 'Joan's Blood'

Alpine pink

Although generally short-lived perennials, alpine pinks are worth propagating every two or three years for their fringed single flowers. These are pink to crimson and hide the cushion of dark green leaves. 'Joan's Blood' has bright magenta flowers with a dark red centre. Hardy.

**Height:** 10cm (4in)

**Spread:** 15cm (6in)

**Site:** Sun. Limy, humus-rich, gritty and sharply drained soil

**Compost:** Soil-based (John Innes No. 1) with added leaf-mould and grit

**Use:** Raised bed, rock garden, scree, trough

**Good companions:** *Armeria juniperifolia, Crocus sieberi* 'Violet Queen', *Daphne cneorum*

3

### 5 Geranium cinereum 'Ballerina'

Cranesbill

Compact evergreen perennial that forms a mound of lobed grey-green leaves. The dark-eyed veined pink flowers are

4

5

7

8

9

borne over many weeks. Hardy.
**Height:** 15cm (6in) **Spread:** 30cm (12in)
**Site:** Sun, partial shade. Well-drained soil
**Use:** Paving, raised bed, rock garden
**Good companions:** *Gypsophila repens* 'Rosa Schönheit', *Lavandula angustifolia* 'Nana Alba', *Muscari botryoides* 'Album'

### 6 Gypsophila repens 'Rosa Schönheit'

Mound-forming perennial with grey-green leaves, above which hover sprays of small flowers in summer. Hardy.
**Height:** 20cm (8in) **Spread:** 45cm (18in)
**Site:** Sun. Well-drained soil, preferably limy
**Use:** Dry wall, raised bed, rock garden
**Good companions:** *Aethionema* 'Warley Rose', *Aubrieta* 'Greencourt Purple', *Convolvulus sabatius*

## yellow, cream and white

### 7 Achillea x lewisii 'King Edward'

Yarrow

Mound-forming perennial with soft, ferny grey-green leaves that often last through winter. For many weeks in summer flat heads of biscuit-yellow flowers top the foliage. Hardy.
**Height:** 15cm (6in) **Spread:** 20cm (8in)
**Site:** Sun. Well-drained soil
**Use:** Front of border, raised bed, rock garden
**Good companions:** *Helianthemum* 'Wisley Primrose', *Linum* 'Gemmell's Hybrid', *Tulipa clusiana* var. *chrysantha*

### 8 Arenaria montana

Sandwort

The glistening white flowers of this evergreen shrubby perennial spangle trailing stems of dark green foliage. Easily grown in a crevice. Hardy.
**Height:** 15cm (6in) **Spread:** 45cm (18in)
**Site:** Sun. Well-drained and gritty soil
**Use:** Dry wall, paving, raised bed, rock garden, ground cover
**Good companions:** *Aubrieta* 'Doctor Mules', *Helianthemum* 'Wisley Primrose', *Sempervivum tectorum*

6

### 9 Helianthemum 'Wisley Primrose'

Rock rose, Sun rose

The dwarf hybrid rock roses are low evergreen shrubs with grey-green or dark green leaves. They bear masses of papery single or double flowers over many weeks. 'Wisley Primrose' has soft yellow single flowers with a more deeply coloured centre, but other rock roses may be yellow, orange, red, yellow, pink or white. Hardy.
**General care:** To keep compact, trim after flowering.
**Height:** 30cm (12in) **Spread:** 45cm (18in)
**Site:** Sun. Well-drained soil. Does well on lime
**Use:** Front of sunny border, paving, raised bed, rock garden, sunny bank, ground cover
**Good companions:** *Aubrieta* 'Greencourt Purple', *Campanula carpatica, Pulsatilla vulgaris*

10

### 10 Lavandula angustifolia 'Nana Alba'

Lavender, Old English lavender

There are several compact cultivars of *Lavandula angustifolia* but most, including purple-flowered 'Hidcote', grow to at least 45cm (18in) in height. 'Nana Alba' is a particularly neat form with short spikes of white flowers over aromatic grey-green foliage. Hardy.
**General care:** Trim plants in early spring.
**Height and spread:** 30cm (12in)
**Site:** Sun. Well-drained soil
**Use:** Edging, front of sunny border, raised bed, rock garden
**Good companions:** *Artemisia stelleriana* 'Boughton Silver', *Hebe cupressoides* 'Boughton Dome', *Helianthemum* 'Wisley Primrose', *Narcissus* 'Jack Snipe'

## silver and grey

11

### 11 Artemisia schmidtiana 'Nana'

Mugwort, Sagebrush, Wormwood

This evergreen perennial makes a tiny foliage plant. The finely divided leaves have a silky texture and are gathered in a silvery tuft. Hardy.
**General care:** To keep compact trim in early spring.
**Height:** 8cm (3in) **Spread:** 25cm (10in)
**Site:** Sun. Well-drained soil
**Compost:** Soil-based (John Innes No. 1) with added grit
**Use:** Raised bed, rock garden, scree, trough
**Good companions:** *Dianthus alpinus* 'Joan's Blood', *Crocus* 'Snow Bunting', *Erodium x variabile* 'Roseum'

## green

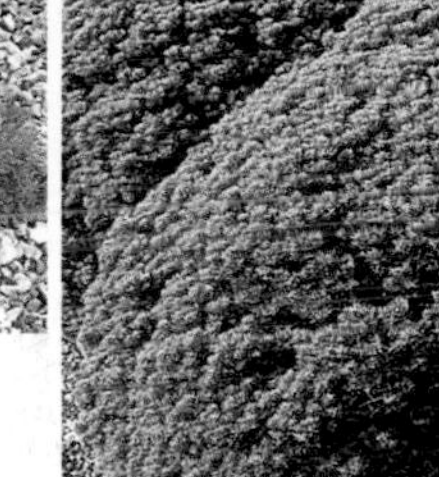
12

### 12 Hebe cupressoides 'Boughton Dome'

The closely packed stems of this slow-growing, dwarf evergreen shrub are covered with scale-like leaves that form a pale green or olive-green dome. Plants rarely flower. Hardy.
**Height:** 60cm (2ft) **Spread:** 1m (3ft)
**Site:** Sun, partial shade. Moist but well-drained soil
**Use:** Front of border, raised bed, rock garden, ground cover
**Good companions:** *Alchemilla conjuncta, Geranium cinereum* 'Ballerina', *Silene schafta*

# water & waterside plants

Most of the plants that relish reliably moist conditions are perennials. Some like the ground really wet and others will even grow in shallow water. Plant in the dormant season.

## purple, blue and violet

1

2

1 **Iris ensata**
Japanese iris
Perennial with fleshy creeping stems (rhizomes) from which grow ribbed sword-like leaves. The flowers are violet-purple. Hardy.
**Height:** 1m (3ft) **Spread:** 20cm (8in)
**Site:** Sun. Lime-free, humus-rich soil, moist or wet during summer but drier in autumn and winter
**Use:** Marginal, waterside
**Good companions:** *Lythrum salicaria* 'Feuerkerze', *Rheum palmatum* 'Sanguineum', *Rodgersia aesculifolia*

2 **Iris laevigata 'Variegata'**
Beardless water iris
The ivory-and-green variegated sword-like leaves grow from fleshy creeping stems (rhizomes). Soft blue flowers are borne from early to midsummer. Tolerates water to a depth of 15cm (6in). Hardy.
**Height:** 60cm (2ft) **Spread:** 25cm (10in)
**Site:** Sun. Humus-rich, wet or reliably moist soil
**Compost:** Soil-based (aquatic)
**Use:** Bog garden, marginal, waterside
**Good companions:** *Iris ensata, Pontederia cordata, Trollius europaeus*

3 **Myosotis scorpioides 'Mermaid'**
Water forget-me-not
This compact perennial spreads by underground stems (rhizomes) to form small carpets of shiny leaves, topped in early summer by blue flowers. Tolerates water to a depth of 8cm (3in). Hardy.
**Height:** 25cm (10in) **Spread:** 30cm (12in)
**Site:** Sun, partial shade. Humus-rich and wet soil
**Compost:** Soil-based (aquatic)
**Use:** Bog garden, marginal, waterside
**Good companions:** *Acorus calamus* 'Variegatus', *Caltha palustris, Pontederia cordata*

## pink and mauve

4 **Nymphaea 'James Brydon'**
Water lily
Perennial water plant with submerged roots and large, rounded floating leaves. These are purplish brown with darker mottling at first but age to brown-green. Crimson-pink floating flowers, with orange-red stamens, are produced throughout summer. Hardy.
**Spread:** 1m (3ft)
**Site:** Sun. Still water 45–75cm (18–30in) deep
**Compost:** Soil-based (aquatic)
**Use:** Pond
**Good companions:** *Pontederia cordata, Iris laevigata* 'Variegata', *Zantedeschia aethiopica*

5 **Primula pulverulenta Bartley hybrids**
Candelabra primula
The large, light green crinkled leaves of these perennials form a rosette from which rise several tall stems powdered with white meal (farina). These carry whorls of dark-eyed pink to purple-red flowers. Flowering starts in late spring. Hardy.
**Height:** 1m (3ft) **Spread:** 60cm (2ft)
**Site:** Sun, partial shade. Humus-rich and reliably moist soil
**Use:** Bog garden, moist border, waterside
**Good companions:** *Filipendula rubra* 'Venusta', *Lobelia* 'Queen Victoria', *Matteuccia struthiopteris*

## red and russet

6 **Rheum palmatum 'Atrosanguineum'**
Chinese rhubarb
The crinkled, jagged lobed leaves of this perennial emerge purplish pink from shiny red buds. By the time the plume of tiny crimson flowers erupts in early summer, the surface of the leaves is dark green. Pink-flushed seed cases follow. Hardy.
**Height:** 2.5m (8ft) **Spread:** 2m (6ft)
**Site:** Sun, partial shade. Humus-rich, fertile and reliably moist soil
**Use:** Bog garden, sunny or lightly shaded border, waterside
**Good companions:** *Astilbe chinensis* var. *taquetii* 'Superba', *Lobelia* 'Queen Victoria', *Rodgersia pinnata* 'Superba'

3

4

## yellow and orange

7 **Nymphaea 'Pygmaea Helvola'**
Water lily
Perennial water plant with submerged roots and olive-green floating leaves that are mottled with purple. Yellow star-shaped flowers with orange stamens are borne freely throughout summer. Slightly fragrant. Hardy.

5

6

7

8

9

10

11

12

**Spread:** 60cm (2ft)
**Site:** Sun. Still water 15-30cm (6-12in) deep
**Compost:** Soil-based (aquatic)
**Use:** Floating aquatic
**Good companions:** *Iris laevigata* 'Variegata', *Myosotis scorpioides* 'Mermaid', *Nymphaea* 'Frobelii'

8 **Primula florindae**
Giant cowslip
This perennial forms a dense clump of rounded leaves. In summer several tall flowering stems each dangle up to 40 fragrant yellow bells, which are lightly powdered with white meal (farina). Attractive seed heads follow. Hardy.
**Height:** 1.2m (4ft) **Spread:** 75cm (2ft 6in)
**Site:** Sun, partial shade. Humus-rich and reliably moist soil
**Use:** Bog garden, moist border, waterside
**Good companions:** *Astilbe* 'Professor van der Wielen', *Hosta sieboldiana* var. *elegans*, *Matteuccia struthiopteris*

9 **Trollius chinensis 'Golden Queen'**
European globeflower
This perennial forms a mound of deeply lobed glossy leaves. Erect stems carry deep orange-yellow cup-shaped flowers, more than 5cm (2in) across, clear of the foliage. Hardy.
**Height:** 75cm (2ft 6in) **Spread:** 45cm (18in)
**Site:** Sun, partial shade. Fertile, reliably moist soil
**Use:** Bog garden, moist border, waterside, wild garden
**Good companions:** *Astrantia major* subsp. *involucrata* 'Shaggy', *Primula florindae, Rodgersia aesculifolia*

## cream and white

10 **Acorus calamus 'Argenteostriatus'**
Sweet flag
Aromatic perennial with sword-like leaves that grow from underground stems (rhizomes). Striped lengthwise with cream and white, the foliage is shown to good effect when reflected in water. Tolerates water up to 20cm (8in) deep. Hardy.
**Height:** 1m (3ft) **Spread:** 60cm (2ft)
**Site:** Sun. Very moist or wet soil
**Use:** Bog garden, marginal, waterside
**Good companions:** *Caltha palustris* var. *palustris*, *Ligularia* 'The Rocket', *Myosotis scorpioides* 'Mermaid'

11 **Zantedeschia aethiopica 'Crowborough'**
Arum lily
Clump-forming perennial with arrow-shaped leaves that survive mild winters. The white spathe swirls around a yellow spadix, on which the tiny true flowers are clustered. Tolerates water to a depth of 30cm (12in). Not fully hardy.
**General care:** In frost-prone areas protect crown in winter with a mulch.
**Height:** 1m (3ft) **Spread:** 60cm (2ft)
**Site:** Sun. Fertile, humus-rich, reliably moist soil
**Compost:** Soil-based (John Innes No. 2)
**Use:** Bog garden, container, moist border
**Good companions:** *Caltha palustris* 'Flore Pleno', *Iris pseudacorus* 'Variagata', *Ligularia* 'The Rocket'

## green

12 **Gunnera manicata**
Deciduous perennial that annually produces massive prickly stems and huge, boldly lobed textured leaves, often more than 2m (6ft) across. A cone-shaped, greenish brown flower spike stands 60cm (2ft) high. Not fully hardy.
**General care:** Protect the crowns in winter.
**Height:** 2.5m (8ft) **Spread:** 4m (12ft)
**Site:** Sun, partial shade. Humus-rich, fertile and reliably moist soil
**Use:** Bog garden, waterside
**Good companions:** *Eupatorium purpureum*, *Ligularia* 'Gregynog Gold', *Lysichiton americanus*

# herbs, vegetables & fruit

Useful plants are often very ornamental, especially when in blossom or making fresh growth, but the first reason for growing early maturing vegetables and fresh herbs is their produce.

## herbs

### 1 Borage
**Borago officinalis**

Hairy-leaved annual with blue star-shaped flowers throughout summer and autumn. Young leaves can be added to salads and dressings; the flowers are used as culinary decoration. Hardy.
**General care:** Sow seed *in situ* from spring to early autumn. Deadhead regularly to avoid over-abundant self-seeding.
**Height:** 60cm (2ft) **Spread:** 45cm (18in)
**Site:** Sun. Well-drained soil, low in fertility
**Compost:** Soil-less
**Use:** Border, large container

### 2 Chervil
**Anthriscus cerefolium**

Feathery foliaged annual with clusters of white flowers from spring to summer. The mild parsley-flavoured leaves are added to salads, soups, sauces and vegetable and egg dishes. Hardy.
**General care:** Sow seed *in situ* monthly from spring to early autumn.
**Height:** 45–60cm (18–24in) **Spread:** 30cm (12in)
**Site:** Partial shade. Light soil with added organic matter to improve moisture retention
**Compost:** Soil-less
**Use:** Border, large container

### 3 Dill
**Anethum graveolens**

Feathery foliaged annual with flat heads of tiny yellow-green flowers. Leaves and seeds are used to flavour soups, fish and lamb. For a regular supply of young foliage, sow successively. Hardy.
**General care:** Sow seed *in situ* in spring and early summer. Water during dry weather. Trim container-grown plants regularly. Self-seeds readily, so remove unwanted seed heads.
**Height:** 1–1.5m (3–5ft) **Spread:** 30cm (12in).
**Site:** Sun. Well-drained soil, low in fertility
**Compost:** Soil-less
**Use:** Border, container

### 4 Hyssop
**Hyssopus officinalis**

Semi-evergreen perennial with long, narrow leaves that can be added to salads, soups, stews, stuffing and meat. Throughout summer and into early autumn it is smothered with small blue flowers. Hardy.
**General care:** To maintain a bushy shape trim the clump in spring and again after flowering.
**Height:** 60cm (2ft) **Spread:** 1m (3ft)
**Site:** Sun. Well-drained soil
**Compost:** Soil-based (John Innes No. 3) with added grit
**Use:** Border, container, low hedge, edging

### 5 Mint, apple
**Mentha suaveolens**

Perennial with apple-and-mint flavoured, oval to rounded mid-green leaves. In summer there are mauve flowers. Very invasive, so grow in a large bottomless container sunk in the ground. Hardy.
**General care:** Trim edges of clump regularly to limit spread.
**Height:** 1m (3ft)
**Spread:** Indefinite
**Site:** Sun, partial shade. Any soil except very dry
**Compost:** Soil-based (John Innes No. 3)
**Use:** Border, container

6

9

10

11

12

6 **Summer savory**
Satureja hortensis
Perennial with long, narrow, dark green leaves and in summer sprays of tiny insignificant flowers. Young leaves are used for flavouring vinegar, cooked dishes and salads. The flavour deteriorates in older plants, so replace them every three years. Half hardy.
**General care:** Protect over winter with deep mulch or a thick layer of straw. Alternatively, grow in a container and move under cover in winter, keeping the compost dry.
**Height:** 1m (3ft) **Spread:** 45cm (18in)
**Site:** Sun. Fertile and well-drained soil
**Compost:** Soil-based (John Innes No. 3) with added grit
**Use:** Border, container

## vegetables

7 **Artichoke, globe**
Cynara scolymus
Large perennial with edible immature flowerheads. Easy to grow but plants take up a lot of space and need to be replaced after three years. Good varieties include 'Green Globe' and 'Gros Vert de Laon'. Hardy.
**Site:** Sun. Preferably fertile, well-drained soil
**How to grow:** Plant rooted offsets in early spring, 60cm (2ft) apart and 75cm (2ft 6in) between rows. Top-dress established plants with fertiliser in early spring and mulch with rotted manure or compost. While the heads are developing, water well during dry weather. Cut the heads when they are fleshy and well formed but while the scales are still closed. After harvest cut down the old stems.

7

8

8 **Beetroot**
Beta vulgaris subsp. vulgaris
Easily grown edible swollen roots with deep red flesh. Choose a bolt-resistant cultivar for early sowings. Hardy.
**Site:** Sun. Fertile and well-drained soil, not recently manured
**How to grow:** At the very end of winter or the beginning of spring sow seed, in rows 30cm (12in) apart, under cloches that have been in place for several weeks. Thin seedlings to 10cm (4in) apart. During dry weather water thoroughly once or twice a week. Harvest as required as soon as the roots are sufficiently large.

9 **Broad bean**
Vicia faba
Broad beans are the earliest outdoor bean to be harvested. For overwintering early plants choose a hardy variety. Sweetly scented flowers. Hardy.
**Site:** Sun. Fertile and well-drained soil
**How to grow:** For an early summer crop, sow seed in late autumn, 15–23cm (6–9in) apart with 45–60cm (18–24in) between rows, depending on height. Choose a sheltered site or protect with cloches. In early spring top-dress with fertiliser and lightly hoe into the soil. Support plants with string stretched between canes. When in flower, pinch out the young top growth to boost pod development. Pick before the pods become tough and fibrous. After harvest, cut stems almost to ground level and dig in the roots.

10 **Cabbage, summer**
Brassica oleracea Capitata Group
Cabbage with a compact rounded head. For an early crop sow under cover. Outdoor sowings, made when the soil is fairly warm at around 7°C (45°F), will mature from late summer onwards. Choose an early maturing variety. Hardy.
**Site:** Sun. Alkaline, fertile, moisture-retentive soil
**How to grow:** In late winter or very early spring sow seed in trays under glass in gentle heat – 13°C (55°F). Prick out the seedlings into individual pots and grow on. Harden off then plant out when around 10cm (4in) high, allowing 45cm (18in) all round. Feed established plants with fertiliser. Harvest as soon as the plants are well hearted, using a knife to cut just above soil level.

11 **Cauliflower**
Brassica oleracea Botrytis Group
Cauliflowers are grown for the white immature flowerheads known as 'curds'. Choose a summer-maturing variety. Can be a difficult crop. Hardy.
**Site:** Sun. Alkaline, fertile and humus-rich soil, that has been deeply dug
**How to grow:** Sow seed in mid-autumn in a cold frame or in midwinter under cover in gentle heat – about 13°C (55°F). Grow on young plants in individual pots in a coldframe then harden off and plant out in early spring in a sunny, sheltered site, allowing 45cm (18in) each way. Keep well watered. Harvest individual curds when firm and well developed but before they open.

12 **Courgette (zucchini)**
Cucurbita pepo
Prolific plant with long green or rounded golden fruits. The large yellow flowers are also edible and can be cooked in batter or used as decoration. Select early maturing varieties. Tender.
**Site:** Sun. Well-drained and fertile soil with plenty of rotted manure or compost
**How to grow:** In early spring sow seed under cover in gentle heat – 13°C (55°F). Place two seeds in an 8cm (3in) pot and thin later to one seedling. Grow on and plant out 1m (3ft) apart, in a sheltered site when all danger of frost is past. Keep well watered and feed with liquid fertiliser once the fruits begin to swell. Harvest regularly as soon as the fruits are large enough.

## vegetables (continued)

### 1 French bean, dwarf

Phaseolus vulgaris

Small bushy annual with long edible pods. Select varieties suitable for early sowing. Tender.

**Site:** Sun. Fertile and well-drained soil

**How to grow:** In mid-spring sow seed under cover individually in small pots or modular trays. Plant out seedlings under cloches that have been warming the soil for several weeks, 10cm (4in) apart with 45cm (18in) between rows; top-dress the soil with fertiliser before planting. Keep plants well watered, especially once flowers appear. Harvest regularly as soon as pods are sufficiently large but before the seeds are prominent.

### 2 Garlic

Allium sativum

The underground bulbs of this strongly flavoured member of the onion family keep for many months if they are ripened in the sun. Garlic produced for cultivation is more reliable than bulbs from the greengrocer, as the latter may not be suitable for cooler climates. Hardy.

**Site:** Sun. Well-drained and fertile soil, not recently manured

**How to grow:** In early to midwinter plant individual cloves 10cm (4in) apart with the tip just showing, and 23cm (9in) between rows; use a trowel or dibber rather than press the cloves into the ground. If drainage is poor, draw up the soil into low ridges and plant the garlic on top. Lift bulbs in mid to late summer, once the leaves have fallen over and begun to yellow. Spread in the sun to dry thoroughly.

### 3 Lettuce

Lactuca sativa

Several different types of lettuce can be grown outdoors for cropping from early summer onwards. Choose from crisp cos or Webb's types; loose-leaf or 'cut-and-come-again' lettuces such as 'Lollo Rosso'; or butterhead varieties like 'Tom Thumb'. For a continuous supply, sow every two to three weeks. Cool season plants, some types tolerant of frost.

**Site:** Sun. Fertile and well-drained soil

**How to grow:** From mid-spring onwards, sow seed in rows 23–30cm (9–12in) apart. Thin to 15–30cm (6–12in) apart, depending on the size of the variety. In cold areas or for a very early crop, sow under cover, prick out into individual pots then harden off and plant out in late spring. Keep plants well watered during dry spells. Harvest when lettuces are sufficiently large.

### 4 Mangetout

Pisum sativum

A type of pea grown for its edible pods and seeds. Tall climbing varieties grow 1.5m (5ft) high, while smaller ones reach 75cm (2ft 6in). Varieties include 'Carouby de Maussanne', 'Oregon Sugar Pod' and 'Sugar Snap'. Tender.

**Site:** Sun. Well-drained and fertile soil with well-rotted compost or manure dug in during winter

**How to grow:** Sow from early spring onwards and grow as for peas (see 6, below). Harvest when the peas are just visible as tiny swellings; pick regularly to encourage the production of pods.

### 5 Onion

Allium cepa

Most onions and shallots are grown from 'sets' planted in spring, but seed sown the previous year gives an early summer crop. Not fully hardy.

**Site:** Sun. Alkaline and well-drained soil

**How to grow:** In late summer to early autumn, sow in rows or in blocks 30cm (12in) apart in an open, sheltered site. Thin to 5cm (2in) apart in spring and feed with general fertiliser. Harvest for eating as soon as bulbs are large enough. For storing, loosen roots with a fork when leaves flop; leave for a week, then lift and dry in sun.

### 6 Pea

Pisum sativum

Easy climbing annuals that can provide a crop in early to midsummer. Choose a suitable variety such as 'Douce Provence', 'Early Onward', 'Feltham First' or 'Kelvedon Wonder'. Hardy.

**Site:** Sun. Well-drained and fertile soil, with well-rotted compost or manure dug in during winter
**How to grow:** For the earliest crops, sow in late winter under cloches, then outdoors from very early spring onwards. Form a drill with a broad hoe 3cm (1¼in) deep and sow seeds 5cm (2in) apart in a triple row. Net freshly sown seed to protect from birds and put up supports such as netting or twiggy branches when the plants are 10cm (4in) high. Harvest pods when they are well filled but still young; pick regularly.

### 7 Potato, first early
Solanum tuberosum
These edible tubers are classified according to when they mature, with 'first earlies' maturing in early to midsummer. They can be grown outside with protection or if 'earthed up' with soil. They are ready when the flowers are fully open, around three months after planting. Not fully hardy.
**Site:** Sun. Acid, fertile and well-drained soil, deeply dug
**How to grow:** Set seed potatoes to sprout, or 'chit', at the end of winter and plant out in early spring, 15cm (6in) deep with 30cm (12in) between tubers and 60cm (2ft) between rows. Before planting, rake in a general fertiliser. Protect with fleece or polythene, or mound the soil over the rows every two to three weeks. During dry weather, water well once a week. Use a fork to lift carefully as needed.

## fruit

### 8 Cherry, sweet
Prunus avium
Compact cherries can be grown in bush, pyramid or fan-trained forms. A number of self-fertile varieties will set a good crop with their own pollen. Best where rainfall is light and in a sheltered position. Hardy.
**Site:** Sun. Deep, fertile and well-drained soil
**How to grow:** Plant trees 3–5m (10–15ft) apart depending on the rootstock. To avoid fruit splitting, keep the soil moist but not overwet. Feed in late winter with general fertiliser and mulch with well-rotted manure or compost. Prune if necessary during the growing season. Net fruit to protect it from birds.

8

### 9 Gooseberry
Ribes uva-crispa
The green or red berries of this prickly bush are the first soft fruits of the summer season. Usually grown as a bush but can also be trained in half-standard and cordon form. Hardy.
**Site:** Sun. Well-drained and fertile soil, with plenty of added well-rotted manure or compost
**How to grow:** Plant 1.2m (4ft) apart with 1.5m (5ft) between rows. In early spring feed each bush with 50g (2oz) sulphate of potash and mulch with plenty of well-rotted manure or compost. Water well while fruit is forming, but stop when it is nearly ripe, otherwise the berries may split. Fruit may need thinning from late spring onwards. Net bushes when the fruit starts to ripen to protect it from birds.

9

### 10 Raspberry
Rubus idaeus
Summer-fruiting raspberries crop at different times depending on the variety. They thrive in sun in cool climates but prefer partial shade in hot areas. Hardy.
**Site:** Sun, partial shade. Fertile and well-drained soil, slightly acid and with plenty of added well-rotted manure or compost
**How to grow:** Grow on a framework of 1.5m (5ft) high posts and horizontal wires, 30cm (12in) apart. Plant dormant canes in autumn or early winter 40cm (16in) apart, with the topmost roots no more than 5cm (2in) below the surface of the soil, and cut back to 15cm (6in) high. In spring feed with general fertiliser and mulch generously with well-rotted manure or compost. Water well in dry weather but not while the fruit is ripening. After harvest, cut old canes at ground level and tie in new ones 10cm (4in) apart, fanning them out if necessary.

10

### 11 Red and white currants
Ribes sativum
Easy and reliable. Grown as bushes, half standards or cordons in warm sheltered sites. Hardy.
**Site:** Sun. Fertile and well-drained soil, preferably slightly acid and with plenty of added compost or well-rotted manure
**How to grow:** Plant 1.2m (4ft) apart with 1.5m (5ft) between rows. In early spring feed each bush with 50g (2oz) per bush of sulphate of potash and mulch with well-rotted manure or compost. In summer pull off any suckers produced from below ground.

11

### 12 Strawberry
Fragaria x ananassa
Strawberry plants crop well for several years and different varieties can provide a succession of fruit throughout summer. Hardy.
**Site:** Sun. Fertile and well-drained soil, preferably slightly acid and with plenty of well-rotted manure
**Compost:** Soil-based (John Innes No. 3)
**How to grow:** Plant in autumn or early spring in deeply dug well-manured ground, containers or raised beds. Space 30–38cm (12–15in) apart with 1m (3ft) between rows. In late winter feed with sulphate of potash. Feed older plants with a general fertiliser if their vigour declines. After flowering, water thoroughly every two weeks in dry conditions. Net to protect the fruit from birds.

12

# the greenhouse

A wide range of tender plants can be grown in a protected environment. In summer many, in particular pelargoniums (see also page 87), can be moved outdoors to give patios and terraces a tropical or sub-tropical look.

## purple, blue and violet

1 **Solanum rantonnetii**
Blue potato bush
Shrubby evergreen with deep green leaves and throughout summer large, yellow-centred violet-purple flowers. Inedible red fruits follow. Tender.
**General care:** Trim lightly in spring.
**Height and spread:** 1.5m (5ft)
**Under glass:** Full light. Soil-based compost (John Innes No. 2)
**Use:** Conservatory or greenhouse minimum 7°C (45°F), sunny patio

## pink and mauve

2 **Begonia x corallina 'Lucerna'**
Cane-stemmed begonia
Fibrous-rooted evergreen with bamboo-like stems and large leaves. The surface is silver spotted olive-green, the underside is wine-red. Single pink flowers in summer. Tender.
**General care:** To encourage low growth, reduce stems to two or three buds in spring.
**Height:** 2m (6ft) **Spread:** 40cm (16in)
**Under glass:** Indirect light. Soil-based compost (John Innes No. 2) or soil-less
**Use:** Container, conservatory or greenhouse minimum 10°C (50°F), houseplant

3 **Bougainvillea glabra**
Bougainvillea
Vigorous, usually evergreen climber that loses its leaves in temperatures below 10°C (50°F) but survives frost-free conditions to make growth in spring. Flowers are produced in regular flushes all summer. Three long-lasting petal-like bracts in vivid purplish pink surround each small white bloom. Half hardy.
**General care:** Prune lightly after each flush of flowers. Hard prune in early spring to check growth or train as standards.
**Height:** 6m (20ft) **Spread:** 4m (12ft)
**Under glass:** Full light. Soil-based compost (John Innes No. 3)
**Use:** Container, conservatory or greenhouse minimum 2°C (36°F), sunny patio

6

7

3

4

8

1

2

5

9

10

### 4 Catharanthus roseus
Madagascar periwinkle

This evergreen perennial, which is widely naturalised in the tropics, is usually grown as an annual propagated from seed or cuttings. It has glossy leaves and tubular pink flowers with five petal-like lobes at the mouth. Selections offer a colour range including white, white with a pink eye, mauve, pale to deep pink and red. Tender.
**General care:** Discard plants grown under glass after two years.
**Height and spread:** 50cm (20in)
**Under glass:** Full light. Soil-based compost (John Innes No. 2)
**Outdoor site:** Sun. Well-drained soil
**Use:** Container, formal bedding outdoors, conservatory or greenhouse minimum 5°C (41°F), sunny patio

### 5 Mammillaria bombycina
The clustered cylindrical or spherical stems of this cactus are covered with white down and hooked spines. In late spring or early summer mature stems bear mauve to purple flowers. Tender.
**General care:** Shade from hot sun.
**Height:** 20cm (8in) **Spread:** Indefinite
**Under glass:** Full light. Soil-based compost (John Innes No. 2) with added grit
**Use:** Conservatory or greenhouse minimum 7°C (45°F), sunny patio

11

12

## red and russet

### 6 Bougainvillea 'Rubyana'
Bougainvillea

In temperatures above 10°C (50°F) the hybrid bougainvilleas flower in frequent flushes, often almost continuously. Their papery bracts can be red, orange, yellow, white, purple or pink; those of 'Rubyana' are wine-red. Tender to half hardy.
**General care:** Prune lightly after each flush of flowers. Prune hard in early spring to check growth or train as standards or other shapes.
**Height:** 10m (30ft) **Spread:** 6m (20ft)
**Under glass:** Full light. Soil-based compost (John Innes No. 3)
**Use:** Conservatory or greenhouse minimum 2°C (36°F), sunny patio

### 7 Cuphea ignea
Cigar flower

Soft-stemmed shrubby evergreen with bright green foliage that shows off the red tubular flowers. Under glass it flowers for much of the year, but has a long season outdoors when grown as an annual for bedding and containers. Tender.
**General care:** Cut back plants under glass by two-thirds in early winter.
**Height and spread:** 60cm (2ft)
**Under glass:** Full light. Soil-based compost (John Innes No. 2)
**Outdoor site:** Sun, partial shade. Well-drained soil
**Use:** Container, formal bedding outdoors, conservatory or greenhouse minimum 7°C (45°F)

### 8 Passiflora antioquiensis
Red banana passion flower

Vigorous evergreen tendril climber with, usually, three-lobed leaves. Dangling red-pink flowers, nearly 15cm (6in) across, are produced throughout summer. Edible fruits occasionally follow. Tender.
**General care:** Prune after flowering or in late winter, cutting back shoots to within a few buds of a permanent framework.
**Height:** 6m (20ft) **Spread:** 3m (10ft)
**Under glass:** Full or indirect light. Soil-based compost (John Innes No. 3)
**Use:** Conservatory or greenhouse minimum 5°C (41°F)

### 9 Pelargonium 'Morwenna'
Regal pelargonium

Regals are shrubby evergreen hybrids with aromatic foliage. In summer they bear clusters of large flowers in a range of colours, often veined and blotched with darker shades. They can be moved to a sunny position outdoors in summer, but need protection from adverse weather. 'Morwenna' has showy red-black blooms. In 'Rimfire' the near black body is edged with scarlet. Tender.
**General care:** Will flower over a long season if the temperature remains above 7°C (45°F).
**Height:** 50cm (20in) **Spread:** 35cm (14in)
**Under glass:** Soil-based compost (John Innes No. 2) or soil-less (coir-based) with added grit
**Use:** Conservatory or greenhouse minimum 2°C (36°F), houseplant

## yellow and orange

### 10 Abutilon 'Kentish Belle'
Evergreen or semi-evergreen shrub with slender arching stems and in summer and autumn dangling bell-shaped flowers. The apricot-yellow petals protrude from the smaller purple-red cup (calyx). Can be grown outdoors in a mild climate if trained against a warm wall. Some stem training is also necessary under glass. Not fully hardy.
**General care:** In late winter or early spring cut back wood that flowered the previous year.
**Height and spread:** 2.5m (8ft)
**Under glass:** Full light. Soil-based compost (John Innes No. 2)
**Outdoor site:** Sun. Well-drained soil
**Use:** Container, conservatory or greenhouse minimum 2°C (36°F), warm wall

### 11 Begonia sutherlandii
Tuberous begonia

Trailing slender stems carry red-veined green leaves. In summer there are cascading sprays of single orange flowers. Tender to half hardy.
**General care:** Shade from hot sun. Start tubers into growth in early spring and in autumn dry off in their container. Store at minimum 2°C (36°F).
**Height:** 20cm (8in) **Spread:** 50cm (20in)
**Under glass:** Full light. Soil-based compost (John Innes No. 2) or soil-less
**Use:** Container, conservatory or greenhouse minimum 10°C (50°F), lightly shaded patio, hanging basket

## cream and white

### 12 Brugmansia x candida 'Knightii'
Angels' trumpets, Datura

The hybrid brugmansias are evergreen shrubs with drooping trumpet-shaped flowers, up to 30cm (12in) long, with turned-back lobes. Powerfully scented in the evening. 'Knightii' has double white flowers. Toxic if ingested. Tender.
**General care:** Prune hard in early to midwinter. Repot annually in early to mid-spring.
**Height:** 4m (12ft) **Spread:** 2.5m (8ft)
**Under glass:** Full light. Soil-based compost (John Innes No. 3)
**Use:** Conservatory or greenhouse minimum 7°C (45°F), sunny patio

# choosing the best plants

The following plant lists draw on all the plants described in the preceding pages of the Plant Selector, but they are grouped together here to help you choose plants for particular conditions, situations and uses.

## plants for clay soil

Although the following plants generally succeed on close-textured clay soils, they do better when the ground has been improved by the addition of grit and organic matter such as well-rotted garden compost.

- *Abelia schumanii*
- *Acanthus spinosus*
- *Alchemilla mollis*
- *Astilbe* (all)
- *Camassia leichtlinii* 'Electra'
- *Cornus alba* 'Elegantissima'
- *Cornus kousa* var. *chinensis*
- *Deutzia* x *rosea*
- *Fargesia murielae*
- *Hemerocallis* (all)
- *Hosta* (all)
- *Humulus lupulus* 'Aureus'
- *Hydrangea anomala* subsp. *petiolaris*
- *Kalmia latifolia* 'Ostbo Red'
- *Kniphofia* 'Early Buttercup'
- *Miscanthus sinensis* 'Zebrinus'
- *Passiflora caerulea*
- *Philadelphus hybrids* (all)
- *Primula florindae*
- *Primula pulverulenta* Bartley hybrids
- *Rheum palmatum* 'Atrosanguineum'
- *Rosa* (all)
- *Thalictrum aquilegiifolium*
- *Weigela* 'Victoria'
- *Wisteria* (all)

*Passiflora caerulea*

## plants for dry chalky soil

A large number of plants are automatically excluded from this list because they do not tolerate alkaline (limy) soil. The improvement of shallow chalky soil by the addition of moisture-retaining organic matter generally improves the performance of the following plants and allows lime-tolerant but moisture-loving plants, notably clematis, to be grown successfully.

- *Acanthus spinosus*
- *Achillea* 'Taygetea'
- *Allium* (most)
- *Antirrhinum* Sonnet Series
- *Anthemis tinctoria* 'E.C. Buxton'
- *Armeria maritima* 'Düsseldorfer Stolz'
- *Campanula cochleariifolia*
- *Campanula latifolia*
- *Centaurea cyanus*
- *Dianthus barbatus*
- *Erysimum* 'Bowles' Mauve'
- *Geranium cinereum* 'Ballerina'
- *Gypsophila repens* 'Rosa Schönheit'
- *Helianthemum* 'Wisley Primrose'
- *Iris* (all bearded)
- *Lavandula angustifolia* 'Nana Alba'
- *Nepeta* 'Six Hills Giant'
- *Papaver orientale* 'Black and White'
- *Philadelphus* 'Belle Etoile'
- *Potentilla fruticosa* 'Tangerine'
- *Salvia* x *sylvestris* 'Mainacht'
- *Salvia viridis* 'Oxford Blue'
- *Verbascum* (all)
- *Weigela* 'Victoria'

*Weigela* 'Victoria'

## plants for sandy or gravelly soil

The following plants require free drainage and are generally drought tolerant. The range of plants that can be grown in dry sunny gardens will be enlarged if the soil is improved by the addition of organic matter.

- *Acanthus spinosus*
- *Achillea* 'Taygetea'
- *Allium* (all)
- *Anthemis tinctoria* 'E.C. Buxton'
- *Artemisia ludoviciana* 'Valerie Finnis'
- *Artemisia* 'Powis Castle'
- *Ceanothus* 'Italian Skies'
- *Cistus* (all)
- *Dianthus* 'Gran's Favourite'
- *Erysimum* 'Bowles' Mauve'
- *Eschscholzia californica*
- *Festuca glauca* 'Elijah Blue'
- *Gleditsia triacanthos* 'Sunburst'
- *Helianthemum* 'Wisley Primrose'
- *Nepeta* 'Six Hills Giant'
- *Papaver orientale* 'Black and White'
- *Philadelphus* 'Belle Etoile'
- *Potentilla fruticosa* 'Tangerine'
- *Robinia pseudoacacia* 'Frisia'
- *Ruta graveolens* 'Jackman's Blue'
- *Salvia* x *sylvestris* 'Mainacht'
- *Tropaeolum majus* 'Empress of India'
- *Verbascum* Cotswold Group 'Gainsborough'

*Dianthus* 'Gran's Favourite'

## plants for acid soils

Plants marked with an asterisk* will grow satisfactorily only on soils that are free of lime. Other plants in the list thrive on acid soils, but may also grow on neutral or slightly alkaline soils.

- *Arisaema candidissimum*
- *Betula pendula* 'Youngii'
- *Cornus controversa* 'Variegata'
- *Cornus kousa* var. *chinensis*
- *Helianthemum* 'Wisley Primrose'*
- *Kalmia latifolia* 'Ostbo Red'*
- *Lithodora diffusa* 'Heavenly Blue'*
- *Lupinus* 'Chandelier'
- *Meconopsis betonicifolia**
- *Primula florindae*
- *Primula pulverulenta* Bartley hybrids
- *Rhododendron* (all)*
- *Schisandra rubrifolia*
- *Styrax japonicus**

## plants for ground cover

The following plants can be used to create an attractive weed-excluding cover. Effective cover can only be achieved by planting in soil that is free of perennial weeds.

- *Alchemilla mollis*
- *Arenaria montana*
- *Armeria maritima* 'Düsseldorfer Stolz'
- *Artemisia* 'Powis Castle'
- *Festuca glauca* 'Elijah Blue'
- *Geranium* (most)
- *Hebe cupressoides* 'Boughton Dome'
- *Hebe* 'Youngii'
- *Helianthemum* 'Wisley Primrose'
- *Hosta* (most)
- *Lithodora diffusa* 'Heavenly Blue'
- *Nepeta* 'Six Hills Giant'
- *Parthenocissus henryana*
- *Rhododendron* (small and medium evergreens)
- *Rosa* 'Bonica'

## plants for moist shade

The following plants tolerate or, more commonly, thrive in moist shade, although many will also grow in full sun provided the soil is moist. Plants marked with an asterisk* will grow in boggy conditions.

- *Aconitum* 'Ivorine'
- *Alchemilla mollis*
- *Arisaema candidissimum*
- *Astilbe* (all)*
- *Astrantia major* subsp. *involucrata* 'Shaggy'
- *Cornus alba* 'Elegantissima'
- *Cornus kousa* var. *chinensis*
- *Fargesia murielae*
- *Fuchsia* (all)
- *Geum rivale* 'Leonard's Variety'
- *Gunnera manicata**
- *Hosta* (all)
- *Kalmia latifolia* 'Ostbo Red'
- *Myosotis scorpioides* 'Mermaid'*
- *Persicaria bistorta* 'Superba'
- *Phalaris arundinacea* var. *picta* 'Feesey'*
- *Primula florindae**
- *Primula pulverulenta* Bartley hybrids
- *Rheum palmatum* 'Atrosanguineum'*
- *Rhododendron* (all)
- *Tiarella wherryi*
- *Viola cornuta* Alba Group
- *Viola* (all)

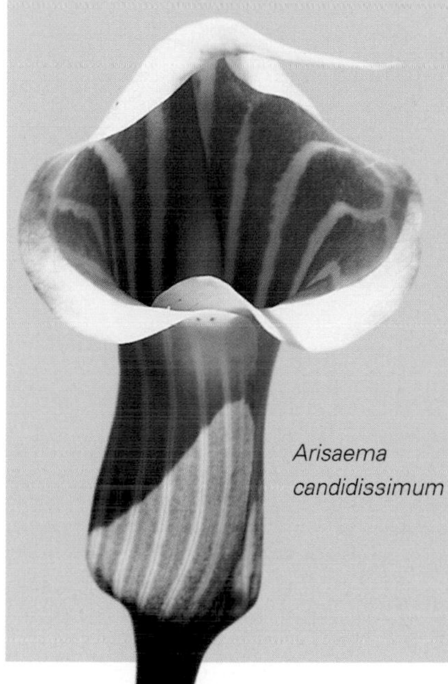

*Arisaema candidissimum*

## plants for coastal sites

Where windbreaks and hedges give protection from salt-laden winds, a wide range of plants can be grown in coastal gardens. Many benefit from the sea's moderating influence on temperatures.

- *Anthemis tinctoria* 'E.C. Buxton'
- *Armeria maritima* 'Düsseldorfer Stolz'
- *Artemisia ludoviciana* 'Valerie Finnis'
- *Artemisia* 'Powis Castle'
- *Campanula cochleariifolia*
- *Centaurea cyanus*
- *Cistus ladanifer*
- *Cistus* 'Silver Pink'
- *Clarkia amoena* Satin Series
- *Dianthus* (all)
- *Erysimum* 'Bowles' Mauve'
- *Eschscholzia californica*
- *Festuca glauca* 'Elijah Blue'
- *Fuchsia* (most)
- *Hebe* (all)
- *Helianthemum* 'Wisley Primrose'
- *Kniphofia* 'Early Buttercup'
- *Nepeta* 'Six Hills Giant'
- *Papaver rhoeas* 'Mother of Pearl'
- *Papaver somniferum*
- *Petunia* (all)
- *Potentilla fruticosa* 'Tangerine'
- *Ruta graveolens* 'Jackman's Blue'
- *Salvia viridis* 'Oxford Blue'
- *Sisyrinchium striatum* 'Aunt May'
- *Veronica austriaca* subsp. *teucrium* 'Kapitan'
- Veronica gentianoides

*Cistus* 'Silver Pink'

# choosing the best plants/2



## trees for small gardens

None of the following is suitable for very small gardens, where climbers on structures such as arches are a better way of creating height and shade.

- *Betula pendula* 'Youngii'
- *Buddleja alternifolia*
- *Cornus controversa* 'Variegata'
- *Cornus kousa* var. *chinensis*
- *Gleditsia triacanthos* 'Sunburst'
- *Styrax japonica*

## summer-flowering plants for containers

As well as the plants listed here as suitable for general container gardening, a number of rock garden, or alpine, plants are suitable for troughs. In addition, all the greenhouse plants described on pages 114–115 can be grown in containers.

- *Ageratum houstonianum*
- *Antirrhinum* Sonnet Series
- *Clematis* 'Bee's Jubilee'
- *Clematis* 'Gillian Blades'
- *Clematis* 'The Vagabond'
- *Fuchsia* 'Lady Thumb'
- *Fuchsia* 'Margaret'
- *Lilium regale*
- *Lobelia erinus* 'Cascade'
- *Matthiola incana* Ten Week Series
- *Pelargonium* (all)
- *Petunia* (all)
- *Tagetes* (all)
- *Tropaeolum majus* 'Empress of India'
- *Verbena* 'Imagination'
- *Viola* x *wittrockiana* 'Bambini'
- *Viola* x *wittrockiana* 'Jolly Joker'

*Petunia* 'Fantasy'

## flowers for cutting

In addition to the following, many other plants provide material for small, sometimes short-lived, displays. The flowers of plants marked with an asterisk* are suitable for drying.

- *Achillea* 'Taygeta'*
- *Aconitum* 'Ivorine'
- *Allium* (all)*
- *Astilbe* (all)*
- *Centaurea cyanus*
- *Consolida ajacis* Giant Imperial Series
- *Dianthus barbatus*
- *Dianthus* 'Gran's Favourite'
- *Eschscholzia californica*
- *Gladiolus* 'The Bride'
- *Iris* 'Pearly Dawn'
- *Iris* 'Jane Phillips'
- *Lathyurus odoratus* (all)
- *Leucanthemum* x *superbum*
- *Lilium candidum*
- *Lilium regale*
- *Matthiola incana* Ten Week Series
- *Nigella damascena* 'Miss Jekyll'
- *Paeonia lactiflora* (all)
- *Papaver nudicaule*
- *Rosa* (most)
- *Salvia viridis* 'Oxford Blue'*
- *Tulipa sprengeri*
- *Verbascum* (most)
- *Zantedeschia aethiopica* 'Crowborough'

*Rosa* Mountbatten

## plants with aromatic foliage

In the case of many aromatic plants the scent of the leaves is only detectable when they are bruised.

- *Acorus calamus* 'Argenteostriatus'
- *Artemisia arborescens*
- *Cistus ladanifer*
- Dill (*Anethum graveolens*)
- Hyssop (*Hyssopus officinalis*)
- Mint, apple (*Mentha suaveolens*)
- *Lavandula angustifolia* 'Nana Alba'
- *Nepeta* 'Six Hills Giant'
- *Pelargonium* 'Chocolate Peppermint'
- *Pelargonium* 'Copthorne'
- *Ruta graveolens* 'Jackman's Blue'
- Tarragon, French (*Artemisia dracunculus*)

## plants with fragrant flowers

The age of a flower, time of day, and temperature all affect the strength of floral scents. These plants are all worth siting carefully so that their perfumes can be enjoyed.

- *Brugmansia* x *candida* 'Knightii'
- *Buddleja alternifolia*
- *Dianthus* 'Gran's Favourite'
- *Hemerocallis* 'Catherine Woodbery'
- *Hemerocallis lilioasphodelus*
- *Iris* 'Jane Phillips'
- *Jasminum officinale*
- *Lathyrus odoratus* (most)
- *Lilium candidum*
- *Lilium regale*
- *Lonicera periclymenum* 'Belgica'
- *Matthiola incana* Ten Week Series
- *Paeonia lactiflora* (most)
- *Papaver nudicaule*
- *Philadelphus* 'Belle Etoile'
- *Primula florindae*
- *Rhododendron luteum*
- *Rosa* (most)
- *Tropaeolum majus* 'Empress of India'
- *Wisteria floribunda* 'Multijuga'

## shrubs and trees for autumn colour

In most years the foliage of the following plants colours well in autumn, but the display is more reliable in a continental climate.

- *Betula pendula* 'Youngii'
- *Cornus kousa* var. *chinensis*
- *Gleditsia tricanthos* 'Sunburst'
- *Rhododendron luteum*
- *Robinia pseudoacacia* 'Frisia'

## plants with variegated foliage

The leaves of the following plants are edged, spotted or otherwise marked in white, cream or yellow.

- *Acorus calamus* 'Argenteostriatus'
- *Actinidia kolomikta*
- *Cornus alba* 'Elegantissima'
- *Cornus controversa* 'Variegata'
- *Hakonechloa macra* 'Alboaurea'
- *Helichrysum petiolare* 'Limelight'
- *Hosta* 'Francee'
- *Hosta* 'Ginko Craig'
- *Hosta* 'Gold Standard'
- *Iris laevigata* 'Variegata'
- *Iris pallida* 'Argentea Variegata'
- *Miscanthus sinensis* 'Zebrinus'
- *Parthenocissus henryana*
- *Pelargonium* 'L'Elégante'
- *Phalaris arundinacea* var. *picta* 'Feesey'
- *Sisyrinchium striatum* 'Aunt May'

*Hosta* 'Francee'

## evergreen shrubs

The evergreen foliage of the following plants helps to create a year-round structure for the garden.

- *Ceanothus* 'Italian Skies'
- *Cistus ladanifer*
- *Cistus* 'Silver Pink'
- *Hebe* 'Youngii'
- *Kalmia latifolia* 'Ostbo Red'
- *Melianthus major*
- *Rhododendron* 'Britannia'
- *Rhododendron* 'Loder's White'
- *Rhododendron* 'Vanessa Pastel'
- *Ruta graveolens* 'Jackman's Blue'

## plants with colourful foliage

The following plants have foliage with distinctive colours other than green. For other colourful foliage see Plants with Variegated Foliage and Shrubs and Trees for Autumn Colour.

- *Actinidia kolomikta*
- *Festuca glauca* 'Elijah Blue'
- *Gleditsia triacanthos* 'Sunburst'
- *Hosta* 'Halcyon'
- *Humulus lupulus* 'Aureus'
- *Pelargonium* 'Bird Dancer'
- *Pelargonium* 'Chocolate Peppermint'
- *Rheum palmatum* 'Atrosanguineum'
- *Robinia pseudoacacia* 'Frisia'
- *Ruta graveolens* 'Jackman's Blue'
- *Thalictrum flavum* subsp. *glaucum*
- *Tropaeolum majus* 'Empress of India'
- *Vitis vinifera* 'Purpurea'
- *Weigela* 'Victoria'

*Pelargonium* 'Chocolate Peppermint'

## plants with ornamental fruits, berries and seed heads

The plants in the following list are of great garden value because they have more than one ornamental feature.

- *Acanthus spinosus*
- *Allium* (all)
- *Astilbe* (all)
- *Cornus kousa* var. *chinensis*
- *Gleditsia tricanthos* 'Sunburst'
- *Passiflora caerulea*
- *Primula florindae*
- *Rheum palmatum* 'Atrosanguineum'
- *Rosa* 'Madame Grégoire Staechelin'
- *Styrax japonica*
- *Vitis vinifera* 'Purpurea'

## plants with large or boldly shaped leaves

The leaves of the following plants are of architectural value in the garden and useful as cut foliage for indoors.

- *Acanthus spinosus*
- *Acorus calamus* 'Argenteostriatus'
- *Gleditsia tricanthos* 'Sunburst'
- *Gunnera manicata*
- *Hosta sieboldiana* var. *elegans*
- *Humulus lupulus* 'Aureus'
- *Iris laevigata* 'Variegata'
- *Iris pallida* 'Argentea Variegata'
- *Lupinus* 'Chandelier'
- *Melianthus major*
- *Miscanthus sinensis* 'Zebrinus'
- *Paeonia lactiflora* (all)
- *Parthenocissus henryana*
- *Primula florindae*
- *Rheum palmatum* 'Atrosanguineum'
- *Rhododendron* 'Loder's White'
- *Robinina pseudoacacia* 'Frisia'
- *Trachycarpus fortunei*
- *Vitis vinifera* 'Purpurea'
- *Wisteria* (all)
- *Zantedeschia aethiopica* 'Crowborough'

*Zantedeschia aethiopica*

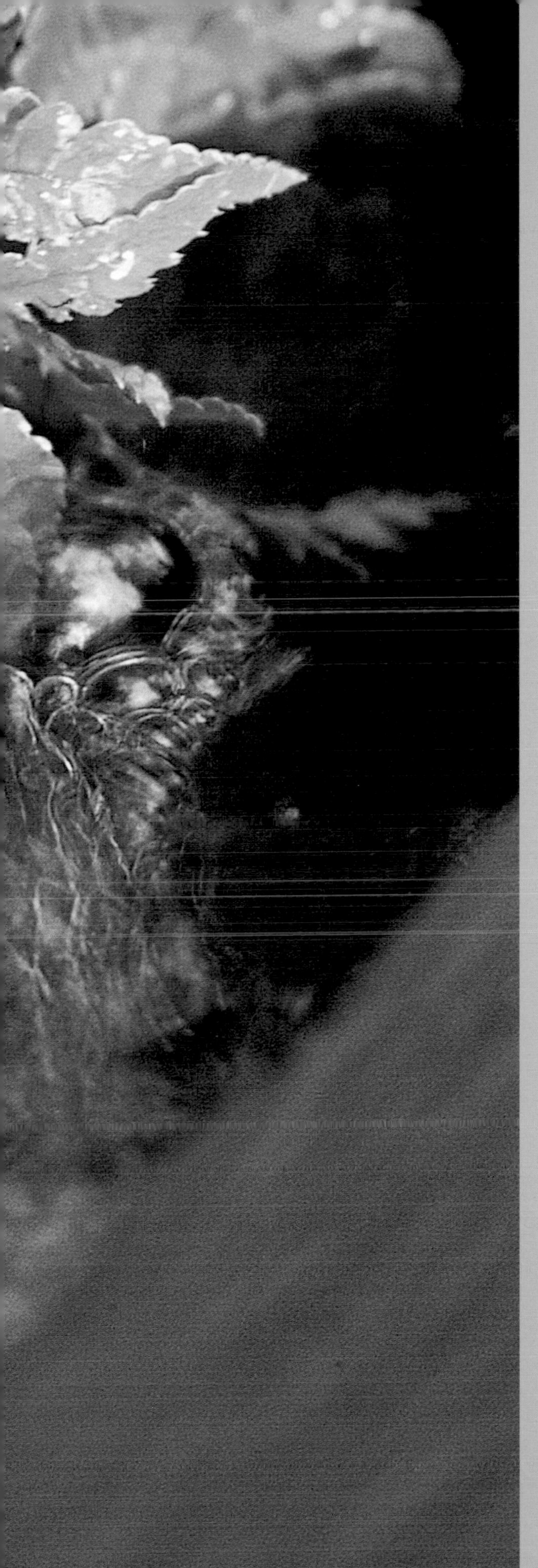

# garden projects

Since the days are long and the weather warm, this is a good time to embark on a major development. How about laying a brand new patio, installing a decked seating area or, perhaps, building an ornamental pond? If these projects seem too ambitious, why not try something simpler and less expensive? You could set up a half-barrel pond in an afternoon or, if you want to save yourself time and effort, install an automatic watering system for container plants. This is the season for relaxing and enjoying the summer outdoors, so make sure you place a seat wherever the garden looks beautiful and make the most of those al-fresco cooking facilities.

# designing a patio

A patio is essentially an outside 'room' where you can sit, play and eat, surrounded by lush foliage and flowers. It can look sophisticated, or relaxed and informal, depending on your choice of materials, plants and furniture.

## planning a patio

The term 'patio' originally referred to an inner courtyard, either open or covered. It was surrounded by the rooms of the house, which had windows looking out onto it. Today its meaning has evolved to describe a paved surface in the garden, usually with outdoor furniture.

The patio's atmosphere will be largely influenced by your choice of flooring, with timber, bricks and natural stone giving a more welcoming feel than gravel or concrete. The choice of materials will be dictated to some extent by situation and local conditions, and that includes factors such as the weather and nearby trees. In very wet climates, for example, gravel surfaces

**Small brick paviors** have been used in this compact garden (below), while a larger town house has room for a second patio at the end of the garden to catch the evening sun (right).

are popular because they provide extra grip under foot, while decking is preferable in warm, dry areas. Bear in mind that leaves falling from any overhanging trees will make most surfaces slippery in a wet autumn, and shade will encourage the formation of mosses, which, again, can be slippery. An otherwise plain, functional surface can easily be embellished by an imaginative choice of plants and pots.

When you have chosen the flooring, give some thought to privacy and harmony. A sense of seclusion makes the area more relaxing to sit in, and you may find that some form of screening is essential to provide some privacy. For a harmonious look, choose furniture, features and plants in colours that complement each other.

**Bricks can be laid** in a variety of decorative patterns: here, herringbone is framed by a single row of straight, end on bricks (below). Old York stone provides a mellow finish. In this small town garden (below left), it perfectly sets off the potted plants framing the route to the outdoor dining area.

## position, shape and size

While a patio is often built next to the house, this is not critical. If, for example, you use a patio mainly in the evenings, and the sun stays longer in another part of the garden, site the patio there. If the best site is at the far end of the garden, it will need good access if you are ferrying food to and fro.

Patios positioned close to the house tend to be square or rectangular, continuing the lines and dimensions of the house. Where the patio is sited away from the house, it can be any shape – circular, octagonal, square or rectangular. The determining factors are the shape of the space available, what you will use the patio for and what furniture it must accommodate.

Ideally, the dimensions of a patio should be in scale with its surroundings. That includes the house and the part of the garden where the patio is to be sited. A common mistake is to make the patio so large that it dominates the area, but it should never be so small that it looks mean.

## creating colourful displays

The patio is more than a place to relax; its hard, all-weather surface makes it an ideal place to grow plants in pots. Gardeners with limited mobility often rely on a patio area because it has a level, even surface. And that surface provides the perfect stage for an array of colourful plants in containers and for raised beds, large and small.

- **plants in containers** of all shapes and sizes are an integral part of most patios. They are invaluable for seasonal displays and add warmth, character, colour and scent to soften the starkness of a flat paved area.
- **raised beds** are excellent for more ambitious, long-term displays. They are also the ideal place to grow larger plants, which provide shelter and shade. They will grow much bigger where there is plenty of room for their roots to develop than in the relatively confined space of a container.
- **shade and shelter** must be considered. Most patios are sited in a warm, sunny position and there are times when the site gets too hot and some shade or shelter is required. Pergolas are the traditional solution: they have an open roof and sides, with a mesh of supports for climbers to grow up. These will provide dappled shade, and with the right choice of climbing plants, plenty of colour and scent.
- **screens** have two functions. If the patio is in a windy, open site, a screen provides a degree of shelter. It also helps to create a sense of seclusion and privacy, especially useful if the patio is overlooked by neighbouring properties.
- **water features for patios** come in all shapes and sizes, varying from wall-mounted fountains to a raised pond with aquatic plants (see page 136). The sound of running water furnishes the ultimate soothing, relaxing atmosphere.

# constructing a patio

A patio surface can be constructed using a wide range of materials, and the determining factors are usually cost and looks. Choose materials and overall appearance to blend in with the immediate surroundings.

## *making a brick and stone patio*

YOU WILL NEED

• paving materials • string • wooden pegs • spade • rammer or post • spirit level • heavy post or vibrating plate compacter • hardcore or crushed stone • dry sand • straight-edged board or plank • spacers • mortar • brush • hammer or board and mallet • trowel

1 **Roughly mark out** the patio area, then strip off the lawn or surface debris within the area. Dig out the soil to a depth of about 15cm (6in), then compact the base with a post or rammer. Measure and mark out the patio area using a string line and wooden pegs. Use a spirit level and pegs to establish the final level of the patio surface, ensuring it has a slight slope (see Practical essentials, opposite).

2 **Make the foundations** by covering the excavated area with a 10cm (4in) layer of hardcore or crushed stone. Spread it evenly until the surface is level.

3 **Compact the hardcore** using a vibrating plate compacter (these can be hired). For awkward corners or a small area, use a heavy post (see inset). Once this layer has been well firmed, cover the area with a layer of dry sand 8cm (3in) deep. Level and compact it, using a board or plank with a straight edge.

4 **Starting in one corner,** set out the perimeter bricks in a stacking or soldier bond, as used below. Insert ready-made or improvised spacers, such as clothes pegs, to keep the gaps even. The short end of the bricks forms the edge of the patio. Set a straight-edged plank to use as a guide.

5 **Bed the bricks** onto a damp mortar mix (or a bed of sand), and check with a spirit level to keep the edges level. Tamp the bricks into the mortar or sand using a board and mallet or a hammer, until they are level.

6 **Now bed the paving slabs.** Spread more sand topped with dry mortar mix so the slabs will be level with the surface of the bricks. Check for levels.

7 Sprinkle a dry mortar mix or sand over the bricks, and brush it into the spaces between them. A dry mortar mix will give a firmer finish and help to avoid weeds in the cracks. You may have to do this several times to fill the gaps completely. Do the same with the paving slabs.

8 When the area is finished, brush out the excess sand or mortar from the cracks. Leave the paved area for a day or two before walking on it, to allow the surface to settle.

**Granite setts** laid along the edges finish off the paved area, which will provide a hard-wearing surface all year round.

## practical essentials

Whatever material you choose, note two important practical points.

- **the finished surface** must have a slight slope, or 'fall' (about 2–3cm/1in for every 2m/6ft), so that surface water runs off to drain away. If the patio is next to the house, angle the fall to carry the water away from the building.
- **the top of the patio** should be at least 15cm (6in), or about two brick courses, below the house damp-proof course. If it is any higher, surface moisture can be absorbed straight through the wall and will cause problems inside.

## materials

Bear in mind not only the cost and appearance, but also the ease of laying if you are building your own patio.

- **paving slabs** Various kinds can be bought, the cheapest being made from pre-cast concrete. The colour range includes grey, blue-grey, pink, yellow and red. The colours tend to fade with age. Baked clay tiles, imported from Asia, are becoming increasingly popular and are often sold in shades of terracotta, sandy yellow or pale grey. Most slabs come in a variety of small to medium sizes, although some larger sizes are also available.
- **bricks** New or recycled bricks can be laid in a variety of patterns to make an attractive surface. Use frost-resistant bricks or they will crumble during the winter. Blocks, or 'paviors', made from pre-cast concrete, are very resilient and are a good choice for a surface that will be heavily used.

LAYING TIP Patterns of brick can be used to fool the eye and make the patio's dimensions look different. If bricks run lengthways they will give the impression of extra length, while bricks that run across a patio will make it look broader. In both cases, keep patterns clear and simple, and avoid mixing them.

- **natural stone slabs** These 'flags' are the most appealing form of stone. They tend to be expensive, especially if recycled, and give a worn, mellow look. Bear in mind that recycled flagstones do not come in standard sizes or thicknesses, and they can be extremely heavy to handle. The use of crazy paving, i.e. broken slabs bedded into mortar or cement, was once the height of fashion. When skilfully laid it can look interesting, but the design must be carefully planned to ensure that you use stone sizes evenly over the whole area, while the arrangement should still appear to be random.
- **wooden decking** Timber boards can be used as an outdoor flooring surface and have a warmer, more natural look when compared with many other materials. Decking lasts longer when it is not in contact with the soil (see page 127).

# the decking option

**Decking is a practical and attractive garden surface for patios, verandahs and roof gardens. It is lightweight, easily maintained and will last for many years. It provides a comfortable transition between house and garden, and a level surface for garden furniture and groups of containers.**

## the advantages of wood

Wood makes an excellent flooring material for outdoor use, and good quality timber can last for years if it is well seasoned or treated with a preservative. Wood is versatile enough to be made into a wide range of structures and shapes. Narrow decking boards can give the impression that an area is larger than it really is, while conversely, fewer, broader boards will make an area appear smaller.

A raised deck is a good way to create a horizontal surface when the ground is sloping. By cutting the support posts to the required length, they compensate for any dips and bumps in the ground.

## the right type of deck

Wooden decking lends itself to several kinds of structure.

- **decking 'islands'** are often built close to water or on wet, muddy sites to create a dry, weatherproof area.
- **split-level decks** are useful on steeply sloping sites, where a series of platforms can be created at different levels. If the structures are well built and linked together, only minimal excavation work is required for the foundations.
- **low-level decks** are usually the easiest to build because they may be laid on roughly levelled ground. Use a low-level deck to cover an old concrete patio or to floor a roof garden (see Early Spring).
- **raised decks** of 60cm (2ft) or more above ground level require more engineering know-how, and you may need to consult a structural engineer to calculate the weight they can support. With large, free-standing decks it is not necessary to concrete upright support posts into the ground. You will only need to use foundation 'pads' because the weight of the wood will keep the deck stable. These pads can be pieces of paving slab or concrete blocks: set them into holes the depth and width of

**Timber decking** around the raised beds provides built-in seating in this harmonious patio area (below). Ridged boards give a non-slip surface.

a spade on a bed of dry mixed sand and cement (mix one part cement to five of sharp sand). Raised decks 1.2m (4ft) above ground need safety hand-rails.

- **walkway decks** make excellent timber paths over uneven ground. They are easier and cheaper to construct than other surfaces, needing less excavation.

## decking materials

- **softwood** is the most inexpensive timber but it must be pressure-treated with a preservative. The chemicals penetrate deep into the wood to give long-term protection from rot and decay.
- **hardwood,** such as iroko and oak, or decay-resistant wood such as western red cedar, will last for many years. It is expensive, even when recycled. Only use wood from a sustainable source.
- **rotting** is the main enemy of any outdoor timber structure. This danger applies especially to decks on, or very close to, the soil. A deck made of untreated softwood will last only about five years.

PRESERVATIVE TIP Paint a wooden deck with preservative every two to three years to extend its life.

**Decking makes** the ideal surface for a rooftop garden (left), with the weight of the pots and plants distributed around the perimeter.

**This decked walkway** and verandah run around the house (below left). The shallow steps are an integral part of the structure, shaped to accommodate the trunk of a tree.

## decking boards and tiles

For outdoor use, decking boards should be at least 5cm (2in) thick to combat the twisting and warping caused by constantly fluctuating temperatures and moisture levels, with the wood being alternately rained on and drying out. Ready-made wooden 'tiles' are a good alternative. Up to 1 x 1m (3 x 3ft) square, they can be laid on a supporting framework to form a surface deck.

## bespoke decking

Where the deck is very large or an irregular shape, the structure is often made to measure on site by specialist contractors. Larger decks tend to be built in several sections, then fitted together, which gives easy access under the deck without causing damage.

SAFETY TIP Give the decking a slightly roughened finish so that it does not become too slippery after rain.

**A low-level deck** is a cheap and quick way to transform a seating area outside the house (below right). The style of the garden furniture echoes the wooden decking.

# ornamental ponds

A water feature brings an extra dimension to a garden – it changes the light, introduces gentle movement and sound, and increases the range of planting opportunities. The style of the pond should complement the overall garden design.

## siting the pond

When installing a pond, the most important decision is where to place it. It needs to be sited where it can be most enjoyed, but there are practical considerations too.

- **choose an open site in good light,** or at least one that receives direct sunlight for part of the day. A little shading will help to keep the water clear and sweet, but dense shade is not suitable. Full sun in summer raises the water temperature and encourages the growth of algae. If a site in full sun is the only option, plants such as water lilies will eventually shade the water, to the benefit of pondlife.
- **avoid large, deciduous trees,** if possible, as excessive quantities of falling leaves in autumn may cause problems. Although it is possible to rake the majority of these out of a small pond or to cover the pond with a net during leaf fall, careful siting can eliminate this extra work and the need to disturb the pond habitat.
- **consider the 'lie of the land'.** A formal, geometric pond will always look better when set into the ground or into paving; as part of a formal design it can be retained by a raised wall or by high sides. An informal pond looks most natural if it is placed where you might expect water to lie – either in a dip, or at least on low-lying, level ground.

## choosing a style

Formal ponds usually have severe edges and suit gardens planted along symmetrical lines. They are built in geometric shapes – rectangles, circles, half circles or squares. Planting works better if it is somewhat severe, but a carefully designed and well-sited formal pond can be almost as wildlife-friendly as a truly natural one.

Ponds with a natural-looking outline look more attractive in an informal setting than those with carefully measured symmetrical lines. They can be almost any shape, from oval or roughly rounded to ribbon shaped, or might even make up a long meandering

**A geometric pool** with corner fountains is a focal point in this all-green garden (top). The restrained planting suits the pond's formality.

**Even on a small scale,** a pond brings interest and soothing qualities to a town garden (above). The brick edging overhangs the pond slightly, concealing the liner.

**A wooden deck** blends naturally with a pond, aided by mature plantings. The pond's surface is partially shaded by water lilies (left).

stream. An area for marginal plants can be incorporated in the design, perhaps with a shallow area making a gradual transition between land and water.

WILDLIFE TIP All ponds, whether formal or informal, need access and escape points for animals, and to allow birds to stand and drink. Either incorporate a shallow end or fix a paving slab or piece of wood at water surface level.

## edging materials

The way a pond is edged, and the materials used, makes all the difference to its final appearance.

### paving

Formal ponds are often finished with a paved edging. There is a wide variety of paving materials to choose from, ranging from inexpensive concrete slabs to costly dressed stone. Make sure that paving slabs are large enough to be laid firmly. In ponds with a flexible liner, the slabs can hold the liner in place. Lay the slabs as for patio slabs (see page 124); to ensure the liner is out of sight, set the slabs just clear of the water surface – no more than 2–3cm (1in) – and to overhang it by a few centimetres. For a rigid liner, slabs can either overhang the edge or be wedged beneath it.

### turf

Where an informal pond is laid in a lawn, the grass can be left to grow right up to the water's edge and be used to anchor the liner. The turf will have been folded back before the hole was dug. Once the liner has been installed, replace the turf, trimming the edges as you go; take care not to puncture a flexible liner. If the grass is allowed to grow long around the edges, marginal plants such as irises or rushes will make the pond look more natural.

### decking

An interesting alternative edging for an informal pond set in grass might be to create a raised decked area or a decking surround, rather like a boardwalk. This would allow marginal plants to develop unfettered, but ensure an attractive walkway, or even a seating area. Such a construction requires a sturdy framework of posts to support the decking above the ground.

## *shape* and dimensions

Space and budget are likely to be limiting factors, but it is worth building the largest pond you can afford or accommodate. The bigger the pond, the easier it is to develop the right ecological balance, and the less likely you are to experience problems with algae or blanket weed. Larger ponds give wider scope for varied planting and are capable of accommodating a larger collection of fish or other creatures.

- **surface area** There is no lower or upper size limit for a man-made pond, but it should be in scale with the garden. In a 10 x 15m (33 x 50ft) garden, for example, a 2 x 4m (6 x 12ft) rectangular pond would be about the right size. It would be large enough to form a main feature, but would leave plenty of room for the rest of the garden design.
- **depth** To sustain an ecological balance that will keep the water sweet and clear, a pond requires sufficient volume. Depth is also a consideration for plants. For most water lilies, a depth of roughly 60cm (2ft) is necessary, and for marginals 20cm (8in) is ideal. Thus, for a 2 x 4m (6 x 12ft) pond, a central depth of 45–60cm (18–24in) would be adequate, with a shallower rim about 20cm (8in) deep and 30cm (12in) wide for a planting ledge.

# ornamental ponds/2



## constructing a pond

Ornamental ponds can be made by lining the hole with concrete or natural clay, but the quickest and most popular method is to use a rigid or flexible man-made liner.

• **rigid liners,** or moulds, are made of reinforced plastic and are available in a variety of shapes and sizes for small to medium ponds and as streams or waterfalls. They are durable and come in dark or neutral colours, which makes them inconspicuous once in place.

Symmetrical, geometrically shaped liners are relatively easy to install (see right), but those of an asymmetric or inorganic shape must be stood upright in position to mark out their form – or you will get a mirror image. Prop the liner upright, sticking canes in the ground to hold it in place and indicate its outline, before excavating the soil.

• **flexible liners** are made from strong but highly malleable materials and are suitable for constructing larger ponds and individually designed shapes and watercourses in any size or style. The design can incorporate waterfalls, streams or other features as well as ledges for growing marginal plants. The size of the liner is virtually unlimited, but the best quality materials are expensive (see Late Spring). Ponds can also be connected by lesser water courses, each one being lined with a flexible liner.

• **concrete** may seem a stronger and more permanent material, but it is more prone to problems than a flexible liner. It can take several years for the alkaline effect of the cement to wear off in the water, and in a hard winter, a concrete pond may crack and then leak.

• **natural ponds** are made by lining the hole with raw clay, which is smeared or 'puddled' all round the bottom and sides until a waterproof layer several

## *installing a rigid geometric liner*

**YOU WILL NEED**

• rigid liner • coarse sand and sand for marking out • spade • spirit level • hardcore or crushed stone • straight-edged plank • edging material e.g. paving slabs

1 **Mark out the shape** of the pond. Lay the liner upside down on the site and, using sand, trace the outline of the liner onto the ground. Remove the liner.

2 **Cut the outline** of the pond into the soil using a sharp spade to ensure straight lines.

3 **Dig out the pond cavity** just inside the cut lines, but only as deep as the shallow marginal shelf. Check across the edges using a spirit level and straight-edged plank to ensure that they are level.

4 **Place the liner** in the hole the right way up and mark around the base of the deep part of the pond with sand. Remove the liner.

5 **Cut the outline** for the deep part of the pond in the soil, then dig out the hole to the correct depth. Clear away all loose stones or root fragments. On stony soil, make the hole slightly deeper, and place a 5cm (2in) layer of coarse sand on which the liner can rest.

6 **Check that the liner** fits in the hole. Dig out more soil if necessary.

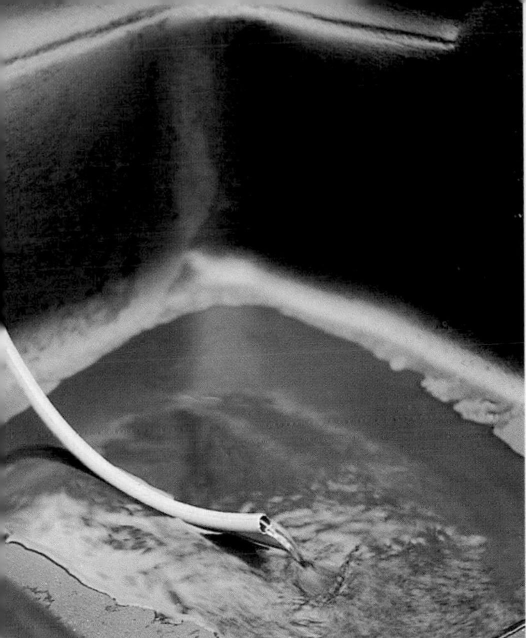

**7** **Ensure the liner is level** in each direction by placing the spirit level along each edge. Make any necessary adjustments and back-fill with soil or sand. Slowly fill the liner with water, allowing the mould to settle under its increasing weight. Check for level as it fills and adjust the liner if necessary, otherwise one edge will stand above the water line and be unsightly.

**8** **As the liner is filling up,** back-fill the gaps with soil or sand. When it is level, prepare the ground for paving around the liner, if you are having paved edges. Place a 10cm (4in) layer of hardcore or crushed stone and ram down with a post (see page 124) to compact it.

**9** **Bed each paving slab** onto the hardcore, overhanging the edge of the liner slightly. Tap each one into position and check for level before mortaring in the gaps.

**Constructed using a rigid liner,** this linear pool is precisely edged with stone slabs, with a slatted wooden bridge across one end.

centimetres thick has been formed. A clay lining should last indefinitely, provided it isn't punctured, or stirred up by rapid currents.

REPAIR TIP A concrete pond that has developed a leak can be repaired simply and quickly by installing a flexible liner.

## laying a flexible liner

Mark out the dimensions of the pond accurately before you begin excavating. For a rectangular pond mark out the design with canes and string. Make sure the corners are exactly 90°. For an informal pond, lay a hosepipe or length of rope on the ground and move it around to form the outline you want – or draw 'real' curves, especially for a circular pond. When you have the right shape, mark it out with sand and cut the outline as shown in steps 2–3. Leave shallow shelves for marginal plants and dig the centre of the pond deeper.

Before laying a flexible liner, make sure there are no sharp stones or roots left in the soil, as these could puncture the liner, or line the hole with a 5cm (2in) layer of damp sand.

Flexible liners are easier to lay on a warm day and with help. Drape the liner in position, then start to fill the pond. As it fills, pleat the liner neatly round curves and corners. The pond edge must be level, firm and stable enough to support the paving surround. Trim the liner to within 10–15cm (4–6in) of the hole and lay the surplus on the ground, under the edging. When the pond is filled with water, check the level and adjust if necessary with dabs of mortar slipped under the edging slabs.

## calculating the liner size

To find the size of liner required, multiply the pond length by its width as follows. The formula works for all ponds, regardless of size or shape.

**length** = maximum overall length + (2 x maximum depth) + 30cm (12in)

**width** = maximum overall width + (2 x maximum depth) + 30cm (12in)

The extra 30cm (12in) is to allow for an adequate overlap around the edges.

# creating a healthy pond

A pond has a dynamic ecology that needs to develop its own natural balance. This can be achieved fairly easily, but success – as seen in clarity of water, a healthy population of invertebrates and flourishing pond plants – will depend on careful plant choice, and on allowing enough time for the various populations to stabilise. In some situations, this may take more than a year, or even two.

## pond plants

Several different kinds of plant are essential for a pond, not only for their decorative value, but also for the positive effect they have on the water. They absorb the nitrogenous waste that is produced by fish, amphibians and other life forms, which in turn helps to prevent too much algae from multiplying and turning the water green. Invasive weeds, however, may need to be kept to a minimum.

### oxygenating plants

These are submerged, green plants that give off a constant supply of oxygen, which is dissolved in the water and sustains many small organisms. These in turn provide food for other creatures and process nitrogenous waste. Although underwater plants may not be spectacular to look at, they serve a vital function. If carefully chosen, however, many add subtle beauty, especially if the water is clear enough for them to be seen. Some have feathery, ferny or finely divided foliage. Others, such as the beautiful water crowfoot or water violet, produce flowers above the water's surface.

### *good oxygenating* plants

- canadian pondweed (invasive) • hornwort (*Ceratophyllum demersum*)
- potomogeton, starwort (*Callitriche*) • water crowfoot (*Ranunculus fluitans*)
- water violet (*Hottonia palustris*)

### deep-water plants

These plants absorb large amounts of nitrogenous waste and their floating leaves help to shade the water. This reduces light levels and temperature, which inhibits the growth of algae. The best deep-water plants are water lilies (see page 134), but there are others of great value:

- **golden club** (*Orontium aquaticum*) has narrow, blue-green leaves and horn-like yellow flowers (see below).
- **pond crowfoot** (*Ranunculus aquatilis*) has palmate, floating leaves as well as feathery submerged foliage and little white flowers in spring and early summer.
- **spatterdock** (*Nuphar advenum*), for larger ponds, has big, heart-shaped leaves, some of which float while others stand clear of the water, and showy green-tinged yellow flowers.

### marginal plants

These also absorb dissolved nutrients and waste and so help to keep down algae and blanket weed (see pages 47 and 134).

*Orontium aquaticum* is known as golden club for its slender yellow flowers.

### floating weeds

Some people dislike such plants as duckweed – a tiny species that grows on the surface of the water and which can be invasive if not controlled. But it is not difficult to control in a small area, and it brings beneficial shade. As fresh, green duckweed is very rich in protein absorbed from the water, removing large amounts is a good way of taking nitrogen from the pond water; furthermore it will benefit your compost heap. Other floating plants include *Azolla caroliniana*, whose ferny leaves will sometimes invade a whole pond, but which may not survive a cold winter. Even less hardy is the water chestnut (*Trapa natans*). This produces 'chestnuts', which can be overwintered in water in a greenhouse, for use the following year.

## fauna

Even if you plan not to have any fish in your pond, the water cannot help but attract many different species. Insects like dragonflies or damselflies will arrive, as will birds. At night, hedgehogs and bats will be attracted to the water.

If you are able to encourage the development of this habitat, you will be helping with bio-diversity, but even if wildlife conservation is of no interest to you, your pond will still be more

**In a healthy, well-stocked pond** the plants and wildlife are in balance and the water is clear.

pleasant if it supports a well-balanced ecosystem. The water will be clearer and sweeter; therefore, the plants that surround it and grow in it will look all the better. Furthermore, with sufficient predators in the water – such as frogs, toads or newts – you will be less likely to be troubled by pests like mosquitoes.

## stocking with fish

For fish to thrive, the pond needs to be balanced, with well-established water plants. Fountains or waterfalls are not vital, but they help to oxygenate the water, particularly in the early stages while the plants are settling in. Fish add to the burden of nitrogenous waste, and it is therefore essential that the pond is very well stocked with vegetation, and that you do not overstock with fish.

If you build and plant the pond in spring, allow the plants a month or two to establish before you introduce any fish. Early to midsummer would be an ideal time.

## *releasing fish*

1 **When releasing fish** into your pond, float the whole bag in the water for a while before you open it, so that the temperature change is gentle. Fish are usually purchased in plastic bags, sometimes with a little oxygen added before it is sealed.

2 **Submerge the bag** only when you are ready to release the fish.

3 **Carefully unseal** the bag and allow the fish to swim out into their new home.

# planting up a pond



One of the key elements of a successful pond is judicious planting. For any pond to succeed, deep-water and oxygenating plants will be necessary as well as those with floating leaves, but the choice of plants and how they are arranged will depend on the style of the pond wanted.

## formal ponds

Planting for a formal pond is likely to be more sparing than in a naturalistic pond, with an emphasis on softening hard lines. Take care not to spoil the pond's symmetry or that of its surroundings. Use restrained colours.

### marginal plants

These are not essential to a formal pond's welfare, but they will do more to enhance its appearance than other types. Limit them in number, to retain a severe look, or plant more densely so that they create a continuous margin, softening the hard, straight edges.

Marginal plants will grow happily in submerged plastic mesh baskets (see Late Spring), provided these are lifted out and the plants divided or thinned every few years. Good garden soil is a satisfactory planting medium, but aquatic compost is widely available. Place a thick layer of gravel on the soil surface after planting, to deter fish.

Concentrate on plants with a good outline, like the upright forms of iris and reeds, with some that flower but do not spread vigorously.

**Restrained use of plants** in this small pool suits its formality. Water lily leaves shade part of the water surface.

### deep-water plants

Water lilies are the most suitable deep-water plants for formal pools, because of their elegant leaves. They come in a range of colours that covers yellow, pink to near red, and white. *Nymphaea* 'Chromatella' has pale yellow blooms set off by leaves splashed with bronze and green. *N.* 'James Brydon' has wine-pink blooms. If your water is lime-free, you could try the lovely water violet (*Hottonia palustris*); its submerged foliage is feathery and, in early summer, the delicate stems that rise above the surface carry pale lilac blooms.

For floating leaves consider water hawthorn (*Aponogeton distachyos*), with oval leaves and scented white blooms. There are several submerged plants too, for example common bladderwort (*Utricularia vulgaris*) which has yellow snapdragon flowers in summer.

### *marginals* for a formal pond

• bowles' golden sedge (*Carex elata* 'Aurea') – yellow and green stems and leaves that arch gracefully over the water • *Equisetum japonicum* – tall stems, 1cm (½in) thick, punctuated with black markings • *Equisetum scorpioides* – attractive rod-like, dark green naked stems • *Iris* 'Holden Clough' – brown-veined, yellow flowers • *Iris pseudacorus* 'Variegatus' – bright cream and green leaves from early spring to midsummer, when they subside to a more subtle range of hues • kingcups (*Caltha palustris*) – yellow flowers • pickerel weed (*Pontederia cordata*) – glossy leaves and blue flower spikes • small reedmace (*Typha angustifolia*) – brown flower spikes in midsummer • *Typha minima* – cylindrical spikes of dark brown flowers in mid and late summer • water forget-me-not (*Myosotis scorpioides*) – blue flowers

**Colourful irises and kingcups** enliven the margins of an informal pool, with large-leaved *Rheum* in the adjacent bed.

## informal ponds

Plants that tend to look best in informal ponds are those you might expect to see growing in the wild. Natives and hardy wildflowers from other parts of the world will look superb in an informal pond. Yellow flag irises with plain green leaves, for example, make more natural looking marginal plants than the variegated kind, and if you decide to plant kingcups (*Caltha palustris*), the single-flowered wild form is more appropriate than the more readily available cultivated double form.

### planting around the pond

Growing conditions adjacent to an artificial water feature are frequently as dry as in a normal border, and yet the pond's appearance will always be enhanced if its surrounding vegetation is lush and prolific. Try, therefore, to select plants that look luxuriant but are in fact happy growing in relatively dry soil. Bearded irises, hostas, a good many ferns and the large-leaved *Rheum palmatum* are all suitable around medium-sized pools, while the giant, vigorous *Gunnera manicata* is best kept for large pools and planting beds only.

### marginals for informal ponds

• arrowhead (*Sagittaria sagittifolia*) – arrow-shaped leaves and showy white flowers with dark centres • arum lily (*Zantedeschia aethiopica*) – a natural water or bog plant with a succession of white blooms and shapely bold leaves • candelabra primulas – yellow or orange flowers in slim spires • *Darmera peltata* – big, disc-shaped leaves follow the pretty pink and white flowers borne on naked stems in spring • frogbit (*Hydrocharis morsus-ranae*) – trails of floating stems with large, white, three-petalled blooms • kingcups (*Caltha palustris*) – yellow flowers • *Ligularia dentata* – luscious growth and towers of orange flowers in late summer • water forget-me-not (*Myosotis scorpioides*) – pale blue flowers for much of the summer; try a form such as 'Mermaid' and allow it to grow in or half out of the water • water plantain (*Alisma plantago-aquatica*) – big sprays of small white flowers • yellow flags (*Iris pseudacorus*) – plain green leaves and yellow flowers

PLANT SELECTION TIP Some native water plants can be too invasive for a small pond. The wild white water lily (Nymphaea alba), for example, is too big and vigorous for a small pond, as is great spearwort (Ranunculus lingua), whose big, golden blooms are a delight in wild marshland. Although planting in baskets limits the spread of invasive species, some are too aggressive even for these and can be too invasive for a small pond.

*Ligularia dentata* (in the background)

## immersing deep-water plants

1 **After planting** a deep-water plant such as a water lily in a lined basket, cover with a layer of fine gravel to stop the compost being disturbed by fish.

2 **Place one or more** bricks on the bottom of the pond to raise the basket to the correct planting depth. Soak in a bowl of pond water to get rid of most of the trapped air bubbles.

3 **Lower the basket** into the water gradually and allow the air bubbles to disperse at each stage before lowering in further.

# patio water features

If space is restricted, there may not be room for a large pond, but that does not mean you cannot have a water feature. A small fountain, a miniature raised pond or even a half-barrel filled with water and planted with aquatic species will enrich the experience of relaxing on your patio.

## *installing a wall-mounted water fountain*

YOU WILL NEED:
• plastic water tank • length of rigid tubing • flexible piping • small pump • low-voltage transformer • wall-mounted spout • spirit level • wall plug and screw • electric drill and masonry bit • bricks or slabs to disguise tank • outdoor waterproof paint and paintbrush

1 **Lift a paving slab** next to a wall to insert a ready-made 20–23 litre (5 gallon) plastic water tank (available from builders' or plumbers' merchants). Sink the tank into the hole and check the levels.

2 **Place garden walling blocks** round the three exposed sides to disguise the tank and butt them together.

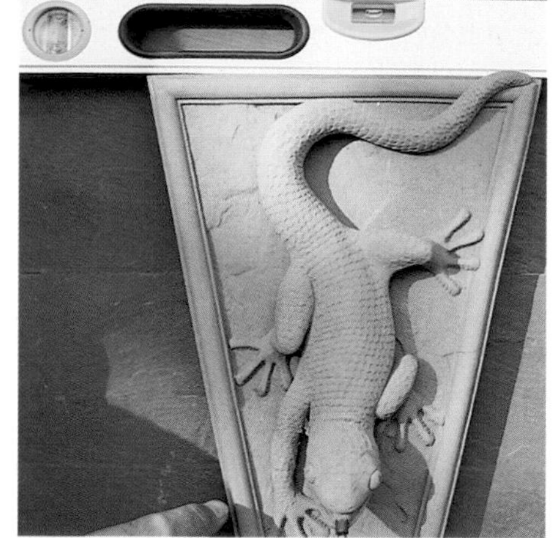

3 **Drill a hole or holes in the wall** and insert a plug and screw on which to hang the water spout. After hanging, use a spirit level to check that it is level. Fit a water pump in the tank following the manufacturer's instructions.

4 **Attach the flexible** piping to the base of the spout and check the pump is working before cutting the piping to fit.

5 **Paint the rigid tubing** to match the wall and feed the flexible piping into it. Attach the other end to the pump.

6 **Tuck the electric cable** from the pump to the electricity supply along the back of the patio paving.

## wall fountains

Wall fountains are easy to install if you choose a low-voltage pump, and the electricity can be fed through a wall from an interior supply. They have a small reservoir fitted with a pump that feeds water up to the fountain. The water pipe can either be left visible, as here, or concealed behind a wall and fed through to the fountain head.

## half-barrel ponds

A half-barrel is large enough to make a tiny patio pond, but it should not have been treated with toxic chemicals such as creosote and it must be waterproof. Line an older, more porous container with a plastic membrane to prevent leaks. Place it in a spot that does not receive direct sun and make sure the base is perfectly level, so the water surface can be close to the top all round.

Place a layer of washed gravel in the base to help to keep the water clear, or install a tiny fountain, with its jet above the water level. Fountains are available in kit form, either powered by a low-voltage transformer inside the house or solar powered.

With such a small volume of water, it is important to adjust the fountain jet correctly to prevent it from draining the container. In windy conditions, water can fall on the ground around the feature instead of back into the barrel. Evaporation will lower water levels more quickly than with a big pond, so during hot weather you may need to top up the water almost daily.

## other water features

A simple cascade over cobbles or a wall fitting that dribbles water into a tank or trough makes a simple but effective water feature. It has movement, makes a soothing noise and it will, to a limited extent, attract birds and other wildlife. It is also much safer than a pond if young children use the garden.

- **cobble or millstone cascades** are available as kits. When constructed, they consist of a concealed reservoir, in which you place a submersible pump, with a grille across the top. Lay cobbles on top of this, so water can flow from a central jet and bubble over the stones.

The pump is wired to a low-voltage transformer inside the house, and the cables should be concealed beneath the patio paving. In most kits, the reservoir is like a small rigid pond. If you prefer to make the feature yourself, dig a hole and line this with a flexible pond liner (see page 130) then set the pump, grille and fountain in place. The mesh must be strong enough to take the weight of the cobbles. Smooth off the edges to prevent puncturing the liner.

- **raised ponds** constructed from brick or concrete blocks housing a rigid liner, possibly with a seat or bench on top of at least one of the sides, allow water to be enjoyed at close quarters. A suitable size would be 1 x 2.2m (3 x 7ft) and 450mm (18in) high. Make the seat top of timber planks 5–7½cm (2–3in) thick, screwed to battens or directly to the brick or blockwork, with a slight overhang on either side. Make sure the 'seat' is wide enough to sit on. Rendering the concrete blocks on the outside will enhance their appearance.

Those inexperienced at bricklaying may prefer to employ a professional tradesman. If the pond is to be built on an existing concrete surface, further foundation work should not be needed.

**Stand pots of moisture-loving plants** such as ferns in the tank to soften its appearance.

## sustaining the balance

The same principles apply to tiny ponds as to large ones (see page 132), but with small volumes of water, a healthy balance is harder to achieve and you will often have to intervene. With the right plants and careful siting – preferably in partial shade, but not beneath deciduous trees or shrubs – it should be easy to keep the water clean, but be ready to replace it occasionally, especially in hot weather. Use only a limited number of plants and control their size. Select the smallest and least vigorous water lily (*Nymphaea* 'Pygmaea Helvola') or float a water hyacinth and plant a single marginal like flowering rush (*Butomus umbellatus*) on the bottom. Oxygenating weed is also important, though you must thin it down during the growing season.

# garden lighting

**Lighting extends the life of the garden into the evening. Apart from enabling you to see, lighting can create all kinds of special effects. Try highlighting ornamental trees and statues, creating extra shadows, and lighting up the most colourful part of a border.**

## the lighting options

Cleverly deployed lighting brings a special beauty to the garden at night. It can be used to highlight certain features, which gives them an extra nuance, while distracting the eye from unsightly areas. Beware of getting carried away and placing lights all round the garden, pointing in every direction; this can be counter-productive and minimise the lighting effect. Be restrained and aim to create atmosphere, with a few magical contrasts between light and dark.

**The discreet placement** of uplighters among these ornamental grasses casts exaggerated shadows on the wall behind them.

Choosing the right coloured light can make a huge difference. White or soft blue enhances the surroundings while other colours such as red, green and orange often make plants appear discoloured and unhealthy.

## decorative lighting

There are five types of lighting:

- **downlighting** When you light specific features or garden areas from above you are imitating nature, suggesting filtered sunlight or moonlight. This creates an enticing contrast between the soft shadows at the base of the feature and the shining bright light above.
- **uplighting** If a light is placed on or near the ground, and angled upwards, it throws the subject's outline into sharp relief, creating a silhouette around it, and provides a focal glow in the garden. Used sparingly, this can be one of the most dramatic of garden lighting effects.
- **spotlighting** Use this to make individual plants or garden structures stand out in the darkness. To be most effective, spotlight very sparingly.
- **wash lighting** This angles a spreading beam of light to cover a structure or feature, picking out special details, such as surface texture, which might go largely unnoticed in daylight.
- **underwater lighting** When subtly used beneath fountains, waterfalls or bubble fountains, underwater lighting can create magical effects.

**Uplighters,** partially obscured by being set into gravel (right), provide subtle effects at ground level while lighting up the edge of a flower bed for safety.

**Discreet lighting** beneath the boards of decking (below right) illuminates the change of level at night.

## functional lighting

**safety** Use garden lighting to illuminate paths and drives at night, especially where there are potential hazards and sudden changes of level, such as steps. **security** Lighting the immediate area around the house can help with security, especially if any hidden corners are lit. Security lighting can be subtle and decorative although it is all too often brash and harsh. A dazzling security light that casts deep shadows is actually intruder-friendly because the darker areas provide somewhere to hide.

### *safety* first

- **unless you are using** low-voltage lights, call in a qualified electrician to carry out the installation.
- **all outdoor electric lights** must be sealed in waterproof units. Most have a spike or plate fitting so that they can be firmly anchored into the ground or against a structure.
- **many fittings** have a swivel mounting so the lights can be angled.
- **keep lights that get hot** well away from children.

### *pond* lighting

A wide range of interesting effects can be created by lighting water features. Lights that are submerged in deep, still water tend to create a moody atmosphere, while lighting in moving water conveys a sense of energy and action. Try varying the depth at which the lights are submerged to emphasise or exaggerate the depth of the water. Underwater lights are sealed in specially made waterprooof casings.

**Underwater lights** create a slightly ghostly ambience and highlight the three water jets where they touch the surface.

## lighting systems

There are a number of systems using either high or low-voltage electricity.

- **mains electricity** With a 240-volt rating, mains electricity can be used to power all your garden lighting, but there is always a risk that the cable might be severed. When choosing mains electricity, employ a qualified electrician who will use armoured cable, giving a high level of protection.
- **low-voltage electricity** For safety reasons, many gardeners prefer to take a low-voltage, 12-volt supply from the mains via a transformer. Although there may be some loss of energy, low voltage is far safer than high voltage. Position the transformer indoors close to the power supply or on an outside wall in a weatherproof box. Connect it to a mains cable. Follow the manufacturer's instructions to connect the low-voltage cable to the transformer.
- **electrical safety** It is an essential practice when working with mains electricity in the garden to use a circuit breaker plug (often called a residual current device or RCD). If the light fittings or cable are damaged, this will automatically cut off the power, which eliminates the danger of electric shocks.

**Fairy lights** for outdoor use (above) are on dark green cable, inconspicuous in daylight.

**A combination of permanent** and portable lighting brings a garden to life at night (left).

**Placing light fittings** in among plants (below) enhances flower and foliage colours at dusk.

## permanent lighting

This involves laying and burying a cable to supply a series of fixed, mounted lights around a circuit. Installing more than one circuit allows lights to be switched on and off in a timed sequence, to create different effects. A good quality lighting system will have a working life of up to 25 years.

It is essential to hide the electric cables and fittings, for safety as well as because they detract from the garden's appearance. There is less likelihood of someone tripping over a cable, or an inquisitive child trying to play with it if

**Extend the hours** of pleasure you can have from water features or sculpture (right) by illuminating them at night.

**A row of neat column lights** (above) illuminates the approach to the house.

it is buried. Dig a trench at least 20cm (8in) deep, running along the most direct route from the power supply to the light. Make sure it lies where no subsequent digging is likely to take place. If you are laying low-voltage cables, it is possible to lay them on the surface. Cover them with a thick protective mulch – which will remind you where they are – and make sure that nobody will dig there. You could even run low-voltage cables overhead to a post or tree, provided that no pruning will need to be carried out nearby.

SAFETY TIP A length of thick hosepipe provides excellent underground protection for low-voltage cables buried in the garden. Use a rigid PVC conduit for mains-voltage cables.

## alternative lighting

There is an ever increasing range of battery and solar-powered lighting equipment for garden use and this is particularly useful where it is difficult to provide a cable power supply.

You can buy single, stand-alone units mounted on a spike pushed into the ground; these have a small integral solar panel and light which enables them to store energy during the day. They can then be switched on via a manually controlled switch at night, as required. Or you can have a cluster of lights linked to a solar panel which harnesses and stores energy. While this type of lighting has many sound environmental qualities, it also has drawbacks. Solar lighting works well only in a bright, sunny location where plenty of energy is available for storage. And although solar panels are becoming more efficient, their storage life is limited. The sensors and circuitry within the panels are also delicate and easily damaged, so must be handled with care. In the right location, they are ideal for lighting remote paths and to use where children are playing, as there is no risk of electrocution.

Lighting in the garden does not have to involve electricity. It can include the use of candles, flares and lanterns for an alfresco touch, though these tend to be used mainly around seating areas. Portable lighting may be set up almost anywhere in the garden, but wind can be a problem, not least when it blows smoke in people's faces. Many candles and flares release scented oils, which add to the ambient mood. They can even be impregnated with chemical repellents, released as they burn, to deter insects attracted by the light.

- **candles,** while they will not provide a great deal of light, create a wonderful atmosphere with their gentle flickering. Protect the flame so that it does not blow out and so that no one gets burnt.
- **flares** resemble large candles; they are often on sticks that can be stuck into the soil. They burn for six to eight hours, and cast a warm, romantic glow.
- **lanterns,** lit either by candle or oil, can be hung around the garden to give a gentle, golden light.

# outdoor living

**Rattan furniture** is lightweight enough to be moved outdoors when the weather permits but will not withstand rain.

Garden furniture is an essential part of the garden, transforming it into a pleasant place to sit, eat or relax – or take a well-earned break. There is a huge range of styles, designs and materials available now, so it is well worth considering a few important practical points before you buy.

## choosing garden furniture

First and foremost, choose furniture to suit the surroundings. Wood in simple designs is a safe bet for almost any garden, though more intricate designs, such as a Lutyens-style bench, look best in a formal or sophisticated setting. While stone can look beautiful in a formal or cottage-style garden, it can look out of place next to a small modern house. Metal in sleek, clean designs complements the lines of a contemporary town garden while moulded, intricate designs look better in a traditional, informal setting. If you are having trouble deciding which style to go for, it is useful to browse through a selection of catalogues for ideas while sitting in your garden, rather than face difficult decisions when out shopping.

Garden furniture must be comfortable and it is important to try before you buy. Garden centres and large garden shows usually have a good selection on display to try out.

### tables and chairs

Think about furniture for the patio first and consider how many items you will need. Most people opt for a table and enough chairs for the household plus a couple of spares. It can be useful to have some cheap folding seats for extra visitors. You may also want to consider permanent seats around the garden (see page 144). Other options include reclining seats like steamer chairs and garden loungers, as well as swinging 'hammocks', all of which are intended for more luxurious relaxation. Make sure you have sufficient space before you buy – they can take up a lot of room. Fabric cushions add comfort, but they will have to be put away under cover every evening.

### storage space

Storage is an immensely important consideration that is easy to overlook until winter arrives. Furniture that stays outdoors all year round needs to be tough and weatherproof, which gives you the choice of stone, metal or suitably treated wood. Otherwise, you will need plenty of covered space in which to store your furniture, or you can buy tough plastic covers which, although effective, are not attractive to look at all winter.

**Steamer chairs** are made for lounging and enjoying the garden in summer.

Plastic stacking chairs are economical on space while folding wooden chairs and tables take up even less room, as do canvas chairs.

## materials and their care

For permanent furniture you will be choosing for durability as well as for looks and comfort. Maintenance might be another factor for consideration.

### wood

Wood is immensely versatile and comes in a wide range of styles, from 'tailored' seats that suit a formal garden to rustic ones that look more at home in a rambling cottage garden. Comfort will vary according to the design. As well as wooden chairs and bench seats for sitting upright, there are swing seats and reclining steamer chairs. Shaker-

**On a rooftop garden,** folding metal framed wooden chairs take up minimal space and can easily be brought indoors for winter.

**Ornate metalwork furniture** painted a vibrant colour turns a small balcony into an enticing place to sit.

style boot benches have a box under the seat that can be used for storage. Most wooden furniture is heavy and hard to move, with the exception of folding seats and tables or those made with metal frames that are more lightweight.

Choose sustainable hardwoods like teak and iroko or tough softwoods like Swedish pine if the furniture has to stay outside all year. With hardwood furniture, check its origins in case it is from a country where illegal logging is commonplace. Buy timber approved by the Forestry Stewardship Council wherever possible.

Clean hardwood furniture twice a year with warm soapy water and a soft brush. If you need to scrub off dirt, work in the direction of the grain. After drying, apply a light coat of wood oil to reduce cracking and restore colour.

You will need to treat softwood furniture with preservative every spring. First clean it thoroughly by scrubbing to remove dirt or mould, as described above, then lightly sand with fine sandpaper and apply clear preservative. For painting, use microporous paint, which is more weatherproof than other types. If you wish to apply a wood stain, do this before coating with preservative. All wooden furniture lasts longer if it can be taken inside for the winter, ideally into an outbuilding.

### resin

Moulded plastic or resin furniture is reasonably priced as well as fairly comfortable, and is often sold with padded cushions. Lightweight and easy to move, it may be left outside for the summer months but needs to be stored under cover for the winter as frost causes the material to discolour and become brittle.

Resin needs very little care. Simply wash down thoroughly two or three times a year with a cloth or soft brush, using warm water to which a mild detergent has been added. Avoid using abrasive cleaning materials, which would scratch the surface.

### metal

Metal comes in many designs, ranging from heavy and costly cast iron to cast aluminium, which is much lighter and cheaper but also less sturdy and durable. Cushions are useful as metal is hard to sit on for any length of time.

Clean metal furniture in the same way as resin (see above). Cast iron needs yearly attention to prevent rust taking hold: clean with a wire brush and repaint using a paint that is suitable for metal.

### stone

Stone is handsome and very durable, but also expensive and difficult to move due to its weight. While high on style, stone is low on comfort and is often better regarded as a permanent feature of the garden than a piece of furniture. But it is virtually trouble-free and requires only an occasional scrub-down with soapy water to remove dirt and algae.

# creating seating areas

Even if a patio provides the main seating place outdoors, additional seats around the garden will allow you to enjoy many different aspects.

## choosing a site

Before positioning any permanent seating consider the advantages and disadvantages of each potential site and how you can make the most of it. Take the following points into account.

- **all seating areas** should be hardstanding, on level ground such as brick or paving slabs laid on firm foundations. Decking is also suitable, but neither grass nor gravel make an appropriate base for tables and chairs.
- **seats facing vistas** across the garden will allow you to enjoy different views. If there is an attractive prospect beyond the garden, make the most of it by placing a seat to face it.
- **areas of sun and shade** can be exploited at different times of day. Position a seat where you can enjoy the warmth of early morning sun and another to take advantage of late afternoon sunshine. In high summer, a seat positioned in shade is welcome during the heat of the day.
- **a garden's design** can combine a seat with a pergola, arbour or trellis to create a peaceful spot away from the house.

## seats as focal points

Every garden needs enticing features placed at strategic viewpoints, such as the view from a main window and at the end of a lawn or path. Such focal points are a visual way of taking someone by the hand and leading them around the garden. A seat can make the best focal point of all, as it will draw all but the hastiest of folk towards it. Instead of placing a seat out in the open, where it would look rather lost, 'anchor' it visually by placing it next to a tree, hedge, wall or fence.

All seating needs to fit the style of the garden, but this is especially important when using seats as focal points. Though most other garden furniture should be chosen with comfort in mind, with seats that are part of the structural design appearance must always take priority.

Choose or decorate a focal seat to contrast with its background. A white or lightly coloured bench set against a dark hedge of yew or Leyland cypress, or a dark wooden fence, makes an eye-catching contrast. Similarly, you could stain or paint a seat a dark colour to make it stand out against golden or silver-foliaged plants or a pale stone wall. A wide range of wood stains and exterior paints makes it possible to introduce a theatrical touch.

## wayside seats

While a seat sited at the end of a viewpoint acts as a rapid draw, one placed alongside a path has the effect of slowing people down. This enables the garden to be enjoyed at a more leisurely pace. Tuck a seat a little off the path, where the pleasure of its unexpected discovery will give it a charm of its own. If it is set a little way into a border, you can enjoy the surrounding fragrant plants to the full. Where a path runs close to a wall, fence or hedge, make the seat more inviting by setting an arch above it and training a vigorous climber over the top.

**A built-in turf seat** can be constructed in the same way as a chamomile seat (see below). This one has been made using willow stems woven around upright stakes.

### *a chamomile* seat

A living seat of chamomile (*Chamaemelum nobile*) is a lovely feature for a sunny spot, although it is suitable only for occasional use and during dry weather. The non-flowering form 'Treneague' is the best variety to use, especially as the foliage releases an apple-like fragrance when gently bruised.

Make the seat about 45cm (18in) high and wide and 1m (3ft) long. The retaining wall around it can be constructed from timber, brick or stone – whatever fits in with the style of garden. Half-fill the seat with stones or rubble and top up with free-draining topsoil. Plant the chamomile 10–15cm (4–6in) apart and keep well watered until established. Trim the plants regularly to encourage bushy growth.

**Wooden table and chairs** positioned beneath a shade-giving pergola (left) make a pleasant eating area on a patio.

**Placed against an arch** in a dark yew hedge (above), this white-painted bench seat cannot fail to act as an eye-catching focal point.

## a secret corner

A well-designed garden should always contain an element of surprise, and few discoveries are more delightful than an intimate seating area where you can relax in perfect peace, away from the demands of the doorbell or telephone. Such a seating area can be as simple as a hidden bench tucked behind plant-clad trellis screens, with a couple of paving slabs beneath to keep feet warm and dry. Extending the trellis to each side of the seat would create even more privacy.

On a larger scale, you can construct a vertical feature over one or more seats. Choose a ready-made arbour – various designs and materials are available – or make your own using timber. It is practical to cover the ground underneath with paving or gravel, as grass tends to get worn away under regular foot traffic, especially in the shade cast by such a structure.

### *Scented plants* for seating areas

Fragrance has a powerful attraction and, while appreciating scented plants in passing is pleasant, sitting down and being drenched in perfume is an even more enjoyable experience. These are some of the best plants for scented flowers or aromatic foliage.

#### SCENTED FLOWERS

ANNUALS • mignonette (*Reseda odorata*) • night-scented stock (*Matthiola bicornis*) • sweet peas • tobacco plant (*Nicotiana affinis*) •

BIENNIALS • sweet william (*Dianthus barbatus*) • wallflower (*Erysimum cheiri*) • sweet rocket (*Hesperis matronalis*)

BULBS • hyacinth • lily (many varieties) • narcissus

CLIMBERS • honeysuckle (*Lonicera periclymenum*) • jasmine (*Jasminum officinale*) • trachelospermum

SHRUBS • broom (*Cytisus*) • lavender • mahonia • mexican orange blossom (*Choisya ternata*) • mock orange blossom (*Philadelphus*) • rose (many varieties)

#### AROMATIC FOLIAGE

lemon verbena (*Aloysia triphylla*) • mint • scented-leaved pelargoniums • thyme

**Aromatic lavender** surrounds a rustic garden bench.

# outdoor entertaining

Al-fresco entertaining is one of the pleasures of summer in the garden and a barbecue is almost essential for this. A built-in barbecue gives you a custom-made cooking area designed to fit your garden, but there are many other options on offer.

**A kettle-style barbecue on wheels** is practical as it can readily be moved.

**The chimenea,** fuelled by wood, gives cooked food a wonderful flavour.

## types of barbecue

There is a wide choice of barbecues, ranging from basic to sophisticated models complete with tools and gadgets – or you may prefer to make your own. The main differences are in the price and the fuel: charcoal or gas.

Charcoal barbecues are cheaper to buy than gas ones, but less convenient, and a DIY barbecue can work out cheaper still. If you plan to barbecue a lot or at short notice, bear in mind that a gas model is much quicker and easier to use than a charcoal one. In most cases, a barbecue is not a thing of beauty and needs to be tucked out of the way when not in use. Check how portable a model is and, if it has to be put away after use, see that you have space to store it in a shed or garage.

### charcoal barbecues

These use solid fuel in the form of charcoal or briquettes. Check the construction is sturdy and that it has a removable lid to cover the barbecue while it cools, or to quench flames. The main drawback is that charcoal barbecues take time to get going: the coals must be lit about an hour before you want to start cooking. Also the only way to regulate heat is by raising or lowering the grill. However, many people find lighting and cooking over charcoal great fun, and an essential part of outdoor entertaining. Remember that a charcoal barbecue can get smoky; site it where smoke will not billow into neighbours' windows.

### gas barbecues

Fuelled by bottled propane gas, these are, essentially, outdoor cookers. They are quick and easy to use and have adjustable controls. Gas barbecues are more substantial pieces of equipment than charcoal models and, with the weight of the gas bottle, are heavy to move around. When buying, check the size in relation to what you wish to cook (larger models roast a turkey) and how easy it is to clean.

### chimeneas

These Mexican clay ovens make handsome outdoor fireplaces that can be used for cooking. Buy from a retailer who supplies grills and other cooking accessories to fit.

# building a permanent barbecue

**YOU WILL NEED**

• spirit level • bricks sufficient for 10 courses • builders' square • chalk • dry-mix mortar • pointed trowel • plumb line • grill and charcoal pan, or a built-in barbecue kit

1 **Use the spirit level** to check the ground is level. Without mortar, lay out the first course of bricks in a double L shape. With the builders' square, check the corners are at exact right angles and ensure that the charcoal pan will fit correctly (see step 4). Draw around the bricks with chalk and move them out of the way.

2 **Mix the mortar** and, using a pointed trowel, put a layer of mortar on the ground. Place the first course of bricks on top. Use the builders' square to check the corners are still at right angles, and ensure the bricks are level.

3 **Place a layer** of mortar on top of the bricks and lay the second course of bricks so that the joints are staggered. Lay further courses of bricks in this way, frequently checking for level. Check the walls are vertical using a plumb line.

4 **Once you reach the height** convenient for the charcoal pan (about six courses), lay three bricks so they stick out at right angles on each side. These bricks will support the charcoal pan. Lay a further one or two courses of bricks, then repeat the right-angled bricks to provide support for the grill. If you wish to vary the grill height, set short metal bars in the mortar between two or more courses of bricks.

5 **Add a further** one or two courses of bricks above the highest grill setting. If your barbecue is in an exposed position you could raise the top by two or three more courses to create a partial windbreak.

## barbecue safety

- **for lighting charcoal,** use only products tailor-made for barbecues.
- **do not pour lighter fluid** onto hot coals and never use petrol.
- **keep matches** and any combustible materials well away from a barbecue.
- **keep the garden hose** and/or a bucket of sand close by, just in case.
- **buy a barbecue** with a hood or lid to quench flames if food catches fire.
- **use long-handled tools** and wear oven mitts to protect skin from burns
- **never leave a lit** barbecue unattended.

## building a barbecue

Before you start to build, think long and hard about the right size, the best site and the most suitable design. The dimensions of a barbecue are dictated by the size of the grill and the ash pan. So purchase these first, or buy a built-in barbecue kit to use as a template.

Try to site a barbecue on or near the patio. For convenience it should also be fairly close to the kitchen. Pick a spot that is out of direct view of the house windows, if possible, unless you want to look at the barbecue all year, and avoid having any potential fire hazards nearby, like fences, trellis or pergolas. A firm, level base is essential. If a suitable area of concrete, slabs or brick is not available, lay a concrete foundation before you start to build.

The instructions above show how to build a simple barbecue with a grill. If you wish, you can add a work surface at one side by duplicating the basic structure to build an 'E' shape. The extra space is useful for standing food and accessories, and if the surface is tiled (use frostproof tiles) it will be easy to clean. The space below the work surface could house charcoal and tools.

# summer watering

All plants need adequate water to survive, which means that artificial watering is usually necessary during dry spells. With supplies often running low in summer, it makes sense to use water as wisely as possible in the garden, both for environmental reasons and to save money on metered supplies.

**An oscillating sprinkler,** though it tends to be somewhat wasteful of water, is useful to cover a large area of vegetable garden.

## conserving water

Well-established plants in the ground should be able to survive all but long periods of drought without extra water, so concentrate watering on those plants that must not be allowed to dry out (see right). However, the key to successful plant survival starts way back at the soil preparation and planting stage, with the addition of organic matter to the soil; this improves its water-holding capacity as it acts like a sponge.

You should also 'lock in' valuable moisture by mulching the ground every spring to reduce evaporation from the soil. Apply a 5–8cm (2–3in) layer of organic material such as chipped bark, garden compost or well-rotted manure (see Late Spring). Work in co-operation with nature: if you garden on free-draining, fast-drying soil, opt for drought-tolerant plants that thrive in such sites. Conserving water also brings labour-saving benefits for the gardener, as artificial watering takes up valuable time.

## watering techniques

Timing is all-important to make maximum use of water and keep plants looking their best. In hot weather, water in the evening or early morning, which is when less moisture is lost by evaporation, and when plants can take up water more efficiently. This also avoids the danger of water-splashed leaves becoming scorched in bright sunshine. In cooler seasons, water early in the day so that the foliage then has a

### *priority* plants

In dry weather, concentrate on watering those plants that need it most.

- **new plants** Do not allow these to dry out during their first year, as they are unlikely to have established enough of a root system to take up sufficient moisture.
- **new lawns** Whether they have been made from seed or turf, new lawns need to be kept moist for several months until established. Fine, bowling green-type lawns also need watering regularly throughout their lives. Existing general-purpose lawns can be left to their own devices – despite turning brown, they will green up surprisingly quickly once rain arrives.
- **annuals and newly sown seed** These must not dry out for the first few weeks after planting; after that you can get away with an occasional soaking during dry spells, with the exception of thirsty varieties like sweet peas that prefer regular watering.
- **plants in containers** You will need to water these frequently, even daily, in summer (see page 150).
- **vegetables** To produce good crops, all vegetables benefit from regular watering, particularly leafy vegetables such as salad crops and spinach, and those with large or succulent fruits such as tomatoes or courgettes.
- **soft fruit** Strawberries and raspberries, especially, need watering while the fruit is developing.

chance to dry out, as moist leaves provide an attractive environment for disease. This is particularly important for plants growing under cover.

How to water is also important. Remember to water the soil – not the plant. During the growing season, always give plants a thorough soaking as a sprinkling of water can be more harmful than none at all, encouraging roots to quest towards the surface.

## watering equipment

There is an extensive range of watering equipment, varying from simple watering cans to more technical and costly equipment such as sprinklers and automatic watering systems.

- **watering can** At least one can is essential: choose a size that you can lift comfortably when full. Although galvanised cans look handsome, plastic ones are lighter and easier to use. For watering seedlings and young plants, fit a rose attachment. Never use the same can for applying weedkiller, but buy another one just for this purpose.
- **plastic bottle** While a small can is useful for watering raised containers such as hanging baskets, a large plastic bottle does the job more easily and costs nothing at all. Such bottles can be fitted with special 'bottle top waterers' for more effective watering.
- **garden hose** A hose is essential unless your garden is very small. Check how long it needs to be as hoses come in a variety of lengths from 15–60m (50–200ft). Cheaper hoses have a tendency to 'kink' readily, while good quality types have reinforced or double walls and are much less trouble.

To keep your hose tidy and out of the way, store it on a wall-mounted reel or trolley – it is usually best to buy this complete with hose. Hose end attachments allow the water to be

**A rotating sprinkler** is a convenient way to water a small flower garden at regular intervals.

delivered in a variety of ways, and a lance or a rigid extension is useful for watering hard-to-reach plants like those in hanging baskets.

- **garden sprinklers** These are fixed to hose ends and automatically deliver a fine spray of water over a large area. A static sprinkler is the simplest design and waters a circular area, though it usually needs to be moved around for an even coverage. Oscillating and rotating sprinklers give better coverage.
- **soaker or seep hose** Large areas of new plants, rows of vegetables or lawns can be watered easily and efficiently with a soaker hose. Made of plastic or rubber, these hoses have small perforations all along their length, which let the water seep out gently. For temporary watering, lay the hose on the soil covered with a 2–5cm (1–2in) layer

**Mircobore tubes** deliver water to individual plants in a window box.

of mulch. Alternatively, bury the hose about 10cm (4in) deep if it is to be a permanent fixture, but mark its position to avoid accidental damage.

- **microbore watering systems** These are perfect for watering container-grown plants in the garden or greenhouse, and automatic water timers can be used with any watering system (see page 151).
- **capillary matting** This thick matting holds water, which is taken up by the plants in pots standing on it. It is useful in the greenhouse to ensure thorough watering; remove it in winter to avoid making the atmosphere too humid.

## recycling and saving water

Collecting rainwater in a water butt is one way to reduce your use of mains water – and many plants prefer it. Models range from inexpensive standard plastic butts to dearer wooden ones or slim wall-mounted models. If looks do not matter, any large watertight container will do, like plastic barrels thrown out from factories or an old water tank. Make sure it has not previously contained anything toxic that could harm your plants.

**Position a water butt** where the downpipe from a gutter can direct rainwater into it.

You can use recycled or 'grey' water from baths and sinks on the garden provided it is reasonably clean and free from strong detergents. Water from washing machines and dishwashers, however, is not suitable.

# easy patio watering

A patio packed with container-grown plants is a glorious sight in summer, but regular watering is absolutely essential to their survival. Fortunately, there are now many different ways to make watering less labour-intensive and provide precious water even when you are not there.

## watering patios

Plants in pots obviously have a limited root area from which to take up moisture, and the situation is compounded by an 'umbrella' of foliage that keeps most rainfall off the compost. Although watering is a relaxing and enjoyable job, it can become a really time-consuming chore in summer when plants can need attention once or even twice a day.

The frequency of watering can be reduced by using water-retaining gels, self-watering containers and large pots. Even better, you can cut the workload dramatically by installing a watering system; the addition of a timer will make the system completely automatic.

### *compost* and water-retaining gel

Soil-based compost dries out more slowly than soil-less types and provides more of a buffer against drought. This is therefore the best type to use for all permanent plants, although its weight makes it an impractical choice for suspended containers such as hanging baskets.

Improve the water-holding capacity of soil-less compost by using water-retaining gel, which is made up of granules that swell to many times their own size when wet (see before and after adding water to the pots, above). Mix just a small quantity of the dry granules into the compost before potting – or you can buy compost that already contains the gel. However, make sure you water whenever necessary, because once the gel has given up its store of moisture, the compost dries out very quickly as air replaces the spaces previously occupied by the swollen gel. Do not use gel for containers that will be outside during autumn, winter or early spring, as the compost would become too wet and cold.

**The drip nozzle** (below) delivers a fine spray of water to plants in containers.

**An effective watering system** (left) involves running lengths of microbore tubing, fitted with drip nozzles, to all your pots.

## choosing containers

The size and type of container, along with the amount of plant growth it has to support, influences how quickly the compost dries out. Hanging baskets dry out fastest of all, as the whole of the container is exposed to sun and wind. Pots made of porous material like terracotta also dry out quicker than other materials, though you can reduce water loss by lining the inside of the container (not the base) with polythene.

Large containers are best at retaining water as there is more compost to hold the moisture, whereas small pots have only a tiny amount by comparison. If you don't want to bother with a watering system, opt for generous containers and put a selection of plants in each one, rather than having lots of smaller pots.

Self-watering containers are a simple way to reduce the amount of watering required as they incorporate a built-in

**Self-watering containers** incorporate a reservoir to top up water as needed.

reservoir. The plant can take up water as necessary, but without the roots becoming waterlogged. This design is particularly useful for hanging baskets.

## patio watering systems

You can plumb your patio containers into a microbore watering system, and tailor it to your own patio. A basic design consists of a rigid hose running to the area to be watered. Flexible microbore tubing travels from the hose to the containers, delivering water to each pot by means of an attached drip nozzle (see below). There are some variations, depending on the kit you buy. The hose itself connects to a tap which you turn on manually as needed, or you can fit a water timer to make the system fully automatic (see above).

A watering system is perfect for containers as the water is delivered slowly and gently, rather than in a rush from a hose. Although fairly costly and time-consuming to set up, such a system can last for years, save time and keep your plants in glowing good health all summer – even during holidays.

### *automatic* watering

- **make your watering system fully automatic** by fitting an automatic timer or computer-controlled timer, both available from garden centres. Both types are battery-powered: a timer is designed to water once a day and is relatively inexpensive, while a computer gives much greater flexibility of watering times but costs almost twice as much.
- **frequency and length of the watering period** will vary, depending on the site and weather conditions. If you are planning to go on holiday, set up the timer at least a week in advance and monitor the amount of watering required to keep the container compost evenly moist but not waterlogged. The best time to set up a watering system is during hot weather when the pipes will be soft and flexible.
- **in winter,** make sure the system is drained of water, which could otherwise freeze and cause damage. Ideally, it should be dismantled and stored under cover, with open ends of pipes sealed with tape to prevent insects crawling in and creating blockages next year. Timers should be dried and stored with their batteries removed.

## *constructing a watering system*

1 **First stand your containers** exactly where you want them. From the tap, run a length of rigid hose where it will be least obvious, for example, along the base of a wall. Measure the distance from your hosepipe to the first container, then measure the distances between the pots. This will give the number and lengths of microbore tubing needed.

2 **Cut lengths of tubing,** using scissors or the tool provided with the kit. Fit a drip nozzle to the end of the first tube and peg it into a container before joining the next length of tubing up to it. Fix the other end of the first length of tubing to the hosepipe, using the attachment supplied.

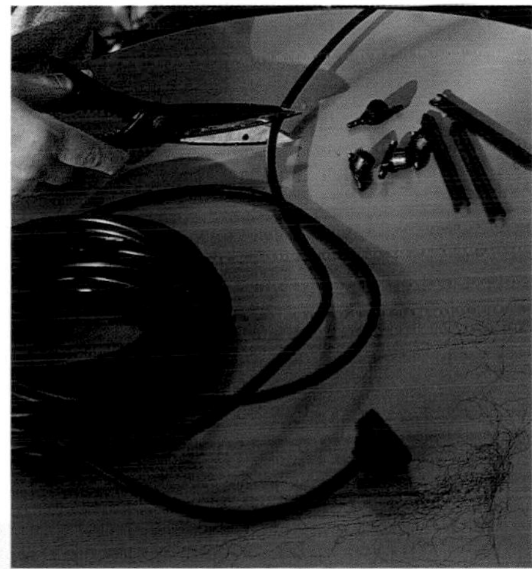

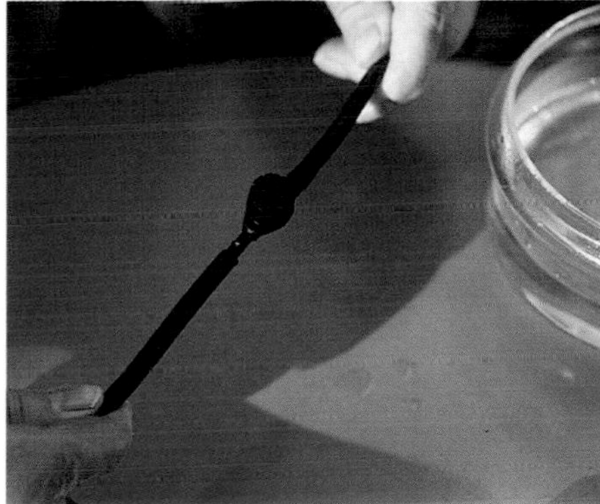

3 **Continue to fit** tubes and drip nozzles to all containers. The easiest way to fit the tubes to the drip nozzles is to dip the ends of the tubing into a bowl of hot water. This makes the plastic more flexible to work with.

# summer feeding

All plants need feeding in order to perform at their best and remain healthy. In a garden plants grow closely in a limited space, which takes more out of the soil than goes back in naturally. The situation is compounded by the removal of untidy plant debris and cut grass, which would otherwise rot down and return nutrients to the soil.

## nutrients

Knowing what plants need makes it easier to choose and apply fertiliser correctly. The nutrients required by plants divide into three groups: major nutrients that need to be added to all soils, and secondary and trace nutrients that only need to be applied on soils that are very poor or have extreme pH levels (too acid or too alkaline). All these nutrients are chemical elements and have a chemical symbol, which is given in brackets.

The three main nutrients required for healthy growth are nitrogen (N), phosphorus (P) and potassium (K). Most general-purpose, or compound, fertilisers contain all three. The actual balance of each nutrient does vary, so check the packet before buying. Fertilisers are also available 'straight' – that is, supplying only one nutrient. These are used to correct deficiencies rather than for general feeding. Do not confuse fertilisers with soil improvers like manure and garden compost, which contain only limited nutrients.

- **nitrogen** encourages strong growth and should be applied early in the growing season. Do not use high-nitrogen fertiliser on permanent plants after midsummer as the resulting soft, young growth could be frost-damaged.
- **phosphorus** boosts strong root growth and is particularly important when planting all permanent plants.
- **potassium** improves both fruiting and flowering. Apply a high-potassium fertiliser (such as a tomato feed) in spring and early summer.
- **secondary nutrients** such as calcium (Ca), magnesium (Mg) and sulphur (S) are needed in relatively large amounts, but are present in sufficient quantities in most soils. In some cases, deficiency is actually caused by insufficient water in the soil, making it hard for plants to extract all they need.
- **trace nutrients** include iron (Fe), boron (Bo) and molybdenum (Mb). While important, they are required only in small amounts and rarely require artificial application. One common exception is lime-hating plants growing on soil that is insufficiently acid, where they often become deficient in iron.

### *easy* fertiliser application

For easy and accurate distribution of nutrients, make your own applicator using two small plastic pots of the same size, placed one inside the other with the drainage holes just offset to leave small gaps. Fill with granular fertiliser and simply shake the pot to distribute the fertiliser evenly.

**Mix a combination** of granular fertiliser and water-retaining granules into the compost when planting up containers.

## applying fertilisers

Whatever the fertiliser, always follow the manufacturer's instructions. Never be tempted to apply more on the basis that double the feed will do twice as much good – over-feeding can do more harm than giving nothing at all.

### granular fertiliser

Fertiliser granules or powder are scattered on the soil surface around plants and hoed or raked into the soil. Apply at the recommended rate by weighing out the amount per metre, then marking a pot or small container at this level for future reference.

Plants can only take up fertiliser when it becomes dissolved in water, so in dry weather water well after feeding.

- **ideally, apply** when the ground is moist but plants are dry, or fertiliser could stick to and scorch damp leaves.
- **always wear gloves** and take care not to breathe in any dust.

*Magnolia* x *soulangeana*

## *specialist* fertilisers

Certain fertilisers are formulated for specific plants in order to achieve their best performance.

- **lawn fertiliser** is usually labelled according to the time of year it should be applied, spring or autumn, as this affects the balance of nutrients.
- **lime-hating or ericaceous plants** like magnolias benefit from an ericaceous fertiliser that contains iron, in which they often become deficient.
- **some specific fertilisers** can be used for a wide range of plants – rose or tomato fertiliser can also be used on all flowering plants.

### controlled-release fertiliser

These polymer-coated granules or tablets are designed to release nutrients gradually over a period of months, as and when conditions are sufficiently warm and moist for the plant to utilise the food. While more expensive than other types, controlled-release fertilisers are also more effective. They are particularly useful for feeding plants in containers as they do away with the time-consuming weekly job of liquid feeding.

### liquid fertiliser

Soluble or liquid fertiliser is dissolved before application, then watered onto the soil around the roots. The plants take up the nutrients rapidly as they are already in solution. But regular feeding is needed as the nutrients quickly leach away through the soil, particularly on light, free-draining ground.

- **water liquid fertilisers** onto the soil using a watering can. Over a large area, a hose end diluter (see above right) cuts down a lot of work – just attach the filled applicator and turn on the hose.
- **apply morning or evening** to avoid the risk of sun scorch on splashed foliage.

**You can buy liquid fertiliser** in an applicator that clips onto the end of a hose. This is invaluable for feeding plants over a large area.

- **do not apply on dry soil** as scorching could occur, and avoid applying before rain which would wash off the fertiliser.

### foliar fertiliser

This liquid fertiliser is designed to be absorbed through a plant's leaves. Spray onto the leaves using a pump-action hand sprayer. The plant absorbs the nutrients very quickly, which is particularly useful if it is showing signs of nutrient deficiency such as pale, yellowing or discoloured leaves. Follow the guidelines for applying liquid fertiliser (left), and never spray when the sun is on the leaves or it could cause severe scorching.

## *feeding* guidelines

| TYPE OF PLANT | TYPE OF FERTILISER | WHEN TO FEED |
|---|---|---|
| NEW PLANTS IN BORDERS | Slow-release, high in phosphorus to aid root growth | On planting |
| ESTABLISHED PLANTS IN BORDERS | Slow-release (general) or controlled-release | Late winter and late spring |
| PERMANENT PLANTS IN CONTAINERS | Controlled-release, along with a top-dressing of fresh potting compost | Early spring |
| ANNUALS IN CONTAINERS | Controlled-release followed by high-nitrogen liquid fertiliser. Add controlled-release fertiliser to compost when planting | Liquid feed from midsummer |
| VEGETABLES | Balanced compound fertiliser | Scatter on the soil, several days before sowing |
| FRUIT | Compound fertiliser high in potassium | Spring and early summer |
| LAWNS | Lawn fertiliser suitable for the time of year | Spring and autumn |

# summer index

Page numbers in *italic* refer to the illustrations and captions.

# acknowledgments

Photographs were supplied by the following people and organisations. Where relevant, the number of a picture as it appears on a page is given. Abbreviations are used as follows: t top, c centre, b bottom, l left, r right. JB Jonathan Buckley, MB Mark Bolton, MBr Martin Brigdale, CB Chris Burrows, HSC Harry Smith Collection, EC Eric Crichton, SC Sarah Cuttle, JD Jacqui Dracup, RE Ron Evans, RD Reader's Digest, FH Fran Harpur, GH Gil Hanly, JH Jerry Harpur, MH Marcus Harpur, NH Neil Holmes, GPL Garden Picture Library, JG John Glover, AL Andrew Lawson, MM Marianne Majerus, S&OM S & O Mathews, CN Clive Nichols, MLS Mayer Le Scanff, MN Mike Newton, JP Jerry Pavia, LP Laslo Puskas, HR Howard Rice, GR Gary Rogers, JS J Sira, GGS Georgia Glynn-Smith, RS Ron Sutherland, SSP Sea Spring Photos, MT Maddie Thornhill, JW Justyn Willsmore, JWh Jo Whitworth, MW Mark Winwood

**Front cover** JH **Back cover tl** MW, **tcl** SC, **tcr** MT, **tr** MW, **br** MT, **bl** SC **1** SC **2-3** GPL/HR **4-5** RD **8-9** GPL/JG (Mills Dean Garden, Glos.) **10 tl** S&OM (The Lawrences' Garden, New Zealand), **tr** RD, **bl** S&OM (Rathmoy, New Zealand), **br** GPL/MLS **11 l** JB (Design: S Raven), **tr** GPL/JS, **br** JH (Weihenstephan Horticultural Garden, Germany) **12 tl & tr** SC, **b** GR **13 tl** MT, **tr** SC, **cl** JH, **cr** GPL/NH, **bl** AL (Alderley Grange, Glos), **br** JH (RHS Chelsea 1993, National Asthma Campaign, Design: L Huntington) **14 t** S&OM, **b** JH (Gunilla Pickard) **15 tl** SSP, **tr** GPL/M Heuff, **cl** S&OM, **cc** MT, **bl** GPL/RS (RHS Chelsea 1995, Design: R Golby), **br** GPL/RS (RHS Chelsea 1996, Design: S Woodhams) **16 tl** MT, **tcl** JB (Design: D & M Seeney), **tcr** MT, **tr** GPL/M O'Hara, **b** MN **17 t** C Boursnell/Homes & Gardens/IPC Syndication, **bl** JH, **br** GPL/C Carter **18 tl** S&OM, **tr** AL, **bl** AL (Design: S Shire), **br** MH (HCFS 2001, Design: P Dyer) **19 tl** JH (Design: S Brown), **tr** A Jones/New Eden/IPC Syndication, **b** GR **20 t** MN, **c** JH (Sun House, Suffolk), **b** S&OM **21 tl** S&OM (Closewood House, Hants), **tr** GPL/HR, **bl & br** JH **22 l** S&OM, **tr** JB (Design: C Lloyd), GPL/HR **23 t** MH (HCFS 2001, Design: E Munro & A Henn), **c** MB (Design: M Payne), **bl** GPL/JG, **br** GPL/JG (H Dillon, Dublin) **24-5** MBr **26** SC **27** MW except **br** MB (Design: M Payne) **28** MW except **t** SC **29** MW except **b** SC **30 l** MT, **tr & br** SC **31 t** MW, **b** MT **32** GPL/RE **33 tl & tr** MW, **33 b** GPL/JG **34** FH **35** MW except **tl** SC **36 l** MN **36-7** S&OM, **37 r** MW, **bl & br** SC **38** JWh, **39 t & b** MT **40 t** JW, **c & b** SC **41 t** GPL/JS, **c & b** SC **42-43** MW, **44 l** MB (RHS Chelsea, Lifetime Care Garden, Design: P Stone), **r** MN **45** SC **46** MB (Design: M Payne) **47 t** MW, **b** GPL/JG **48 t** GPL/JG, **b** MT **49 t & b** MN **50** GPL/GH **51** MW **52** SC **53 t & br** MT, **bl** SC **54** MW **54-55** MT **55-56** MW **57 t** MB, **b** MW **58 l** CN (Design: S Irvine), **r** MT **59 t** MW, **c** JB (Design: M Crosby-Jones), **b** GPL/JP **60** MT **61** MW **62 t** MW, **b** MN **63 t** MN, **b** SC **64 tl** SC, **tr** MW, **b** MBr **65** SC **66** MW **67 t** MN, **b** MW **68-69** MW **70** GPL/M Heuff **71 t & bl** MW, **71 br** GPL/CB **72** SC **73 l** JB (Design: V Kennedy), **73 r** MW **74-5** MN **76-77 (1, 9)** MB, **(2, 5, 6, 8, 10)** JWh, **(3)** GPL/JG, **(4, 7, 11)** RD, **(12)** HSC **78-79 (1, 5, 7, 8, 9, 11)** RD, **(2)** MB, **(3)** HSC, **(4)** GPL/HR, **(6, 10)** JWh, **(11)** RD, **(12)** CN **80-81 (1, 11)** MB, **(2, 3)** GPL/JS, **(4, 6, 7, 12)** RD, **(5)** SC, **(8)** GPL/JG, **(9)** JD, **(10)** AL **82-83 (1, 4)** AL, **(2, 3, 9, 11, 12)** RD, **(5, 6, 7, 8)** JWh, **(10)** HSC **84-85 (1, 2)** GPL/JG, **(3, 12)** AL, **(4, 11)** RD, **(5)** GPL/Lamontagne, **(6)** CN, **(7)** MB, **(8, 10)** HSC, **(9)** GPL/MLS **86 (1, 4, 6)** JWh, **(2, 3)** MB, **(5)** GPL/MB **87 (1, 2, 4, 5)** JWh, **(3)** GPL/EC, **(6)** AL, **(7)** GPL/D Askham, **(8)** GPL/CB **88-89 (1, 4, 5, 7, 8, 9, 10, 11)** MT, **(2)** GPL/JS, **(3, 12)** HSC, **(6)** GPL/JG **90-91 (1, 11)** GPL/HR, **(2, 3, 4, 5, 6, 7, 12)** MT, **(8)** GPL/J Hurst, **(9)** RD, **(10)** GPL/CB, **92-93 (1, 2, 3, 5, 6, 8)** RD, **(4)** GPL/RS, **(7)** GPL/J Wade, **(9)** GPL/JS, **(10)** GPL/JG, **(11)** GPL/HR, **(12)** GPL/RE **94-95 (1)** RD, **(2)** S&OM, **(3)** GPL/C Fairweather, **(4)** SC, **(5)** GPL/JS, **(6)** JW, **(7, 8, 10)** MT, **(9)** MB, **(11)** GPL/R Wickham, **(12)** AL **96-97 (1)** RD, **(2, 8)** GPL/HR, **(3)** HSC, **(4)** MT, **(5)** MN, **(6)** CN, **(7)** JH **98 (1, 2, 4, 5, 6)** MT, **(3)** AL, **(7)** RD **99 (1)** S&OM, **(2, 4, 6)** RD, **(3)** GPL/D England, **(5)** GPL/NH **100-101 (1, 4, 5)** HSC, **(2, 6, 7, 9, 11, 12)** RD, **100 (3)** GPL/Lamontagne, **(8)** GPL/MB, **(10)** GPL/JG **102-103 (1, 5, 6, 7, 8, 9)** RD, **(2, 11)** AL, **(3)** MB, **(4)** GPL/B Thomas, **(10)** HSC, **(12)** S&OM **104-105 (1)** GPL/JG, **(2, 4)** MB, **(3)** JH, **(5, 9)** GPL/LP, **(6)** GPL/EC, **(7)** GPL/D Clyne, **(8)** RD **106-107 (1, 3, 4, 5, 7, 9, 11)** RD, **(2)** GPL/NH, **(6)** HSC, **(8, 12)** GPL/HR, **(10)** GPL/B Carter **108-109 (1)** GPL/K Blaxland **(2, 7)** GPL/HR, **(3, 4, 8, 9)** RD, **(5)** S&OM, **(6)** GPL/RE, **(10)** MH, **(11)** AL, **(12)** MB **110-111 (1)** MB, **(2, 4)** GPL/J Hurst, **(3)** GPL/C Boursnell, **(5, 7, 10)** MT, **(6, 11)** HSC, **(8, 12)** SSP, **(9)** GPL/M Howes **112-113 (1)** HSC, **(2, 4, 5, 7)** SSP, **(3, 9)** GPL/JG, **(6)** GPL/M Howes, **(8)** SC, **(10, 11)** MT, **(12)** GPL/M Watson **114-115 (1)** GPL/JS, **(2)** GPL/NH, **(3, 5, 7, 8, 10, 11, 12)** RD, **(4)** GPL/JP, **(6)** GPL/D Askham, **(9)** GPL/CB **116-117** RD **118 l** MT, **r** GPL/LP, **119 l** GPL/JG, **c** JWh, **r** AL **120-121** MW, **122 t** JH (Design: C Masson), **bl** MN, **br** JH (Design: S Fraser) **123** JH (Design: Oehme Van Sweden), **124-125** MW **126** CN (Furniture Design: S Layton) **127 t** CN (Design: P Thompson & T McDowell) **bl** AL, **br** S Dalton/ Living etc/IPC Syndication **128** GPL/ J Wade, **128-129** JH (Design: M Balston), **129** JH (Design: I & M Hughes) **130-131** MW except **tr** JB (Design: D Buckley), **132** AL, **133 t** JH (Design: B Hicks, Australia), **b** MW **134** JH (Design: R Hartlage, USA), **135 tl** MH, **tr** GPL/M Paul, **b** MW **136-137** MW **138** CN (Design: P Thompson & T McDowell) **139 t & c** CN (Garden & Security Lighting),**139 b** CN (HCFS 1997, Natural & Oriental Water Gardens, Garden & Security lighting) **140 t** JH (Design: V Nelson, NYC, USA), **bl** JH (Design: K Corlett, NYC, USA), **br** CN (Garden & Security Lighting) **141 l** J Mitchell/Living etc/IPC Syndication), **r** MM (Sculpture fountain by S Percival, Lighting by J Brett) **142 l** JH (Design: P Causer, Roja Dove, Brighton) **r** MT **143 l** A von Einsiedel/Country Homes and Interiors/IPC Syndication, **r** MH (Design: J Baillie), **144** JH (Helmingham Hall, Suffolk) **145 tl** JB (Design: G Wilson), **tr** JH (Tintinhull, Somerset), **b** JH (Design: S Hopkinson) **146 l** JWh ( HCFS 2000, Design: A Sargent & D Domoney), **r** MB, **147** MW **148** S&OM **149 t** GPL/GGS, **c** GPL/M Watson, **b** GPL/A Jones 150 **t** MW, **c** GPL/GGS, **b** GPL/J Sorrell **151 t** GPL/F Strauss, **b** MN **152** MW **153 tl** RD, **tr & b** MW

**Front cover:** *Rosa* Bonica. **Back cover,** clockwise from bottom left: *Lathyrus odoratus* 'Sicilian Pink'; cutting out blackberry canes; *Echinops ritro*; *Lobelia erinus* Cascade Series; fixing flexible hose to wall-mounted water feature; *Papaver nudicaule*

Amazon Publishing would like to thank Adrian Hall Garden Centres and Lotus Water Garden Products Ltd (www.lotuswatergardens.com). Thanks also to the following individuals who allowed us to use their gardens for photography: Bridget Heal, Gaye Prescott, Jenny Raworth.

**Summer** is part of a series of gardening books called the **All-Season Guide to Gardening**. It was created for Reader's Digest by Amazon Publishing Limited.

**Series Editor** Carole McGlynn
**Art Director** Ruth Prentice

**Editors** Barbara Haynes, Jackie Matthews; also Norma MacMillan, Richard Rosenfeld
**Design** Jo Grey, Mary Staples; also Alison Shackleton
**Photographic art direction** Ruth Prentice
**Special photography** Sarah Cuttle, Mark Winwood, Martin Brigdale
**Writers** Steve Bradley, Andi Clevely, Nigel Colborn, Sue Fisher, David Joyce
**Picture research** Clare Limpus, Mel Watson, Sarah Wilson
**Consultants** Jonathan Edwards, Mike Lawrence
**DTP** Claire Graham
**Editorial Assistant** Elizabeth Woodland

FOR READER'S DIGEST
**Project Editor** Christine Noble
**Pre-press Accounts Manager** Penny Grose

READER'S DIGEST GENERAL BOOKS
**Editorial Director** Cortina Butler
**Art Director** Nick Clark

First Edition Copyright © 2002
The Reader's Digest Association Limited
11 Westferry Circus, Canary Wharf,
London E14 4HE

**www.readersdigest.co.uk**

Reprinted with amendments 2003

Copyright © 2002 Reader's Digest Association Far East Limited
Philippines copyright © 2002 Reader's Digest Association Far East Limited

All rights reserved. No part of this book may be reproduced, stored in a retrieval system or transmitted in any form or by any means, electronic, electrostatic, magnetic tape, mechanical, photocopying, recording or otherwise, without permission in writing from the publishers.

® Reader's Digest, The Digest and the Pegasus logo are registered trademarks of The Reader's Digest Association, Inc., of Pleasantville, New York, USA.

We are committed to both the quality of our products and the service we provide to our customers. We value your comments, so please feel free to contact us on **08705 113366**, or via our website at **www.readersdigest.co.uk** If you have any comments about the content of our books, you can email us at **gbeditorial@readersdigest.co.uk**

**Origination** Colour Systems Limited, London
**Printed and bound** in the EEC by Arvato Iberia

ISBN 0 276 42709 2
BOOK CODE 621-002-2
CONCEPT CODE UK0087